The UNIX
Command Reference Guide

The UNIX†
Command Reference Guide

KAARE CHRISTIAN

The Rockefeller University
New York, New York

†UNIX is a trademark of Bell Laboratories.

A Wiley-Interscience Publication
JOHN WILEY & SONS
New York   Chichester   Brisbane   Toronto   Singapore

Library of Congress Cataloging in Publication Data:

Christian, Kaare, 1954-
    The UNIX command reference guide.

    "A Wiley-Interscience publication."

    Bibliography: p.
    1. UNIX (Computer operating system) I. Title.
QA76.76.063C46 1987   005.4'3   87-20969
ISBN 0-471-85580-4 (pbk.)

Printed in the United States of America

10 9 8 7 6 5 4 3 2 1

This book was prepared for phototypesetting by the author using the typesetting tools of the UNIX system.

CONTENTS

`.`	`:`	`eval`	`exec`
`exit`	`export`	`newgrp`	`read`
`readonly`	`shift`	`times`	`trap`
`ulimit`	`umask`	`unset`	`wait`

PREFACE

In the first edition of my book *The UNIX Operating System* I included a brief manual describing forty of the most useful UNIX commands. This book is an expansion of that material. It includes more information on more commands, and it has been revised to cover both the System V UNIX system and the Berkeley UNIX system.

Although the UNIX system has been constantly evolving since I wrote the first edition of *The UNIX Operating System*, the command descriptions that I wrote in 1981 accurately describe modern versions of those commands. The UNIX system is changing, but those changes mostly alter what test pilots call the outside of the envelope. The inside of the envelope, the core commands used in the course of everyday work, has changed very little.

Today my intention is the same as it was in 1981. This manual focuses on the basic commands that everyone must master to use the UNIX system effectively. I have chosen to focus on the commands that almost everyone needs. Covering only the core commands makes it easier for a novice to separate the essential from the extraneous; providing many examples makes it easier for intermediate users to discover the common uses of these commands; providing summaries of several key subsystems—vi, awk, sed, the shells, text processing—makes it easier for advanced users to find important information. Moreover, organizing the book topically makes it easier for all users to understand which commands work together to perform standard tasks, such as file management.

The major change in this manual since its 1981 version is that this book contains half a dozen long manual pages that detail major UNIX subsystems. The coverage of awk, sed, the Bourne shell, and the C shell is intended both as an introduction to their features and as a reference. However, the coverage of the ex/vi editor, the -ms and -mm macro packages, and the eqn and tbl text preprocessors is intended primarily as a reference.

Readers unfamiliar with the UNIX system should start by reading the Introduction, which gives a thumbnail sketch of the system and some of the most important UNIX ideas. Those who are new to the UNIX system should also read the introductions to each of the sections in this manual. The introductions explain which commands are covered in each section and which of those are the most important. The Introduction plus a crutch (a friend, a good introductory book, prior experience with computers) should get beginners over the initial hurdle of learning the UNIX system.

The three Appendixes are an important resource for those people who are just starting to use the UNIX system, but are familiar with another computer system. They provide UNIX roadmaps for MS-DOS users, RT-11 users, and VAX/VMS users. Those who are not familiar with the UNIX system but are familiar with one of these systems should read the Introduction and then the appropriate Appendix.

Although this manual may replace the standard manual for a few users, the intention is not to replace but to complement. Of necessity the official UNIX manual is thorough and complete. It describes all commands, the wheat and the chaff, with equal vigor. Some users may need to use the standard manual occasionally or not at all. When there are discrepancies between the usage cited here and the usage in your local manual you should probably assume that your local manual should usually take precedence.

Each manual page in this book follows the format established by the original UNIX system manuals. The first part of a citation is the command's NAME and a one-line description. Next comes a SYNOPSIS that summarizes how to type the command line to invoke the command. The third section of each citation is the DESCRIPTION, which provides most of the detailed information. Wherever possible, the citation ends with an EXAMPLES section to show how things work in practice. Early examples usually demonstrate the normal use of the command; later examples often demonstrate advanced usage. The long citations—awk, sed, ex, vi, sh, csh, -mm, -ms, tbl, and eqn—have a more detailed structure to make them better references.

The syntax of the command SYNOPSES also follows the lead of the original UNIX Programmer's Manual: square brackets surround optional command line arguments, and ellipses (...) follow arguments that may be repeated.

The organization of this book differs slightly from that of traditional UNIX manuals in they way that commands are listed. The standard user's manual lists commands alphabetically, whereas I have organized the commands into seven groups within which the commands are listed alphabetically.

The **General Utility Commands** section covers the basic commands for finding out about the system and for communicating with other UNIX users.

The **File Management Commands** section covers the standard UNIX commands for listing information about files (copying, renaming, deleting) and the commands for creating and removing directories.

The **Text File Commands** section discusses the famous UNIX filters for analyzing and reformatting text files. It also discusses sed, a scripted text file editor, and awk, a simple programming language for text files.

The **Process Management Commands** section covers the commands that help to manage processes (executing programs).

The **UNIX Shells** section covers the two most common UNIX shells: the Bourne shell and the C shell.

The **The Ex/Vi Text Editor** section covers this powerful UNIX editor.

The **Text Processing Commands** section discusses the nroff/troff text formatter and its important collaborators: the -mm and -ms macro packages and the tbl and eqn preprocessors.

My original intent was to simplify the manual pages by presenting only the most important options for each command. It proved to be difficult to omit the obscure options. For example, although I rarely use the cat options, others assure me that they are often useful. Occasionally, I omitted an option that was present only in System V or in Berkeley, but more often I presented every option.

Of course, there are some areas where System V and Berkeley differ. There is only one command, `ps`, that differs so completely that I provide two separate manual pages. There are also several common functions that are provided by separate programs. System V uses the `lp` command for printing; Berkeley uses `lpr`. System V uses `pg` for viewing a file on the terminal's screen; Berkeley uses `more`. And, of course, there are a few commands that exist only on one system or the other: System V is in sole possession of `cut` and `paste`, while Berkeley claims `head` and the C shell. Hybrid UNIX systems, such as Xenix and Ultrix, usually choose which of the `ps`, `stty`, and `lp[r]` subsystems to use, and then provide as many as possible of the commands that are traditionally found on only one of the two systems. The ten manual pages mentioned above all have a DIS-TRIBUTION section that details their availability.

The typography has been designed to provide maximum clarity.

`monospace`	Command or argument names.
italics	Emphasis or user-supplied values.
`'/usa/jim/james'`	Filenames.
`<Ctrl-A>`	Control characters, formed by holding down the *Ctrl* button and striking *A*.
`<CR>`	Carriage Return.
`<NL>`	Newline.
`<BS>`	Backspace.
`<SP>`	Space.
`<ESC>`	The escape character.
`<TAB>`	The tab character.

Most examples are shown as dialogues, with one monospace typeface used for the computer's output and a variant monospace typeface used for the user's input. Dialogues use the Bourne shell interpreter, except where the C shell is explicitly mentioned, or those on the C shell manual page.

In my day-to-day work I use the Berkeley version of the UNIX system. I have tried nonetheless to present a balanced view of both Berkeley and System V. My efforts at assimilating the occasional System V differences were aided by the Santa Cruz Operation's (SCO) donation of a copy of Xenix 2.2 System V for the PC/AT. In particular, the examples on the `ps`, `lp`, and `stty` manual pages were produced using Xenix, and my understanding of `pg`, `ls`, and a few other commands was enhanced by exposure to Xenix. My thanks go to Bruce Steinberg and Bridget Fuller at SCO for making Xenix available.

The original idea for this manual was given to me by Norma Paley after she read an early draft of the first edition of my book on the UNIX system. She thought that a simple command reference guide would be useful to many readers. Many readers have since expressed the same thought. In June of 1986 I discovered that my revision of the UNIX book was getting far too large. With the assistance and encouragement of Maria Taylor, then my editor at John Wiley and Sons, Inc., I liberated this material from the UNIX revision and turned it into a separate book. Now that I see the material standing on its own, it looks like the correct decision. At the time it seemed risky. During the latter part of the work on this book, my editor at John Wiley was Diane Cerra. I gratefully appreciate her help and support.

Because of the density of information in this book, I felt compelled to solicit criticism from a variety of users. I tried to get experienced System V and Berkeley users to pick nits, and I tried to get several people with user training experience to suggest ways to make the UNIX system more approachable for beginners. The final result was that over a dozen people scrutinized the manuscript. My sincere thanks go to the following reviewers: Rick Adams, Bruce Barnett, Scott Berger, David Elliott, Tony Hansen, Andrew Koenig, Phil Margolis, Barbara McGuire, Susan Richter, Roy Smith, and Dan Ts'o. Each has made valuable contributions.

I encourage readers to contact me with any comments on this book. I am especially interested in comments, examples, or suggestions that will help me to prepare the second edition. I can be reached at The Rockefeller University, Neurobiology Laboratory, RU Box 138, 1230 York Avenue, New York, N.Y. 10021, or at my address on the UUCP network, cmcl2!rna!kc. I always appreciate hearing from readers.

KAARE CHRISTIAN

New York, New York
April 1987

Alphabetical List of Commands

The UNIX
Command Reference Guide

INTRODUCTION

The UNIX system is a multiuser, multitasking operating system that runs on a wide variety of computers. Multiuser means that several people may use the system simultaneously, although the UNIX system is widely used on personal computers or workstation computers where only one user at a time is the norm. Multitasking means that several activities may be processed simultaneously. This makes it easy to work on one task interactively, such as text editing, while other jobs, such as mail forwarding or printing, are proceeding unattended.

The UNIX system has many features that you should understand. For example, it has a hierarchical file system, which means files are grouped in directories, directories can have subdirectories, etc. This structure resembles the organizational chart of a big corporation or a person's genealogical tree. The UNIX system has a line-oriented command system that is both a user interface and a programming language. You can enter single commands to perform straightforward tasks, or you can use the command programming language to automate repetitive tasks. The UNIX system comes with over two hundred utility programs, many of which are described in this manual. The traditional UNIX manual is organized alphabetically, but this manual is organized topically to make it easier to find related information.

Logging In and Out

You must log in before you can actually use the UNIX system. The login process identifies you to the system so that it knows who you are, which files you may access, where you should be placed in the filesystem, and perhaps who should be charged for your system usage.

Your first step in logging in is to acquire a fresh login message. On most directly connected terminals you can simply strike <CR>. On dial-ups you may have to strike <CR> several times, or send the system a break to force it to change serial I/O speeds. These issues vary from system to system, and you should get advice from experienced users.

Once you have a login message, you can enter your login name. Your login name is assigned to you when you set up your account. Typically it is your first or last name, your initials, or a nickname. After entering your login name you should hit <CR>.

1

The system will then ask you to enter your password. Your initial password is usually assigned when you set up your account. Good passwords are at least six characters long and memorable to you. Your password should not be something found in a dictionary or something obvious like a proper name, a birthdate, an address, or a ZIP code. While you are entering your password, the UNIX system will not echo it to the screen. This simple security precaution is unnerving, so type carefully. Strike <CR> when your password has been completely entered. You can change your password using the `passwd` command.

Once your password has been accepted, the UNIX system will print any message of the day and then eventually print your prompt. The prompt means that the UNIX system is ready to perform your chores. The standard UNIX prompt is a $ (the Bourne shell), although a % (the C shell) is also common.

At the conclusion of your session you should log out. Logging out is a courtesy to other users, and if you are using a dial-up line it also frees the line for others. Of course on systems that charge for usage logging out is essential to prevent others from spending your money. There are several ways to log out. One way is to use the `exit` command, which is built into most shells. You can also log out by striking <Ctrl-D> at the beginning of a line. Once you have logged out, a new login message will be printed on most directly connected terminals, or the carrier will be dropped on most dial-up connections. (From a dial-up simply hanging up the phone will usually log you off.)

Executing Programs

You can run a program by typing its name and then striking the <CR> key. (The *Keyboard Conventions* section describes how to fix typos while you are typing.) Each command is usually entered on a separate line. The first word of a command is always the *name*, and subsequent words are called *arguments*. Some arguments are called *options*. They often elicit variant behavior of a command. For example, the `ls` command will list your files. If you want to know the size, date, etc., for your files, you use the `-l` (hyphen, ell) option to tell `ls` to produce a long format list. Most UNIX system options consist of a single character preceded by a hyphen. Some commands require that each option be a separate word, but most (like `ls`) allow multiple options to follow a single hyphen. For example, the command `ls -lt` asks `ls` to produce a long format list of files (the *ell*) sorted by time of modification (the *tee*).

Many commands let you enter filenames after the options. Filenames can be simple names of files in the current directory. They may also be pathnames. (Pathnames are described below.) You can enter filenames exactly (remember that the UNIX system is case sensitive: a file named 'John' is not the same as a file named 'john') or you can use simple matching characters. For example, the filename 'jo*' will be replaced by an alphabetized list of all the filenames that start with the letters *jo* because the * matches anything. The rules for matching filenames are described in the *Shell* section below and in the *Argument List Generation* section of the `sh` or `csh` manual page.

Pathnames

A UNIX pathname is a path through the filesystem. There are two types of pathnames: *relative* pathnames, which start in the current directory, and *absolute* pathnames, which start in the root directory. Absolute pathnames are easy to spot because they always start with a / (slash) character. A simple pathname is just the name of a file in the current directory. Longer pathnames list a sequence of directories that lead to a file. The initial elements of a pathname (if present) are always directories, while the final element may be an ordinary file or a directory. Each element in the sequence is separated from the next by a /, and there are no spaces in a pathname. By convention, the directory name . (dot) always refers to the current directory, and the name .. (dot dot) refers to the parent directory.

An example of an absolute pathname is '/usr/janet/letters', which leads from the root directory to the 'usr' subdirectory, to the 'janet' subdirectory, and then finally to the 'letters' file. An example of a relative pathname is 'boots/docs/chqtr.s', which leads from the current directory to the 'boots' subdirectory, to the 'docs' subdirectory, and then finally to the 'chqtr.s' file. You often use the name .. for ascending paths through the filesystem. For example, the pathname '../resrch/lab2' leads from the current directory to its parent directory, and from there to the 'resrch' subdirectory, and finally to the 'lab2' file.

UNIX filenames may be up to fourteen characters long on System V or 255 characters long on Berkeley systems. In the UNIX system many files are named using a basename, which is descriptive, and an extension, which conventionally indicates the type of the file. The basename and the extension are usually joined by a period. For example, C language programs are named using a '.c' extension. The file 'primes.c' is probably a C language program that relates to prime numbers. The tradition of splitting filenames into two parts, a base and an extension, comes from older operating systems. The UNIX system doesn't force you to separate a filename into two parts, although various application programs (such as the C compiler) may impose file naming conventions.

The two most important commands for using the filesystem are cd, which lets you move from one directory to another, and pwd, which lets you print the name of the current directory on the terminal. These and other basic commands are discussed in the *General Utility Commands* section of this manual.

The Shell

The mediator between you and the UNIX system is called the shell. It is a program that reads commands from your terminal and then carries out the actions that you have specified. For example, if you type in the command who to find out who is using the system, it is the shell that reads the letters that you typed, finds out where the who program is located, issues a request to the system to run that program, waits for who to complete, and then prints another prompt to indicate that it is ready for more input.

Since the shell is an ordinary program, you can decide which shell you want to use. Today the two most often used shells are the Bourne shell, which is commonly used on System V; and the C shell, which is widely used on Berkeley systems. There are also more specialized shells, menu shells, etc.

One of the most useful facilities provided by the shell is I/O redirection. Most commands that produce output or read input are attached, by default, to the terminal. For example, the who command normally displays the list of users on the terminal.

```
$ who
kc        tty01    Mar 28 12:00
jane      ttyh7    Mar 28 10:08
james     ttyh2    Mar 27  9:78
$ _
```

I/O redirection lets you route input and output to files instead of to the terminal. For example, the command who > userlist will run the who command and route its output into the 'userlist' file instead of to the terminal.

```
$ who > userlist
$ _
```

Similarly, the shell recognizes the < character as a directive to perform input redirection. For example, the command wc < userlist runs the wc (word count) program with its input attached to the 'userlist' file. This lets wc display a tally of the number of people using the system when the who program created the 'userlist' file.

```
$ wc -l < userlist
        3
$ _
```

The -l (letter *ell*) tells wc to count lines.

A pipe is a specialized form of I/O redirection that connects the output of one process to the input of another. Tying several processes together using pipe connections lets you create sophisticated text manipulation programs. A simple example is who | wc, which pipes the output of who into the input of wc. (The | is the shell's pipe indicator.)

```
$ who | wc -l
        3
$ _
```

Another very important feature of the shell is *filename generation*, which lets you use a simple text-matching language to describe lists of files. For example, if you name the chapters of a book 'chap1.t', 'chap2.t', and so on, you can tell wc to count the words in all of the chapters of your book with the simple command wc chap*. Of course, you could also type each name individually, but the * character, which matches any text in a filename, is easier on your fingers. Another important filename generation character is **?**, which matches any single character. For example, the command **wc ?c?** tells **wc** to count the words in any file whose name has three letters, and a *c* in the middle.

(More information on using the shell can be found in the *UNIX Shells* part of this manual. If you use the C shell, consult the **csh** manual page; if you use the Bourne shell, consult the Bourne shell manual page.)

File Management

In the UNIX system individual users are responsible for managing their own files. Directories should be created so that files are organized. Out of date files should be removed. Occasionally files need to be renamed, moved from one place to another, or copied.

One of the most important parts of file management is creating directories so that related files can be stored together. You can create a directory with the **mkdir** command. When a directory is no longer in use, it can be removed with **rmdir**.

Most file management is accomplished with the **mv**, **cp**, and **rm** command trio. **mv** moves a file from one place to another, **cp** makes a copy of a file, and **rm** removes files. Although **rm** is the official tool for removing files, both **mv** and **cp** let you copy a file over another, thereby erasing the second file. Be careful with this shortcut, however, because it is difficult to recover an accidentally erased file.

The key to learning about your files is **ls**. It lets you simply list the names of the files in your directory, or print a list that includes of file sizes, dates, and ownership. **ls** has many options, but only a few of them are necessary for competent file management.

These and other file management tools are discussed in the *File Management Commands* section of this manual.

Keyboard Conventions

There are several keystrokes that perform special functions that are useful to you while typing. The **<CR>** is probably the first special keystroke that most users learn. While you are entering command lines, the **<CR>** completes the line. However, interactive applications are free to reassign the meaning of the **<CR>** key; for example, the **vi** text editor makes the **<CR>** a "move to the start of the next line" command.

You can use the *erase* character, which is usually assigned to the # key or to the backspace key, to erase the last character that you typed. To erase a whole line, enter the *kill* character, which is usually assigned to the @ key or to the **<Ctrl-U>** key. Two similar characters are available only on Berkeley systems: the *word erase* character, which is usually assigned to the **<Ctrl-W>** key; and the *redraw line* character, which is usually assigned to the **<Ctrl-R>** key.

   You can stop a program while it is running by typing the *interrupt* character, which is usually assigned either to the <DEL> key or to the <Ctrl-C> key. You can type the *end of file* character, which is usually assigned to the <Ctrl-D> key, to indicate the end of the input to some command that is reading from the keyboard. (Doing this when your login shell is waiting for input will usually log you out, so be careful.)

   You can pause programs that are writing lines of output to the terminal by striking the *stop* character, which is usually assigned to the <Ctrl-S> key. Pausing the program lets you read what is on the screen. Strike <Ctrl-Q> to resume the output. On Berkeley systems voluminous output can be discarded by striking the <Ctrl-O> key. The difference between <Ctrl-S> and <Ctrl-O> is that the former is an aid for slowing down output so that you can read it, while the latter is an aid for discarding unnecessary output so that the program will complete execution sooner.

   The stty program allows you to assign any of these special function characters to a particular key.

SECTION I

GENERAL UTILITY COMMANDS

The general utility commands section of this manual includes just over a dozen general-interest commands used to control and manage your sessions with the UNIX system. This section includes general-interest commands that don't manage files. General-purpose file management commands are in Section II, and commands for text files are in Section III.

The most important of these general-interest commands are probably cd and pwd, the commands for moving from directory to directory, and printing the name of the current directory. The other critical command in this section is passwd, which lets you change your password. (Be careful with your password, because other people's files and your own can be lost if your personal password is compromised.)

Some of the commands in this section let you display useful information. For example, who lets you find out who is using the system, and date prints the date and time. On some systems, the man command is available to print the on-line manual pages.

Other related commands included in this section are for communicating with other users. The UNIX system offers two separate flavors of communication: mail, which sends electronic mail to a person, and write, which displays a message on someone's screen and allows you to interact with them in a typed conversation.

Several of the commands in this section are difficult to use, but very important. For example, the stty command, which lets you control how the system manages your terminal, is often set for you by your system administrator to free you from that responsibility. However, you should know at least a little about stty and how to use it to customize your terminal settings. For this reason, I chose to concentrate on the most important options for most people with the stty command, and I have not included a complete manual page for it.

The od command is not for novices, but it is such a generally useful command that I felt compelled to include it here. It prints an unambiguous representation of any file's contents. Most of the text file commands (Section III) can be fooled by files with unexpected values. od is often used to see what information the file really contains.

CD

NAME

cd — move (change) to a new working directory

SYNOPSIS

cd [directory]

DESCRIPTION

Files in the UNIX system are collected into directories. At any given time, you are in one particular directory, which is called the current directory or the working directory. You can use the cd command to move to another directory. If you don't specify a directory on the command line, cd moves you to your home directory, which is where you are positioned initially when you log in.

EXAMPLES

Print the name of the current directory, move to the '/usr/bin' directory, and then print the name of the current directory:

```
$ pwd
 /usa/kc
$ cd /usr/bin
$ pwd
 /usr/bin
$ _
```

Print the name of the current directory, move to the parent directory of the current directory, and then print the name of the current directory:

```
$ pwd
 /usr/bin
$ cd ..
$ pwd
 /usr
$ _
```

Return to your home directory:

```
$ pwd
 /usr
$ cd
$ pwd
 /usa/kc
$ _
```

The C shell and the Korn shell contain a feature called tilde substitution, which replaces a tilde followed by a username with the path of that user's directory. This feature is often used with cd. (The example below uses the C shell.)

```
% cd ~owen
% pwd
/usr1/owen
% cd ~gilbert
% pwd
/usr1/gilbert
% _
```

NOTES

Newer versions of the Bourne shell contain a variable called $CDPATH that provides a list of directories for cd to search. See the sh manual page for more information.

You cannot move to a directory that denies you execute permission. See the chmod manual page for a fuller discussion of directory access rights.

cd is built into the shell. Shell scripts that contain cd commands will change the directory in which the script executes, but this change does not affect the location of your interactive shell. At the conclusion of the script, your interactive shell will still be where it was before the shell script was executed.

DATE

NAME

date — print the date and time

SYNOPSIS

date

DESCRIPTION

The date command is used to display the date and time.

EXAMPLES

Display the date:

```
$ date
Sun Apr 20  17:52:20 EST 1986
$ _
```

NOTE

System V date lets you control the output format.

GENERAL
UTILITIES

ECHO

NAME

echo — repeat command line arguments

SYNOPSIS

echo [arguments]

DESCRIPTION

The echo command copies the words on the command line to the standard output. echo is used for several purposes including printing messages in shell command files, inserting small amounts of known data into a pipe or file, displaying the values of shell variables, and finding out what the shell is doing with command line arguments. Although echo's serious use is mostly in shell command scripts, it is also extremely useful for exploring the command line entry facilities of the UNIX system.

The Berkeley version of echo accepts the -n command line option, which makes echo refrain from printing a newline at the end of its output. This option is useful when you are prompting for input or using several echo commands to construct a single output line.

The System V version of echo understands control codes embedded in the words. These control codes are similar to C language conventions for representing tabs, newlines, etc. Beware that the backslashes must be quoted so that they are actually delivered to echo.

\b	Backspace	\c	Omit trailing newline
\f	Form Feed	\n	Newline
\r	Carriage Return	\t	Tab
\v	Vertical Tab	\\	Backslash
\0n	3 Digit Octal ASCII Code		

EXAMPLES

Print the message "Hello" on the terminal:

```
$ echo Hello
Hello
$ _
```

Place the message ''Processing complete'' in the file 'pmessage':

```
$ echo Processing complete > pmessage
$ cat pmessage
Processing complete
$ _
```

Display the value of the shell variable $PATH:

```
$ echo $PATH
/bin:/usr/bin:/usr/local/bin:
$ _
```

echo can list files:

```
$ ls
EXAMPLE.pro   del        mailos2     prime2
append        mailos     prime       ruleout
$ echo *
EXAMPLE.pro append del mailos mailos2 prime prime2 ruleout
$ _
```

echo is often used to see what arguments are actually passed to a command. In the following example, the expr command is used to compute a value. When expr returns an error, the same expression is given to echo to help diagnose the problem.

```
$ expr \( 5 + 7 \) * 3
syntax error
$ echo \( 5 + 7 \) * 3
( 5 + 7 ) gem1 gem2 gem3 3
$ ls
gem1 gem2 gem3
$ echo \( 5 + 7 \) \* 3
( 5 + 7 ) * 3
$ expr \( 5 + 7 \) \* 3
36
$ _
```

echo's output reveals the problem with expr's expression — the asterisk (expr's multiply symbol) is expanded into a list of the files in the current directory because of the shell's filename generation process. The asterisk in the expression must be escaped to remove its special meaning.

Produce several columns of figures using the System V control codes:

```
$ echo ´10\t20\t30\n40\t50\t60´
10       20       30
40       50       60
$ _
```

When you are writing scripts that ask questions and read in answers, you often want to omit echo's customary trailing newline. This works differently on System V and Berkeley.

Berkeley:

```
$ echo -n "How many pigs in a pot? " ; read n
How many pigs in a pot? 5
$ echo $n pigs
5 pigs
$ _
```

System V:

```
$ echo ´How many minutes till shutdown? \c´ ; read ans
How many minutes till shutdown? 5
$ echo $ans minutes
5 minutes
$ _
```

MAIL

NAME

mail — send electronic mail or read your own mail

SYNOPSIS

mail username ...
mail [-ehrpq] [-f mailfile] [-F usernames]

DESCRIPTION

There are two common interfaces to the UNIX mail system. The one described in
this manual page is the standard System V mail program. However, the Berkeley
mail program is available starting with Release 2 of System V under the name
mailx. The Berkeley interface is much richer, and, consequently, harder to master. This (System V) version of mail may be best for casual users; the Berkeley
version is clearly superior if you use mail often enough to justify the effort of
learning the Berkeley options.

When usernames are mentioned as arguments to mail, then messages are sent to
the named users (as in the first command in the above SYNOPSIS). In all other
cases, the mail command is used to read your own mail.

Let's first discuss sending mail to other users. mail acquires the message from
the standard input. You may either prepare the message in advance using a text
editor and use the input redirection capabilities of the shell to make mail read the
message from a file, or you can type the message interactively and then strike
<Ctrl-D> (EOF) at the beginning of a line (or a period alone on a line) to termi-
nate the message. If the named users cannot be located (i.e., you probably mis-
typed the username), then the message is saved in the file 'dead.letter' to allow
you to determine the correct username and retransmit the message.

The mail command works differently when you use it to read your mail. When
you log in, the shell informs you of the presence of mail by printing the message,
"You have mail". System V mail accepts the following command line options to
help you read your mail:

-e   mail will simply check for the presence or absence of mail, exiting with 0
      if mail is present or with 1 if mail is not present. This option is useful
      when mail is used in a shell script, such as your '.profile' login script.

-h   mail will print the message headers at the beginning of the session.

-f *filename*
> This option specifies that the named file is the source of the mail; ordinarily the file is your mailbox.

-p Print all of the messages without pausing. Ordinarily, the messages are printed one at a time, and you are prompted between messages for a disposition command.

-q Ordinarily, an interrupt merely causes `mail` to stop printing the current message and wait for your next command. However, when the **-q** option is used, `mail` will terminate when an interrupt is received.

-r Print in reverse order, with the oldest messages first; ordinarily, the newest messages are printed first.

-F *usernames*
> This option causes all subsequent mail sent to you to be forwarded to *usernames*. You may only exercise this command when your mailbox is empty. You must quote *usernames* if there is more than one, and you can stop forwarding by using the command

```
$ mail -F ""
$ _
```

> This option is available starting in Release 3 of System V. In earlier versions of System V, you must manually edit '/usr/mail/$LOGNAME' and insert the line "Forward to ..." to forward your mail. On most Berkeley systems you can put a forwarding address in the file '.forward' in your home directory, or you can have your system administrator place an alias in the file '/usr/lib/aliases' (and then run `newalias`).

`mail` ordinarily stops after printing each message and waits for you to enter a disposition command, followed by a carriage return. The following disposition commands are recognized:

<CR> or **+**
> Print the next message.

d   Delete the message.

m *usernames*
> Forward (mail) the message to the named users.

r [*users*]
> Send a reply to the originator of the message and to any named *users*, then delete the message.

p   Print message again.

s [file]
: Save message in the named file ('mbox' is used by default). A header will be placed in front of the message to identify the message.

w [file]
: Save the message, with the header omitted, in the named file.

-
: Go back to previous message.

x
: Exit from `mail` without modifying your mailbox. All of the current messages, plus all new mail, will be available the next time you use `mail`.

<Ctrl-D> or q
: Place undeleted mail back in mailbox and exit.

?
: Print a help message. (Some versions use the asterisk in place of the question mark to produce a help message.)

You can usually read your mail without using any of the command line options and only using the <CR>, d, and s dispositions.

EXAMPLES

Send Tom, Dick and Barry the message in 'msgfile':

```
$ mail tom dick barry < msgfile
$ _
```

Round up some friends for lunch:

```
$ mail samantha jms smitty ralph esr
Hey!
Tomorrow at noon the troops (led by me)
are assembling in front of Smith Hall for
a foray to Ye Goode Olde Tyme Shoppe for
sandwiches and ice cream.
        wwb
^D
$ _
```

Read your own mail:

```
$ mail
From cv Tue Nov 25 22:41:29 1986
Received: by rnc.UUCP (4.12/4.7)
        id AA00519; Tue, 25 Nov 86 22:40:18 est
Date: Tue, 25 Nov 86 22:40:18 est
From: cv (NYC_Vision_People)
Message-Id: <8611260340.AA00519@rnc.UUCP>
Apparently-To: kc


NYC Computer vision meeting Weds.
Lester Raskin from R+R will talk
about recent work in surface recognition.
        NYC vision people


? s cvtalk
From jj Tue Nov 25 22:39:58 1986
Received: by rnc.UUCP (4.12/4.7)
        id AA00511; Tue, 25 Nov 86 22:39:23 est
Date: Tue, 25 Nov 86 22:39:23 est
From: jj (James Jones)
Message-Id: <8611260339.AA00511@rnc.UUCP>
Apparently-To: kc


Torsten is giving a talk tomorrow
at noon in the conference room.
Remind Sam about refreshments.
jj


? d
? q
$ tail -4 cvtalk
NYC Computer vision meeting Weds.
Lester Raskin from R+R will talk
about recent work in surface recognition.
        NYC vision people
$ _
```

MAN

NAME

man — print entries from the on-line manual

SYNOPSIS

man [-t] [section] title

DESCRIPTION

The man command is used to locate and print citations from the UNIX system manual. It is used primarily by users to produce manual sections on the screen when a printed manual is unavailable. A regular printed manual is more convenient but less up-to-date than repeated use of the man command.

The *section* argument specifies which section in the manual to search for the entry. Manual entries describing the commands that most people typically use are in section one. If the section argument is omitted, then all eight sections of the manual are searched, starting in section one. The *title* is the name of the command that you want to see. For example, the command man cat will display the manual page for the cat command.

The -t option produces output using the troff formatter. It will only work on systems where man has been specially installed.

The Berkeley version of man understands the -k *keywords* option, which directs it to print the names of citations that contain the given keywords in the title. Berkeley man also contains the -f *filename* option, which directs man to print the names of commands that reference the given file.

EXAMPLES

```
$ man yes
YES(1)        UNIX Programmer's Manual        YES(1)

NAME
     yes - be repetitively affirmative

SYNOPSIS
     yes [ expletive ]

DESCRIPTION
     Yes repeatedly outputs "y", or if expletive
     is given, that is output repeatedly.
```

```
                    Termination is by rubout.

        Printed 2/5/84    18 January 1983            1
        $ man -k macros
        man (7)        - macros to typeset manual
        me (7)         - macros for formatting papers
        ms (7)         - text formatting macros
        trman (1)      - translate version 6 manual
                         macros to version 7 macros
        $ man -f /dev/tty
        tty (1)        - get terminal name
        tty (4)        - general terminal interface
        $ _
```

NOTES

A few user commands, such as kill, have the same name as a system call or sub-routine. Use the section argument to tell man which citation to print. Since commands are in section one of the manual, the command man 2 kill will print the citation for the kill system call (Section 2), not the kill command (Section 1).

man's availability varies widely. It was originally offered as part of System V, but it is not available in the latest releases of System V. It is available as part of the BSD 4.1, 4.2, and 4.3, but it is not available in all systems that claim to be based on BSD. man is commonly omitted from UNIX systems designed to run on personal computers because of its large disk storage requirements.

OD

NAME

od — print a binary file

SYNOPSIS

od [format] [file] [offset]

DESCRIPTION

The od (octal dump) program is used to display the values in the named file (or the standard input if no file is specified). Although od is primarily used by programmers, it also is generally useful for finding out exactly what values a file contains. For example, you might want to see if tabs or spaces are used in a given file, or you might want to see what codes are stored in a directory file.

The command cat -v overlaps the command od -c. The cat -v command lets you examine files that are mostly text, but have some control codes; od has more flexibility and is much better for binary files.

The format argument allows you to control whether the file is dumped in octal words (the default), octal bytes, ASCII bytes, hexadecimal words, or decimal words. The file is normally dumped starting at the beginning unless an offset is supplied.

The following format control arguments are recognized on System V, Berkeley, and Version 7 systems:

-b   Interpret bytes in octal.

-c   Interpret bytes in ASCII.

-d   Interpret words in decimal.

-o   Interpret words in octal.

-x   Interpret words in hexadecimal.

Berkeley systems have several additional format options:

-f   Interpret long words in floating point.

-h   Interpret words in unsigned hexadecimal.

-i   Interpret words in signed decimal.

-l   Interpret long words in signed decimal.

When bytes are interpreted in ASCII, the following escapes are used to represent certain common nongraphic characters:

\0	null	\b	backspace	\f	formfeed
\n	newline	\r	carriage return	\t	tab

During ASCII interpretation, bytes that are nongraphic and not listed in the above table are represented using three-digit octal numbers.

An output line consisting of an asterisk means that the data on the preceding line is repeated. This condenses the output.

The offset is used to control the distance from the beginning of the file to where the dumping starts. If no file is mentioned, the offset must start with a plus sign. Otherwise, the offset can start with an ordinary number. The offset is interpreted as an octal number of bytes unless a period is attached to the end. Thus, the offset 10 is interpreted as decimal 8 bytes, but the offset 10. is interpreted as decimal 10 bytes. If the offset is suffixed with a b, then the number is taken to mean blocks of 512 bytes; otherwise, the offset is in bytes. Thus, the offset 20 is interpreted as decimal 16 bytes, but the offset 20b is interpreted as decimal 16 blocks (8192 bytes).

EXAMPLES

Dump the '/etc/motd' file in character format:

```
$ cat /etc/motd
4.2 BSD UNIX #63: Tue Apr 15 13:31:03 EST 1986
Today...
        Sir Francis Bacon born, 1561
$ od -c /etc/motd
00000   4   .   2       B   S   D       U   N   I   X       #   6   3
00020   :       T   u   e       A   p   r       1   5       1   3   :
00040   3   1   :   0   3       E   S   T       1   9   8   6  \n   T
00060   o   d   a   y   .   .   .  \n      \t   S   i   r       F   r
00100   a   n   c   i   s       B   a   c   o   n       b   o   r   n
00120   ,       1   5   6   1  \n
00127
$ _
```

Dump the file 'a.out' in octal word format:

```
$ od a.out
0000000  000413 000000 016000 000000 002000 000000 037500 000000
0000020  000000 000000 000000 000000 000000 000000 000000 000000
*
0002000  007400 036421 057320 140532 055004 150120 054520 054720
0002020  152530 011611 010402 150772 064131 001431 002302 150131
         — The remainder of a.out is dumped —
$ _
```

Dump the file 'a.out' in hexadecimal word format starting at block 10 (in decimal):

```
$ od -x a.out 10.b
0005120  5150 4190 8567 00f1 5256 fff1 567c 6594
0005136  303b ae0b e104 5a05 d57a fcac 7513 53d1
0005152  1204 9012 788f e150 5a06 9004 588f 9050
0005168  7150 02d0 9057 7130 5911 8fca 0090 0000
         — The remainder of a.out is dumped —
$ _
```

Notice that the address in the left column is in decimal because the offset was specified in decimal.

The preceding example could also be done like this:

```
$ od -x a.out 12b
0012000  5150 4190 8567 00f1 5256 fff1 567c 6594
0012020  303b ae0b e104 5a05 d57a fcac 7513 53d1
0012040  1204 9012 788f e150 5a06 9004 588f 9050
0012060  7150 02d0 9057 7130 5911 8fca 0090 0000
         — The remainder of a.out is dumped —
$ _
```

The only difference is that the octal address specifier leads to an octal format address column.

GENERAL UTILITIES

GENERAL
UTILITIES

PASSWD

NAME

passwd — change your login password

SYNOPSIS

passwd [name]

DESCRIPTION

The passwd command is used by ordinary users to change their own login passwords. Super-users can use the command to change the passwords of any user.
When invoked by an ordinary user, the program prompts for the old password to
verify that the person running passwd is the authorized owner of the account.
This check prevents a co-worker from changing your password while you are
away from your terminal. Then the program prompts for the new password, and
it prompts again for the new password to make sure that the password was
entered correctly. Echoing to the screen is suppressed during password entry to
improve security.

The super-user uses passwd to install a password while creating an account or to
install a new password for you if you forget your password. On some systems
the administrator periodically changes user passwords to improve security. An
encoded list of passwords and other information about user accounts is kept in
the file '/etc/passwd'.

EXAMPLES

Change your own login password:

```
$ passwd
Old password:
New password:
Retype new password:
$ _
```

NOTES

Good passwords shouldn't be ordinary words or something obvious like your
birthday, middle name, pet's name, or social security number. Your password
must be longer than a certain minimum, which is usually six characters, and
other restrictions may apply.

Memorable passwords can often be constructed from short phrases or fractured words. For example, "4score + 7", "2bor!2b", "DayOfInfamy" or "AlEyeNStyN". Some people substitute numbers or punctuation into common words, such as "Pa77worD" or "Goe..deL!".

GENERAL
UTILITIES

PWD

NAME

pwd — print the name of the current directory

SYNOPSIS

pwd

DESCRIPTION

The pwd command prints the full pathname of the current directory. The current directory, which is also called the working directory, is your current location in the UNIX filesystem. When you first log onto the UNIX system, you are placed into your home directory. From there you can visit other directories using the cd command, and you can always print the name of the current directory by using the pwd command.

EXAMPLES

Print the name of the current directory, move to the home directory, and then print the name of current directory:

```
$ pwd
/usa/kc/drawings
$ cd
$ pwd
/usa/kc
$ _
```

STTY

NAME

stty — set or display terminal handler options

SYNOPSIS

stty [options]

DESCRIPTION

The stty command is used to control the interface between the computer and your terminal. One reason for the stty command is that there are many different terminals that may need slightly different treatment. Another reason for stty is to allow you to customize certain UNIX system features, such as the assignments for the erase and kill control characters. If no options are specified on the command line, then stty will report the current settings of a few key options.

Although both the Berkeley and the System V stty have the same role, they operate slightly differently and have somewhat different options. The Berkeley stty command displays and controls the settings of the terminal attached to its standard output, while the System V stty command displays and controls the settings of its standard input. This difference is only important when you are using stty to display or control the status of some other terminal. For example, you might go to another terminal and then use stty to restore an ordinary mode to your original terminal.

Another difference is where the output is sent. On Berkeley systems, the printed output of stty appears on the standard error output. If you want to collect the information printed by Berkeley stty, you must redirect the standard error, not the standard output. System V stty prints its information on the standard output.

stty is one of the most machine- and version-dependent utility programs. It is also one of the most diverse utilities. Some options are commonly used by most UNIX users, but most are used only by system programmers or system administrators. Only the major user options are described. Most stty options are not described here. Use your standard manual for more information.

On both systems, you can display a brief summary of the current settings by entering the stty command without options. For more information about the current settings on Berkeley systems, you should enter the command stty all. For a complete report on every detail, enter the command stty everything. On

System V, you can get a full list of the current settings using the -a command line option.

Many people use stty in their '.profile' (or '.login') scripts to specify how they want their terminal managed. For example, if you prefer to use <Ctrl-C> as your interrupt character, you might place the appropriate stty command in your login script. The other common use of stty is for disaster recovery. Occasionally, you run a program that leaves the terminal in an unusable state. One remedy is to log off (possibly by killing your shell from another terminal); another is to repair the damage with stty.

The following are some of the more commonly used stty options. This first batch of options is used to set your preferences, or to let stty properly manage your terminal.

tabs (-tabs)
> Preserve tabs (replace tabs with spaces) on output. The -tabs option is used on terminals that don't know how to expand tabs; the tabs option is used on terminals that understand the dynamics of the tab character.

erase c
kill c
intr c
quit c
stop c
start c
eof c Set the specified control character to c, where c stands for any keyboard character. The default values for these characters on System V, Version 7, and early Berkeley systems are:

erase	#	kill	@	intr	<DEL>
quit	^\	stop	^S	start	^Q
		eof	^D		

Modern Berkeley systems have changed erase, kill, and intr to more modern values:

erase	<DEL>	kill	^U	intr	^C

On most systems only the erase, kill, and intr characters are changed often. A control character can be indicated by preceding the ordinary character with a caret, which must be escaped from the shell. (The erase character deletes the previously entered character, the kill character erases current line of input, the intr character terminates the current program, the quit character terminates the current program and causes a core dump for debugging, the stop character suspends output until the start character is entered, and the `eof` character, when entered at the beginning of a line, indicates the end of the input.)

ek   Set the `erase` character to `#` and the `kill` character to `@`. These aren't optimal values, but this command is an easy way to establish known values for these important control characters.

dec   Set the `erase` to `<DEL>`, the `kill` to `<Ctrl-U>` and the `intr` to `<Ctrl-C>`. (Also set the modes `new`, `crt`, and `decctlq`.) Berkeley only.

Some of the new features of the Berkeley tty handler are controlled by the following options. None of these settings will be usable unless the command `stty new` is entered to switch to the new driver. You can return to the old tty driver with the command `stty old`.

The most important feature of the new driver is that it supports job control. Job control lets you run several jobs at once, suspend the current job with a single keystroke, and determine whether background jobs can write to the terminal.

new   Switch to the new driver.

old   Switch to the old driver.

crt   Set options optimally for a crt terminal. This means that `crtbs` and `ctlecho` will be set, as will `crterase` and `crtkill`, if the baud rate is 1200 or above.

crtbs   Echo backspace or backspace, space, backspace (depending on the setting of the `crterase` option) when the erase character is entered.

-crtbs
        Don't try backspacing when the erase character is entered.

crterase
        Echo backspace, space, backspace when the erase character is entered. This option must be used on terminals that have a nondestructive backspace.

-crterase
        Simply echo a backspace when the erase character is entered.

ctlecho (-ctlecho)
        Echo control characters using the `^C` notation. (Echo control characters as themselves.)

tostop (-tostop)
        Stop (don't stop) background jobs when they attempt to write to the screen.

Berkeley's new tty handler has additional special characters.

susp   Suspend the current job immediately.

dsusp Suspend the current job when this character is encountered in the input.

rprnt Reprint the current input line.

flush Discard output until another flush character is entered, or until the shell prints a fresh prompt.

werase
      Erase the last entered word.

lnext Quote the next character.

The (seldomly changed) defaults for these are the following:

susp	^Z	dsusp	^Y	rprnt	^R
flush	^O	werase	^W	lnext	^V

The following **stty** options are often used for disaster recovery—restoring normal functionality to your terminal handler after it has been left in a sorry state by an application.

sane   Reset all modes to reasonable values. System V only.

raw (-raw)
      Enable (disable) raw input mode. In raw input mode, the system doesn't perform the normal input processing. This means that the erase, kill, interrupt, quit, and eof characters are delivered to running programs instead of being interpreted as usual by the tty handler. All characters are delivered with the parity bit in place. Your terminal handler is not usually in the raw input mode, except when you are running an interactive application that wants to perform all character handling itself.

cooked
      Same as -raw.

cbreak
      Input characters can be read one at a time, as they are typed. The erase and kill characters are ineffective, but interrupt, quit, and eof work as usual. cbreak is a middle-of-the-road option. In cbreak mode, a program can get input as each character is typed, although it becomes the program's responsibility to perform input line editing. The advantage of cbreak mode over raw mode is that in cbreak you can kill the current program by striking the interrupt character or specify end of input by striking the end of file key. Berkeley only.

-cbreak
> Input characters are available only when you strike the newline (or return) at the end of the line. Erase, kill, interrupt, quit, and eof all work normally. This is the normal mode for most UNIX system activities. Berkeley only.

-nl
> Allow either carriage returns or newlines to indicate the end of input lines.

nl
> Allow only newlines to indicate the end of input lines. When nl mode is set, the usual carriage return or enter key on your keyboard will echo as ˆM, and striking that key will not complete a line of input. You can return to -nl mode while the nl mode is set by entering the command <NL>stty -nl<NL>. If your keyboard doesn't have a newline key, strike <Ctrl-J> instead.

echo (-echo)
> Echo (do not echo) each character as it is typed. The -echo mode is used mostly during the entry of passwords and other sensitive information on terminals that always echo locally, or inside applications that want to perform all character processing themselves.

lcase (-lcase)
> Map (do not map) upper-case input to lower-case and map (do not map) lower-case output to upper-case. The lcase mode is used only on terminals that don't have lower-case letters; the mode -lcase is used on most terminals that support both upper- and lower-case.

The terminal usually has the settings -raw, -cbreak, -nl, echo, and -lcase.

EXAMPLES

Print the current settings (Berkeley):

```
$ stty
new tty, speed 9600 baud; -tabs crt
$ stty all
new tty, speed 9600 baud; -tabs
crt
erase kill werase rprnt flush lnext susp    intr quit stop    eof
ˆ?    ˆU   ˆW     ˆR    ˆO    ˆV    ˆZ/ˆY   ˆC   ˆ    ˆS/ˆQ    ˆD
```

```
$ stty everything
new tty, speed 9600 baud
even odd -raw -nl echo -lcase -tandem -tabs -cbreak
crt: (crtbs crterase crtkill ctlecho) -tostop
-tilde -flusho -mdmbuf -litout -nohang
-pendin -decctlq -noflsh
erase kill werase rprnt flush lnext susp    intr quit stop    eof
^?   ^U   ^W     ^R    ^O    ^V   ^Z/^Y   ^C   ^    S/^Q   ^D
$ _
```

Display the stty settings (System V):

```
$ stty
speed 4800 baud; evenp hupcl
brkint -inpck icrnl onlcr cr0 nl0 tab0 bs0 vt0 ff0
echo echoe echok
$ stty -a
speed 4800 baud; line = 0; intr = DEL; quit = ^\;
erase = ^H; kill = ^U; eof = ^D; eol = ^@;
parenb -parodd cs7 -cstopb hupcl cread -clocal -ctsflow -rtsflow
-ignbrk brkint ignpar -parmrk -inpck istrip
-inlcr -igncr icrnl -iuclc
ixon ixany -ixoff
isig icanon -xcase echo echoe echok -echonl -noflsh
opost -olcuc onlcr -ocrnl -onocr -onlret -ofill -ofdel
cr0 nl0 tab0 bs0 vt0 ff0
$ _
```

Set the erase character to <Ctrl-H> and the kill character to <Ctrl-U>:

```
$ stty all
new tty, speed 19200 baud; -tabs
crt
erase kill werase rprnt flush lnext susp    intr quit stop    eof
#    @    ^W     ^R    ^O    ^V   ^Z/^Y   ^C   ^    ^S/^Q   ^D
$ stty erase ^h kill ^u
$ stty all
new tty, speed 19200 baud; -tabs
crt
erase kill werase rprnt flush lnext susp intr quit stop eof
^H   ^U   ^W     ^R    ^O    ^V   ^Z/^Y ^C   ^    ^S/^Q ^D
$ _
```

The key line in the dialogue shown above is in the middle, and it works the same on either System V or Berkeley. The ^h shown means that you should type a caret followed by an *h*. stty interprets this two-character string to mean that you want to use <Ctrl-H> as your erase character. Similarly, the ˆu is a caret followed by *u*. Depending on which shell you are using, you may have to quote the caret with a leading backslash. (The option displays are shown for Berkeley.)

NOTES

Occasionally a program will exit without restoring the terminal's state correctly. When this occurs, one remedy is to log out (if you can), or to go to another terminal and kill your login shell with signal nine.

Both System V and Berkeley offer fairly simple methods that often restore functionality. On Berkeley, you can run the reset program. It will reset most modes to reasonable values, and you can then restore your personal preferences with stty. You may have to enter the command <LF>reset<LF> to get reset to run. On System V, you can use stty's sane option. You may have to enter the command <LF>stty sane<LF>. The sane mode will restore basic functionality, which will allow you to restore your personal preferences.

There is also a more manual solution. If the carriage return won't get you a fresh prompt, then try striking the newline on your terminal to get a prompt (<Ctrl-J> will send a <NL> on terminals that don't have a newline button). In most cases, a newline followed by the word "stty" followed by a newline will make stty display the current settings. First get rid of raw mode or cbreak mode. Try the commands <NL>stty -raw<NL> to end raw mode or <NL>stty -cbreak<NL> to terminate cbreak mode. If the carriage return still doesn't work (but the newline does), then enter the command <NL>stty -nl<NL>. If you aren't getting input echoing, enter the command stty echo<CR>. Use the appropriate stty commands to change the erase and kill characters to your preferences.

GENERAL
UTILITIES

TTY

NAME

tty — print the name of the special file for your terminal

SYNOPSIS

tty [-s]

DESCRIPTION

The tty command tells you which tty port you are using. If the standard input is not a terminal (not a special device file), then the tty command prints a message similar to "not a tty". The -s option makes tty silent so that its exit code can conveniently be used in a shell script.

Knowing which tty port you are using is occasionally important. For example, if you occasionally experience noisy dial-up connections, you can use tty to see if it is always the same communication line.

EXAMPLES

```
$ tty
/dev/ttyh3
$ tty < /dev/null
not a tty
$ if tty -s
> then
>    echo input is a tty
> fi
input is a tty
$ _
```

WHO

NAME

who — list the current users

SYNOPSIS

who

DESCRIPTION

The who command produces a list of all the people who are currently logged onto the system. The list contains the login name, the time of login, and the terminal for each user.

The special command who am i usually produces your login name.

EXAMPLES

List the current users:

```
$ who
gilbert    ttyh1    May 3 15:35
jurgen     ttyh3    May 8 21:17
dan        ttyi9    May 8 13:30
$ _
```

The Berkeley who command also lists the remote hostname for remotely logged-in users.

List your login name:

```
$ who am i
kc
$ _
```

NOTES

Numerous options are available in the System V who. Most are intended for system managers, not ordinary users. Two of the more commonly useful are -u, to show how recently each user has been active, and -T, to show if it is currently possible to write to each user's terminal.

Berkeley's `whoami` command prints who you are, instead of your login name. The distinction occurs when you have assumed a new effective user id using the su command.

```
$ who am i
rna!kc          ttyh4    Mar  9 14:12
$ whoami
kc
$ su
Password:
# who am i
rna!kc          ttyh4    Mar  9 14:12
# whoami
root
# exit
$ _
```

Berkeley's `w` command prints a list of everyone who is logged in, what communication port they are using, when they logged in, the amount of time they have been idle, a summary of cpu usage, and their current activity. It takes `w` much longer to prepare its report than `who`.

WRITE

NAME

write — write to another logged-on user

SYNOPSIS

write username [ttyname]

DESCRIPTION

The write command allows you to initiate (or respond to) a conversation with another logged-in UNIX system user on your system. To initiate a conversation with a person whose username is "tom", you should enter the command

    $ write tom

(Usernames are displayed by the who command and the Berkeley finger command. They can also be found by examining the file '/etc/passwd'.) If Tom is logged on several different terminals, then you can use the command

    $ write tom tty50

to write to Tom using the '/dev/tty50' connection.

Once you have entered the command, a message similar to "Message from ralph on tty30" will appear on Tom's terminal. Tom should drop what he is doing (perhaps use the shell escape from within an editor, mailer, or other interactive program) and enter the command

    $ write ralph

to complete the connection. At this point, anything that Tom or Ralph types appears on both of their terminals. To minimize confusion, only one user should type at a time. Usually the person who initiated the conversation types a message and then types an "o" alone on a line to signify "over." The other party then types a response followed by "o". This is similar to the protocol used in CB radio communication. At the conclusion of a conversation, enter an "oo" alone on a line to signify "over and out" and strike <Ctrl-D> to stop the write program.

A line that starts with a ! will be interpreted as a shell command and passed off to a shell for execution. This lets you interrupt a write session to perform standard UNIX chores.

NOTE

The Berkeley `talk` program is superior to `write`, and is recommended for Berkeley UNIX users.

SECTION II

FILE MANAGEMENT COMMANDS

This part of the manual contains commands that let you manage your collection of files and directories. Commands for viewing and manipulating text files are in Section III. Most files are created by applications programs, such as the vi text editor. However, file removal is usually done with the UNIX system's rm command. Be careful because removed files are really gone.

The UNIX system has two commands for copying and moving files: cp and mv. These commands are powerful, but dangerous. They allow you to move (or copy) one file onto an existing second file, thereby losing the contents of the second file. Although erasure of the second file may be exactly what you want, you should be careful because typos and mental lapses can have serious consequences.

The most important command for finding out about your files is ls. It lets you produce a simple list of the files in your current directory, or you can produce a long format listing that contains much more detail. One of the key items listed in a long format listing is the file's access mode, which details who can perform what accesses to a file. Access modes are explained in the chmod manual page, which also explains the chmod command that you use to control file access modes.

UNIX directories are created and removed using mkdir and rmdir. You should learn to use these commands because organizing your files into directories can make your work much more productive. The cd command (Section I) lets you move from one directory to another, and pwd (Section I) prints the name of the current directory.

The most difficult command in Section II is find, which will search through the filesystem to find a file. find isn't too hard to use if you know the file's name, but the difficulty escalates quickly when you use more sophisticated search criteria.

CHMOD

NAME

chmod — change the access mode of a file

SYNOPSIS

chmod mode file ...

DESCRIPTION

The chmod command lets you control the access privileges for your files. The first part of this manual page is a discussion of the UNIX file access system. The USAGE section of this manual page contains information on using chmod.

There are three ways to access a UNIX file: it can be read, written, or executed. UNIX provides three corresponding access modes for a file so that the owner can specify whether reading, writing, or executing is permitted or denied. To provide even more control over access to a file, UNIX implements a three-tiered access system. One set of read, write, and execute permissions is maintained for the file's owner, a separate set is maintained for members of the owner's group, and a third set is maintained for all other users. This makes it possible to control access to a file so that, for example, the owner can read and write the file, the members of the owner's group can read the file, and others can't have any access to the file. You could even implement the opposite, you could make a file fully accessible to others but inaccessible by the owner.

The execute mode for a file controls whether the contents of the file can be executed. The language compilers, such as the cc C language compiler, automatically set the execute mode when they create an executable file. When you write shell scripts, however, you must use the chmod program to set the execute mode for the file so that it can be executed like any other command.

The read, write, and execute permissions for a directory file differ slightly from the permissions of an ordinary file. For a directory, the read permission specifies whether a program can open the directory to read its contents. If read permission for a directory is denied, you can't use the ls program to read its contents. If you try to use ls to read the contents of a directory in which you don't have read permission, you will get the error message ''*name* unreadable.''

The write permission for a directory controls whether you can create, delete, or rename a file in that directory. If the write permission for a directory is denied, you may still be able to modify existing files in that directory, depending on the access modes of the individual files. In fact, you can even truncate a file to zero length in a directory where you don't have write permission, as long as you do have write permission for the file itself. Thus, you can't rely on write protecting your directories to protect the files in those directories.

The execute permission for a directory controls whether you can search the directory in the course of resolving a filename. This is the strictest limitation on access to a directory that UNIX provides. Denial of execute permission for a directory means you can't cd to that directory and you can't access any files in that directory or any of its subdirectories. You can list the files in a directory where you don't have execute permission, but you cannot find out anything about those files, such as their size or access time.

Programs that create files can control their access mode. However, there is a default access mode that is set using the umask command. You can give your files some degree of privacy by setting the mask to limit other users' read or write access. (See the shell manual page for a description of the umask command.)

USAGE

You specify the mode that you want for your files using the *mode* argument on the chmod command line. It is composed of three parts:

who operator permission

The following tables list the key letters used to construct the symbolic mode:

Who		Operator	
u	user (owner)	-	remove permission
g	group	+	add permission
o	other	=	assign permission
a	all (ugo)		

Permission	
r	read
w	write
x	execute
s	set user (or group) id mode
t	the save text (sticky) mode
u	the user's present permission
g	the group's present permission
o	the other's present permission

For example, the symbolic mode g-x means that you want to deny the execute permission to members of your group, or a=rw means that you want the file(s) to have read and write (but not execute) access to everyone.

On System V, if the *who* part of the mode argument is omitted, then all three permissions will be affected. However, on Berkeley systems, if the *who* part of the mode argument is omitted, the result depends upon the value of the umask. If your mode is a+w, everyone will have write access to the file. If your mode is +w and umask is zero, once again everyone will have write access to the file. But if your mode is +w and your umask is 022 (very common), then only you will have write access; the umask will deny write access to group members and others.

Only the owner of a file or the super-user may change the mode of a file. The set user and group id modes and the save text modes, which are generally used by the system manager or systems programmers, won't be discussed here. Modes may also be specified absolutely by mentioning an octal number in place of the symbolic mode. The absolute form of mode expression is discussed below.

To understand the following examples you must realize that the -l option of the ls command lists the full mode for a file in the leftmost word on the line. The first character is the file type, which is d for a directory and - for an ordinary file, and then the next nine characters specify the access mode. The first three letters specify the read, write, and execute mode for the file's owner, the next three specify the access for the members of the owner's group, and the last three specify access for others. The letters r, w, and x are used when the access is allowed; a - is used when the access is denied.

EXAMPLES

Make the file 'arli' readable to everybody:

```
$ ls -l arli
-rw-------   1   kc   1801  Aug  3 14:01 arli
$ chmod a+r arli
$ ls -l arli
-rw-r--r--   1   kc   1801  Aug  3 14:01 arli
$ _
```

or, because a is the default *who* part of the symbolic mode, equivalently:

```
$ chmod +r arli
$ ls -l arli
-rw-r--r--   1   kc   1801  Aug  3 14:01 arli
$ _
```

Make the group and other permissions for the file 'kari' the same as the owner's current permissions:

```
$ ls -l kari
-rw-------   1   kc   2630  Aug  8  9:05 kari
```

```
$ chmod go=u kari
-rw-rw-rw-  1  kc    2630  Aug  8  9:05 kari
$ _
```

Make the file 'newsysdb' unreadable and unwritable by anyone but the owner:

```
$ ls -l newsysdb
-rw-rw-rw-  1  kc   32041  Jun 17 21:30 newsysdb
$ chmod go-rw newsysdb
$ ls -l newsysdb
-rw-------  1  kc   32041  Jun 17 21:30 newsysdb
$ _
```

Make the file 'ptime' and the file 'qtime' readable and writable by everybody, but not executable by anybody:

```
$ ls -l [pq]time
-rwx--x--x  1  kc   18200  Oct 20 19:01 ptime
-rwxr-xr-x  1  kc   18298  Oct 25  8:15 qtime
$ chmod a=rw ptime qtime
$ ls -l ptime qtime
-rw-rw-rw-  1  kc   18200  Oct 20 19:01 ptime
-rw-rw-rw-  1  kc   18298  Oct 25  8:15 qtime
$ _
```

Make the file 'chbeau.sh' executable:

```
$ ls -l chbeau.sh
-rw-rw-rw-  1  kc     930  Dec 21 11:50 chbeau.sh
$ chmod a+x chbeau.sh
$ ls -l chbeau.sh
-rwxrwxrwx  1  kc     930  Dec 21 11:50 chbeau.sh
$ _
```

Make it impossible for anyone to create files in the current directory:

```
$ ls -ld .
drwxrwxr-x  3  kc    1024  Jan 18 15:30 .
$ chmod a-w .
$ ls -ld .
dr-xr-xr-x  3  kc    1024  Jan 18 15:30 .
$ _
```

The effect of **umask** on Berkeley's version of **chmod**:

```
$ ls -l ch1
-r--r--r--  1 kc              8174 Mar 12 23:28 ch1
$ umask
022
$ chmod +w ch1
$ ls -l ch1
-rw-r--r--  1 kc              8174 Mar 12 23:28 ch1
$ umask 2
$ chmod +w ch1
$ ls -l ch1
-rw-rw-r--  1 kc              8174 Mar 12 23:28 ch1
$ chmod a+w ch1
$ ls -l ch1
-rw-rw-rw-  1 kc              8174 Mar 12 23:28 ch1
$ _
```

OCTAL MODES

I mentioned above that the new mode for a file could be specified in octal, rather than in the symbolic form that was described. Because several other programs and facilities in the UNIX system (e.g., find, umask, mv, cp, ln, rm) use octal modes, they are detailed here.

4000 2000 1000	Set user id, group id, or sticky bit.
0400 0200 0100	Owner read, write, and execute.
0040 0020 0010	Group read, write, and execute.
0004 0002 0001	Other's read, write, and execute.

NOTES

Even though UNIX allows you to control the access modes for your files and directories, you should know that this control has very limited ability to truly protect your files. For example, the access controls described here don't constrain your system's super-user, who can perform any access on any file. These protections also don't protect you against a determined, malicious attacker. There are several ways to thwart this system, such as stealing a backup tape and accessing the files on a foreign system. The control that UNIX does provide is adequate in most friendly environments because it does provide limited protection from nosy co-workers or the mistakes of naive users.

For real security you must go beyond the simple access system described here. For example, you can use the crypt program to encrypt sensitive text files. Although there are ways of defeating the security offered by crypt, it is an order of magnitude more secure than simply setting file access modes to deny access to your files.

CHOWN, CHGRP

NAME

chown — change the ownership of a file
chgrp — change the group affiliation of a file

SYNOPSIS

chown newowner file ...
chgrp newgroup file ...

DESCRIPTION

The chown and chgrp commands are used to change the owner and group affiliation of files. You might need to do this when you are inheriting files from another user, changing your user id number, or transferring files from one system to another.

Usernames are found in the file '/etc/passwd' and group names are cataloged in the file '/etc/group'.

EXAMPLES

Change the ownership of the file 'nycal' to the user named "ralph":

```
$ ls -l nycal
-rw-rw-rw-   1   kc      staff  810  Feb 13 17:01 nycal
$ chown ralph nycal
$ ls -l nycal
-rw-rw-rw-   1   ralph   staff  810  Feb 13 17:01 nycal
$ _
```

Change the group affiliation of all the files whose names start with the letters "ch" to the group named "staff":

```
$ ls -l ch*
-rw-r--r--  1 kc    wheel   13493 Mar 11 23:36 ch1
-rw-r--r--  1 kc    wheel   20033 Mar 11 23:36 ch2
-rw-r--r--  1 kc    wheel   18843 Mar 11 23:36 ch3
-rw-r--r--  1 kc    wheel    9207 Mar 11 23:36 ch4
-rw-r--r--  1 kc    wheel   89043 Mar 11 23:36 ch5
$ chgrp staff ch*
```

```
$ ls -l ch*
-rw-r--r--  1 kc    staff    13493 Mar 11 23:36 ch1
-rw-r--r--  1 kc    staff    20033 Mar 11 23:36 ch2
-rw-r--r--  1 kc    staff    18843 Mar 11 23:36 ch3
-rw-r--r--  1 kc    staff     9207 Mar 11 23:36 ch4
-rw-r--r--  1 kc    staff    89043 Mar 11 23:36 ch5
$ _
```

NOTES

On System V, only the owner of a file or the super-user can change a file's ownership or group affiliation.

On Berkeley UNIX systems, only the super-user can change a file's ownership, and only a file's owner who is also a member of the specified group (or the super-user) can change a file's group affiliation.

FILE
MANAGEMENT

CP

NAME

cp — copy files

SYNOPSIS

```
cp file1 file2
cp file ... directory
```

DESCRIPTION

In its simplest form, cp makes a copy of 'file1' using the name 'file2'; 'file1' is not affected by the copy operation. If 'file2' already exists, it will be overwritten although its mode and ownership will be unchanged; otherwise its mode and ownership will be copied from 'file1'.

In the second form shown in the SYNOPSIS, cp copies the file or files into the named directory, which must already exist, while maintaining their original file names. Any existing file with the same name as the cp destination will be overwritten, if allowed by the file access permissions.

It is very important to understand the distinction made in the preceding two paragraphs. When the rightmost argument of cp names a directory, the file(s) are copied into that directory. Otherwise there should be just two arguments, and cp will copy 'file1' into 'file2'. In both cases the original files are not altered.

The Berkeley version of cp allows two options: -i, which prompts you for permission to proceed whenever cp will overwrite an existing file; and -r, which will copy entire subtrees whenever one of the source files is a directory. Copying subtrees with Berkeley cp is very useful; the same operation can be achieved on System V using tar or cpio, but both tar and cpio are overkill for simple subtree copying.

EXAMPLES

Make a copy of the file 'nuk.abm' in the file 'nk.2':

```
$ ls nuk.abm nk.2
nk.2: not found
nuk.abm
$ cp nuk.abm nk.2
$ ls nuk.abm nk.2
nk.2 nuk.abm
$ _
```

Copy all of the files in the 'disarm' subdirectory into the subdirectory 'newlit':

```
$ cp disarm/* newlit
$ _
```

Copy all of the files with the suffix '.doc' in the current directory into the 'disarm' subdirectory:

```
$ cp *.doc disarm
$ _
```

Copy a distant file into the current directory:

```
$ cp /tmp/kermit .
$ ls -l kermit
-rwxr-xr-x  1 kc        91136 Mar 12 00:01 kermit
$ _
```

Create an empty file:

```
$ cp /dev/null newandempty
$ ls -l newand*
-rw-r--r--  1 kc            0 Mar 25 00:15 newandempty
$ _
```

When the destination file exists, its ownership and mode are preserved:

```
$ ls -l ch1*
-rw-r--r--  1 kc        81043 Mar 11 23:36 ch1
-rw-rw-rw-  1 kc         8905 Mar 10 11:57 ch1.bak
$ cp ch1 ch1.bak
$ ls -l ch1*
-rw-r--r--  1 kc        81043 Mar 11 23:36 ch1
-rw-rw-rw-  1 kc        81043 Mar 11 23:49 ch1.bak
$ _
```

When the destination file doesn't exist, its ownership and mode are taken from the source file:

```
$ ls -l ch2*
-rw-r--r--  1 kc        3203 Mar 10 21:26 ch2
$ cp ch2 ch2.bak
$ ls -l ch2*
-rw-r--r--  1 kc        3203 Mar 10 21:26 ch2
-rw-r--r--  1 kc        3203 Mar 11 23:49 ch2.bak
$ _
```

NOTES

cp is one of the most common ways to unintentionally write over a file. If the destination file exists, it will be overwritten. Make sure that your destination file isn't an existing, valuable file.

On Berkeley systems, people sometimes create an alias for cp that automatically engages its −i option.

FILE

NAME

file — guess the type of files

SYNOPSIS

file filename ...

DESCRIPTION

The file command attempts to determine the file type of the named files. For directory files and special files the file command is unnervingly accurate; for other types of files, the file command resorts to educated guessing. For ordinary files that appear to contain ASCII text, the file command attempts to determine the language; the results often are accurate. For ordinary files that contain binary information, the file command attempts to determine if the file is an object file, an ar library, a cpio image file, or any other file. Files that don't fit any of these categories are usually classified as "data".

EXAMPLES

Determine the file types of all of the files in the current directory:

```
$ file *
a.out: executable not stripped
gem.c: c program text
gem.t: nroff/troff input text
$ _
```

NOTE

file's heuristics for recognizing files vary widely, and the System V file has programmable heuristics.

FIND

NAME

find — search for files in a subtree

SYNOPSIS

find pathname ... condition ...

DESCRIPTION

The find command searches the file system subtrees specified by the command line pathnames for files that meet the specified conditions. (A *subtree* is a region of the filesystem that contains all the files in a given directory, all the files in its subdirectories, and so forth.) At least one pathname (often '.' meaning the current directory) and one condition must be specified.

To be complete, I have listed all of the conditions that find knows how to evaluate. However, in my day-to-day usage I use the -name condition about ten times more than the others combined. The rightmost element of the condition is usually -print to display the filename, or occasionally -exec (or -ok) to execute a UNIX command for each found file.

The condition is specified by mentioning one or more of the following:

-atime n
> Find files that were last accessed exactly *n* days ago. *-n* means files accessed within the past *n* days, and *+n* means files that were last accessed more than *n* days ago. The option -atime n is rarely used; use -atime -n to find files accessed recently and -atime +n to find old files.

-exec cmd
> Execute *cmd* when the preceding condition is true. The end of the command is indicated with an escaped semicolon. Within the command, the argument "{}" is replaced by the current pathname. Note that the "{}" must be a separate argument, even though it is tempting to assume otherwise.

-group groupname
> Find files with the specified group affiliation.

-links n
> Find files with *n* links. *-n* means find files with less than n links and *+n* means find files with more than *n* links.

-mtime n
Find files that were last modified exactly *n* days ago. *-n* means files modified within the past *n* days and *+n* means files that were last modified more than *n* days ago. The **-mtime** n option is rarely used; +n and -n are much more useful.

-name filename
Find files with the given *filename*, which may contain escaped shell meta-characters. The difference between the command

```
$ ls *.[cf]
```

and the command

```
$ find . -name "*.[cf]" -print
```

is that the ls command looks only in the current directory, whereas the find command searches the current subtree. Both commands will list any file whose name ends in *.c* or *.f*.

-newer file
Find files that are newer than the named file.

-ok cmd
Same as **exec** except that *cmd* is printed preceded by a question mark and you are given the chance to approve by replying yes or no.

-print
The pathname of the current file is printed.

-size n
Find files that consume exactly *n* blocks. *-n* means files that consume less than *n* blocks, and *+n* means files that are larger than *n* blocks.

-type c
Find files of a specified type: f for an ordinary file, d for a directory, c for a character special file, b for a block special file, p for a fifo (System V only), l for a symbolic link (Berkeley only).

-perm n
Find files that have a specified permission. *n* is the permission, specified in octal as detailed on the chmod manual page. If *n* has a hyphen prefix, then only the bits that are set in *n* must also be set in the file's permissions. Without the leading hyphen the permission *n* must exactly match the file's permission.

-inum n
Find files with the specified i-node number.

-user username
> Find files owned by *username*.

System V has several useful additional conditions:

-cpio *device*
> Copy the matched files to the named *device* in cpio format.

-depth
> find will do a depth first search, descending subdirectories as early as possible. This option is often used in conjunction with cpio archives to allow restoration of files in write protected directories. Only available on newer version of System V.

-mount
> Always true. Restricts find to a single filesystem.

-local
> Returns true if the file resides on the local system (is not on a remote system).

If you specify a string of conditions, each must be met. For example, the command

```
$ find . -size +10 -type f -mtime +100 -print
```

will find files that are larger than ten blocks, ordinary, and that have not been modified in the last 100 days. You can also use logical operators (and, or, and not) to combine the primitive conditions, and conditions may be grouped by surrounding them in escaped parentheses.

-a Logical *AND* operator. The and operation is implied by placing conditions side by side, but it may also be specified explicitly. The following is equivalent to the command shown immediately above:

```
$ find . -size +10 -a -type f -a -mtime +100 -a -print
```

-o Logical *OR* operator. Two ored conditions are usually enclosed in parentheses to achieve the effect *(A OR B) AND C* instead of *A OR (B AND C)*, especially when *C* is -print. See the -o example below.

! Logical *NOT* operator. csh users must escape the exclamation point because it is a csh metacharacter. The following command will print the names of all files in the current subtree that aren't ordinary files.

```
$ find . ! -type f -print
.
./junk
./junk/sysdir
./Letters
$ _
```

Combining a complicated set of conditions in a find command is more akin to writing a program than entering a command. Casual users (if there are any) might try using just one condition at a time followed by -print to print the names of the found files or -exec (or -ok) to perform some simple task when the files are found. Searching the entire file system is very time consuming on large systems, so limit your searches to as small a subtree as possible.

EXAMPLES

Print a list of all of the files in the current subtree:

```
$ find . -print
.
./.exrc
./docs
./text
./xold/docs
./xold/text
$ _
```

The effect of the option -print can be simulated slowly using the echo command:

```
$ find . -exec echo {} \;
.
./.exrc
./docs
./text
./xold/docs
./xold/text
$ _
```

Note the requirement that the curly braces must be an argument, without any attached text. The following example doesn't work as you might want.

```
$ find . -exec echo {}: found today \;
{}: found today
{}: found today
{}: found today
{}: found today
{}: found today
{}: found today
$ _
```

The obvious intent of the command is to list found files, but the result is otherwise because the colon is attached to the braces.

Find all the files in George's subtree that aren't owned by George:

```
$ find /usa/george ! -user george -print
/usa/george/mail/core
$ _
```

The following example demonstrates the importance of enclosing most ored (-o) conditions within parentheses. With the parentheses, the find command prints all files in the current subtree owned by Dan or Owen. Without the parentheses, only those owned by Owen are listed.

```
$ find . -user dan -o -user owen -print
./.gotcha
$ find . \( -user dan -o -user owen \) -print
./.gotcha
./.fooledya
$ ls -l .gotcha .fooledya
-rw-r--r--  1 dan      3471 Mar 13 23:54 .fooledya
-rw-r--r--  1 owen       91 Mar 13 23:54 .gotcha
$ _
```

Find all of the files in the file system that are more than 350 blocks long and print a long format listing for each:

```
$ find / -size +350 -exec ls -ld {} \;
-rw-r--r--  1  bin   194186 Sep 24 1985 /usr/dict/words
$ _
```

The disadvantage of using the -exec option is that it can be very expensive if many files are found because the command will be executed separately for each file. On System V the same functionality can be attained using the xargs program, which will create an argument list from the standard input and only execute the command once (or a few times if there is a lot of input).

```
$ find / -size +350 -print | xargs ls -ld
-rw-r--r--   1   bin    194186  Sep 24 1985 /usr/dict/words
$ _
```

Find all of the files in the current subtree that haven't been accessed in the last 100 days:

```
$ find . -atime +100 -print
./old/text
./review/ch1
./review/ch2
$ _
```

Find all of the special files in the '/usr' subtree or in the '/usr1' subtree:

```
$ find /usr /usr1 \( -type b -o -type c \) -print
$ _
```

Find all of the files in the current subtree with the ".c" suffix:

```
$ find . -name '*.c' -print
./csrc/gem.c
./csrc/gem1.c
./dbmain/main.c
$ _
```

Find all files in the filesystem that have the set user id mode:

```
$ find / -perm -4000 -exec ls -l {} \;
---s--s--x 1 uucp      11264 Feb 14  1984 /usr/bin/uuname
---s--s--x 2 uucp      15360 Feb 14  1984 /usr/bin/uusend
---s--s--x 1 uucp      26624 Feb 14  1984 /usr/bin/uucp
---s--s--x 1 uucp      26624 Feb 14  1984 /usr/bin/uux
---s--s--x 1 uucp      12288 Feb 14  1984 /usr/bin/uulog
-rws--s--x 2 uucp      46080 Jun  1  1985 /usr/bin/tip
^C
$ _
```

(The permission value of 2000 would find all set group id programs.)

LN

NAME

ln — create a pseudonym for an existing file

SYSTEM V SYNOPSIS

```
ln file1 file2
ln file1 . . . dir
```

BERKELEY SYNOPSIS

```
ln [ -s ] file1 [ file2 ]
ln file1 . . . dir
```

DESCRIPTION

The ln command is used to establish a new name (a pseudonym) for an existing file, while retaining the original name. The technical name for creating a pseudonym is linking, hence the name ln for link. The most common usage is probably ln old new, which makes 'new' a new name for 'old'. You can also create several links at once, if the last argument is a directory. Thus, the command ln ../txt/*.t . will create links in the current directory to all of the files whose names end in '.t' in the '../txt' directory.

Berkeley allows you to omit 'file2', which creates the pseudonym in the current directory with the same name as the last component of 'file1'. (The command ln file1 is not valid if 'file1' is in the current directory. 'file1' must be a pathname specifying a file in another directory.)

When a file is known by two (or more) names, both names have equal weight. Even though there are several names, there is only one copy of the data in the file, one owner, and one access mode.

The easiest way to tell if two names are links to a single file is to look at the i-node number for the file using the -i option of the ls command. Each file in a filesystem has a unique i-node number, so if two names are listed by ls as having the same i-node number, then both names refer to the same file. The long format ls listing displays the number of links in the second column. If you want to find all of the links to a file, you can use the -inum option of the find command.

If files 'a' and 'b' are linked together, you can mention either name when you want to modify the file. For example, editing 'a' is the same as editing 'b'. Some programs, however, such as the programming language compilers, don't modify files; they remove and recreate them. If you remove 'a', and then recreate it, 'a' will no longer be linked to 'b'.

On Berkeley UNIX, the -s option is used to create symbolic links. Unlike ordinary links, symbolic links aren't limited to linking files on a single filesystem. Symbolic links can reference directories, and they aren't disturbed if the original file is deleted and then recreated.

EXAMPLES

Create the pseudonym 'soft_rev' for the file 'techrpt302':

```
$ ls -i tech* soft_rev
soft_rev: not found
15204   techrpt302
$ ln techrpt302 soft_rev
$ ls -i soft_rev tech*
15204   soft_rev       15204   techrpt302
$ _
```

Create the pseudonym 'mkjuice' in the current directory for the file 'mkjuice' in a distant directory:

```
$ ls mkjuice
mkjuice: not found
$ ln ../fruit/tropical/mkjuice
$ ls mkjuice
mkjuice
$ _
```

Berkeley symbolic links:

```
$ mount | grep usr
hp0f on /usr
hp0e on /usr/spool
hp0g on /usr1
$ ln -s /usr/sys sysdir
$ ls -ld sysdir
lrwxr-xr-x  1 kc        8 Mar 13 00:13 sysdir -> /usr/sys
$ ls sysdir
GENERIC    conf     h         misc     netinet   sys      vaxmba
RNA        dist     machine   net      netpup    vax      vaxuba
cassette   floppy   mdec      netimp   stand     vaxif
$ ls /usr/sys
GENERIC    conf     h         misc     netinet   sys      vaxmba
RNA        dist     machine   net      netpup    vax      vaxuba
cassette   floppy   mdec      netimp   stand     vaxif
$ _
```

NOTE

The syntax for ln follows that for mv and cp, with the original file mentioned first on the command line.

LS

NAME

ls — list the contents of directories

SYNOPSIS

ls [-option] [name ...]

DESCRIPTION

The ls command is used to list files. In the simplest case, when the options and filenames are absent, ls alphabetically lists all of the files in the current directory. Files whose names begin with a period usually aren't listed.

The names mentioned on the command line can be either the names of directories or the names of files. For each named file, the requested information is printed if the file exists. If the file doesn't exist, then a brief diagnostic message is printed. However, ls responds differently when you place a directory name on the command line. For each named directory, the requested information is printed for each file in the directory.

Because the default directory for ls to examine is the current directory, the command

```
$ ls
```

is equivalent to the command

```
$ ls .
```

When the current directory doesn't contain any subdirectories, the command

```
$ ls
```

is equivalent to the command

```
$ ls *
```

However, the two commands differ when the current directory contains subdirectories because the second command will detail the contents of each subdirectory. (The * will be expanded by the shell into a list of all of the files, including directories, in the current directory.

The following command line options can be used to alter the usual ls behavior:

-l Produce a long format listing (see the description of the long format listing below).

-C Force multicolumn output for simple lists of files. On Berkeley systems, multicolumn output is the default when the output is to a terminal; and single is the default otherwise. On System V, the default is always single column.

-q Display nonprintable characters in filenames as ?. On Berkeley systems, this is the default when the output is sent to a terminal.

-F Place a character after certain files to highlight their usage: mark directories with a /; executable files with a *; and, on Berkeley systems, mark sockets with =; and symbolic links with @.

-t Sort the list of files according to the file modification times rather than alphabetically. Newest files are listed first.

-a List all files in named directories, including files whose names begin with a period.

-R Recursively list all subdirectories and the files they contain.

-s Print the sizes of the files in blocks. On System V UNIX systems, a block contains 512 bytes; on Berkeley UNIX systems, the size is in kilobytes.

-d For each named directory, list the information for the directory itself rather than listing the information for each file in the directory.

-r Reverse the order of the output.

-i List the i-node number of each file.

-u Use the access time rather than the modification time for sorting or for the long format display.

-c Use the time of last modification of the i-node for sorting or output in the long format display.

-f Interpret each named argument as a directory, and list the contents of each slot.

The following options are specific to the Berkeley version of the UNIX system:

-g Include the group field in a long format listing. The group affiliation is printed by default on System V.

-L For files that are symbolic links, list information about the target file rather than information about the link.

-1 Force single column output for simple lists of files. (Numeral *one*, not letter *ell*.)

The following options are specific to the System V version of the UNIX system:

-g Omit the owner field in a long format listing.

-o Omit the group field in a long format listing.

-m List filenames separated by commas.

-x List files in columns, sorted left to right across columns and then from top to bottom. (The default sort is from top to bottom, and then left to right.)

-b Display nonprinting characters in filenames using the \ddd octal notation.

-p Place a / after each directory name.

On Berkeley systems, the standard long format listing of a file contains six fields (if you consider the date to be a single field). On System V, one additional field, the group ownership, is usually present. On both systems, it is possible to display additional fields using the options mentioned above. The following describes the fields in a long format ls listing in left-to-right order.

File Type and Mode
   The first field is always ten characters long: a one-letter file type followed by three sets of three-character access permissions, one for the file owner, one for members of the owner's group, and one for others. The file type codes are - for an ordinary file; d for a directory; c for a character special file; b for a block special file; p for a fifo (System V only); l for a symbolic link (Berkeley only); and s for a socket (Berkeley only). The three-character permission letters are rwx when read, write, and execute access is permitted; and the corresponding letter is - when the access is denied. (Other permission letters are displayed for files that have been assigned special modes by the system administrator; they are not discussed here.) See the chmod manual page for more information about file access permissions.

Number of Links
   The second field is the number of links to the file.

Owner
   The name of the file's owner.

Group Affiliation
   On System V systems, and on Berkeley systems when the -g option is used, the next field specifies the group affiliation of the file.

Size
   The size in bytes of the file. For character or block special files, the size field will contain the major and minor device numbers.

Time

The time the file was last modified. The -u command line option lets you display the access time instead. The -c command line option lets you display the time the file's i-node was last modified. The format of the time information is *month day hr:min* for dates within the last few months, and *month day year* for older files.

Filename

The name of the file. On Berkeley systems, files that are symbolic links are listed as *file -> dest*.

EXAMPLES

List the files in the current directory. (In this display, as in the other short format ls displays in this book, the files are listed in columns, which is the Berkeley default. On System V, the output is listed in columns only when the -C option is used.)

```
$ ls
a.c b.c c.c
$ _
```

See if the file '/usa/bill/kill' exists:

```
$ ls /usa/bill/kill
/usa/bill/kill: not found
$ _
```

List the size in blocks of the file '/etc/passwd':

```
$ ls -s /etc/passwd
  8 /etc/passwd
$ _
```

List the i-node number of the file '/etc/passwd':

```
$ ls -i /etc/passwd
  131 /etc/passwd
$ _
```

List all of the files, including files whose names begin with a period, in the current directory:

```
$ ls -a
.   ..   a.c b.c c.c
$ _
```

List the five largest files in the current directory:

```
$ ls -s | sort -n | tail -5
  21 vi.t
  38 csh.t
  40 ex.t
  60 sh.t
  84 man.orig
$ _
```

List the five oldest files:

```
$ ls -lt | tail -5
-rw-r--r--  1 kc         107 Jan  8 00:36 apviops.pg
-rw-r--r--  1 kc       15977 Jul 23  1986 man.add
-rw-r--r--  1 kc         883 Jul 23  1986 nohup.t
-rw-r--r--  1 kc       79620 Jul 23  1986 man.orig
-rw-r--r--  1 kc          94 May 13  1986 man.x
$ _
```

Show the difference between file modification time, file access time, and file i-node modification time:

```
$ ls -l fmtdate ; ls -ul fmtdate ; ls -cl fmtdate
-rwxr-xr-x  1 kc         539 Feb  1 23:16 fmtdate
-rwxr-xr-x  1 kc         539 Mar 11 23:36 fmtdate
-rwxr-xr-x  1 kc         539 Feb  1 23:17 fmtdate
$ cat fmtdate > /dev/null # access file
$ ls -l fmtdate ; ls -ul fmtdate ; ls -cl fmtdate
-rwxr-xr-x  1 kc         539 Feb  1 23:16 fmtdate
-rwxr-xr-x  1 kc         539 Mar 13 00:27 fmtdate
-rwxr-xr-x  1 kc         539 Feb  1 23:17 fmtdate
$ chmod a+w fmtdate # modify i-node
$ ls -l fmtdate ; ls -ul fmtdate ; ls -cl fmtdate
-rwxrwxrwx  1 kc         539 Feb  1 23:16 fmtdate
-rwxrwxrwx  1 kc         539 Mar 13 00:27 fmtdate
-rwxrwxrwx  1 kc         539 Mar 13 00:28 fmtdate
$ echo >> fmtdate # modify file
$ ls -l fmtdate ; ls -ul fmtdate ; ls -cl fmtdate
-rwxrwxrwx  1 kc         540 Mar 13 00:29 fmtdate
-rwxrwxrwx  1 kc         540 Mar 13 00:27 fmtdate
-rwxrwxrwx  1 kc         540 Mar 13 00:29 fmtdate
$ _
```

FILE
MANAGEMENT

The following is a long format listing of several files in the Berkeley UNIX format.

```
$ ls -l l*.t
-rw-r--r--  1 kc          1630 Jan 11 21:42 ln.t
-rw-r--r--  1 kc          1019 Jul 23 19:38 lp.t
-rw-r--r--  1 kc          4784 Jan 11 22:15 ls.t
$ _
```

The following is a long format listing of several files in the System V UNIX format.

```
$ ls -l l*.t
-rw-r--r--  1 kc      staff    1630 Jan 11 21:42 ln.t
-rw-r--r--  1 kc      staff    1019 Jul 23 19:38 lp.t
-rw-r--r--  1 kc      staff    4784 Jan 11 22:15 ls.t
$ _
```

MKDIR

NAME

mkdir — make a directory

SYNOPSIS

`mkdir dirname ...`

DESCRIPTION

The `mkdir` command is used to create directories. You must have write permission in the parent directory to create a directory.

Newly created directories are empty except for the entry '.' , which refers to the directory itself, and '..' , which refers to the directory's parent directory.

EXAMPLES

Create a subdirectory named 'newsub':

```
$ mkdir newsub
$ ls -a newsub
.      ..
$ _
```

Create a directory named '/usa/kc/games/numoo':

```
$ mkdir /usa/kc/games/numoo
$ _
```

FILE
MANAGEMENT

MV

NAME

mv — move or rename files

SYNOPSIS

```
mv [ -f ] file1 file2
mv [ -f ] file ... directory
```

DESCRIPTION

The mv command is used to move or rename files. In its simplest form, it changes the name of a file without changing its location in the filesystem. mv can also be used to move a file (or a group of files) from one directory to another. Movements within a file system are actually renaming operations; movements from one file system to another involve an actual transfer of data. You must have write permission for the directory files containing 'file1' and 'file2'.

In the first form of the mv command, 'file1' is renamed 'file2'. (Of course 'file1' and 'file2' may be full pathnames.) In the second form, the named files are moved into a directory, retaining their original names.

If 'file2' already exists and is write protected, mv will print the access mode of the file, and ask for permission to overwrite it, and then read a line from the standard input. A "y" response will cause the operation to proceed, while "n" (or anything else) will halt the movement. If 'file2' already exists and is not write protected, mv will replace it with 'file1' without asking.

The -f option tells mv to overwrite 'file2', even if its mode prohibits writing. Berkeley has an additional option, -i, which tells mv to ask for permission to overwrite any existing files.

mv can rename directories. On System V, a directory rename will only work if the directory doesn't change its place in the filesystem. On Berkeley, the rename will only work if the directory stays in the same filesystem.

EXAMPLES

Rename the file 'newdb' to 'olddb':

```
$ ls *db
newdb
$ mv newdb olddb
```

```
$ ls *db
olddb
$ _
```

Move the file named 'rj_stat' from the current directory into the 'rje_files' sub-directory:

```
$ ls rje_files
t5.data t6.data t7.data t9.data zq.data
$ ls *_stat
dd_stat rj_stat     .
$  mv rj_stat rje_files
$ ls *_stat
dd_stat
$ ls rje_files
rj_stat t5.data t6.data t7.data t9.data zq.data
$ _
```

Move the file named 'dd_stat' into the 'rje_files' subdirectory under the new name 'xdd_stat':

```
$ ls *_stat
dd_stat
$ mv dd_stat rje_files/xdd_stat
$ ls *_stat
*_stat not found
$ ls rje_files
rj_stat t5.data t6.data t7.data t9.data xdd_stat zq.data
$ _
```

Move all of the files in the 'rje_files' subdirectory into the 'old_rje' subdirectory of the parent directory:

```
$ mv rje_files/* ../old_rje
$ _
```

NOTES

mv is one of the most common ways to unintentionally delete a file. If the destination file exists, it will be overwritten. Make sure that your destination file isn't an existing, valuable file.

On Berkeley systems, people often alias mv to automatically engage the -i option. (See the Alias section of the C shell manual page.)

FILE MANAGEMENT

RM

NAME

rm — remove files

SYNOPSIS

rm [-fir] file ...

DESCRIPTION

The rm command is used to remove files. To remove a file, you must have write permission in the directory that contains the file, but you do not need to have write permission for the file itself. However, if you don't have write permission for the file, rm will print the file mode and wait for you to enter "y" or "n" to indicate whether you really want to remove the file.

Three options are available:

-f The force option removes files without regard to whether you have write permission on the file—the usual query for approval to remove write protected file does not occur. This option is often used in command script.

-i The interactive option causes rm to ask you whether you really want to remove each named file. Reply "y" or "n".

-r The recursive option is used to remove an entire subtree of the file system. The filename argument should be the name of a directory; that directory and all of its files, subdirectories, and so on, will be removed. The -i option can be used with -r in order to make the recursive remove a bit more controlled.

EXAMPLES

Remove the file 'mydocs':

```
$ ls mydocs
mydocs
$ rm mydocs
$ ls mydocs
mydocs not found
$ _
```

Remove several files:

```
$ rm nicotine caffeine tar
$ _
```

Remove all of the files in the subdirectory 'xyresp':

```
$ rm xyresp/*
$ _
```

Remove all of the files in the subdirectory 'xyresp' interactively:

```
$ rm -i xyresp/*
xyresp/doodleA  n
xyresp/doodleB  n
xyresp/doodleC.old  y
$ ls xyresp
doodleA doodleB
$ _
```

Remove all of the files in the subdirectory 'zzresp' without querying for write protected files:

```
$ rm -f zzresp/*
$ _
```

Remove the subtree headed by the '/usa/kc/nudocs' directory:

```
$ rm -r /usa/kc/nudocs
$ _
```

NOTES

In the UNIX system, removed files are really gone. The best way to recover an accidentally removed file is to restore a copy from a recent backup.

Beware that several older versions of UNIX don't recognize the -i option of rm. On those systems commands such as

```
$ rm -i *
```

will lead to disaster because all of the files will be removed without asking you about them individually. Try interactively removing a single (expendable) file before trusting -i on an older system.

Another common error is to unglue wildcard characters from filename roots.

```
$ rm * .old
$ _
```

The command given above will remove every file in the directory, and then complain that '.old' is not found. Don't use wildcards with dangerous commands until you understand them thoroughly. It is also wise to use echo or ls before using rm to check on your wildcard usage.

One common use of rm -i * is to purge files that have untypable names. Simply respond no for every file except the one with the untypable name.

RMDIR

NAME

rmdir — remove directories

SYNOPSIS

rmdir dirname ...

DESCRIPTION

The rmdir command removes empty directories. By definition, an empty directory is one that contains only two entries, '.' and '..'. To see a list of all of the
files in a directory you should use the -a option of ls.

You must have write permission for the parent of the directory that you want to
remove.

EXAMPLES

Remove the '/usa/kc/games/numoo' directory:

```
$ rmdir /usa/kc/games/numoo
$ _
```

Remove the 'sortsh' subdirectory:

```
$ ls sortsh
sort1   sort1.out   tmp01
$ rm sortsh/*
$ rmdir sortsh
rmdir: sortsh: Directory not empty
$ ls -a sortsh
.    ..    .exrc
$ rm sortsh/.exrc
$ rmdir sortsh
$ _
```

SECTION III

TEXT FILE COMMANDS

The UNIX system has a long heritage of working with text files. The original system development was geared toward producing a document preparation system for the Bell Laboratories patent office, and subsequent use of the system has continued to revolve around flexible text file manipulation.

This section of the book, which contains more command citations than any other, describes the principal text manipulation facilities. The most used text file utility is cat. All it does is read from its input and write to its output, but that simple operation combined with the UNIX system's I/O redirection facilities (see the I/O Redirection part of either shell description in Section V) can perform a host of operations. cat is commonly used to combine (catenate) files, display files on the screen, make copies of files, and capture keyboard input.

The two major versions of the UNIX system have two slightly different programs for viewing a text file on your screen. System V offers pg, and Berkeley offers more. Be sure to read only the citation that is appropriate for your environment. The two versions also have slightly different software systems for printing a file. On System V you use lp; on Berkeley systems, lpr. The pr command separates a file into pages, add page headings, etc.

Some of the standard text file manipulation tools are crypt, which encrypts a file; diff, which summarizes the differences between two similar files; grep, which searches for text patterns in files; head (Berkeley) and tail, which print the beginning or end of a file; and cut (System V) and paste (System V), which cut and paste columns.

Three sophisticated file manipulation programs—sort, sed, and awk—are described in this section. sort can sort a file. It has numerous command line options that let you control the part of each line that is compared and the comparison criteria. Simple sorts are easy, but sophisticated sorts require study and experimentation. sed is a stream editor. It follows an editing script to make changes in its input. sed's editing script is based on the facilities provided by ed, but there are enough differences that you should be attentive to detail when working with this command. sed can change one text pattern to another, combine multiple files, split one file into several pieces, and perform other simple editing tasks that can be described by a script. awk is a more sophisticated text manipulation program. It is a simple interpretive programming language, based in part on the C language's syntax and facilities, based in part on ed's pattern matching facilities, and based in part on text manipulation languages like Snobol and Spitbol. awk programs feature conditional and iterative statements, very flexible associative arrays, variables, and other advanced programming language features. All that, and it is easy to use.

AWK

NAME

awk — programming language to manipulate text files

SYNOPSIS

awk [-Fc] program [file . . .]
awk [-Fc] -f progfile [file . . .]

DESCRIPTION

awk is a programming language developed by Alfred V. Aho, Peter J. Weinberger, and Brian W. Kernighan. Its name is derived from the authors' initials. The goal of awk is to provide a flexible programming language for manipulating text. awk contains a fairly ordinary programming language, with the twist that sections of code are associated with text patterns. Each section of code is executed on those lines of the input that match a given text pattern.

An awk program contains two elements: code blocks and text patterns. Each block of code is executed whenever the associated pattern, which is similar to an ed style regular expression, matches a record in the input. The input records, which are read sequentially, are usually lines, although the record separator can be set within the awk program. Records are composed of fields, which, by default, are separated by white space. The field separator character can be changed within the program or by using the -Fc command line option to change the field separator to c. The individual fields are called $1, $2, etc., and the entire record is called $0.

When a code block doesn't have a pattern, it is executed for every record in the input. When a pattern doesn't have a code block, the default action, copying the record to the output, is performed. Each code block is surrounded by curly braces.

The awk script can either be supplied in a file, or it can be a command line argument. When supplied on the command line, it should usually be surrounded by single quotes so that embedded newlines and other special characters will not be mangled by the shell.

Let's first look at a few simple examples. The first example prints the second field of every line:

```
$ cat lincoln
Fourscore and seven years ago
our fathers brought forth
```

TEXT FILE
UTILITIES

```
on this continent
a new nation
$ awk '{ print $2 }' lincoln
and
fathers
this
new
$ _
```

Since the pattern is missing, the code block is executed for every record in the input.

The following example prints every line that contains the pattern /or/:

```
$ awk /or/ lincoln
Fourscore and seven years ago
our fathers brought forth
$ _
```

Since the code block is missing, the default action, printing the matching input lines, is performed.

The following example script prints the first word of the first record, the second word of the second record, and so on. It also demonstrates the special BEGIN and END patterns that let a code block execute before any input is read, and after the input is exhausted. The built-in variable NR is the record number.

```
$ awk 'BEGIN { print "starting . . ." }
>            { print $(NR) }
> END        { print "done" }' lincoln
starting . . .
Fourscore
fathers
continent

done
$ _
```

PATTERNS

Each code block may be associated with zero, one, or two patterns. If zero, then the code block is executed for every record in the input. If one, then the code block is executed for every line that matches the pattern. If two, then the code block is executed for that range of lines.

The patterns can consist of Boolean expressions and regular expressions. The regular expressions are a superset of the ed regular expression language. (See the

Regular Expressions description on the ex manual page.) The additions are +, which means one or more of the previous, and ?, which means zero or one of the previous, the | to indicate *or*, and parentheses for grouping. (Note that + and ? are related to ed's *, which means zero or more of the previous.)

The Boolean expression can use any of awk's relational operators, it can reference individual fields, and it can reference variables (including the built-in variables). Here are some examples:

/awk/	Matches any line that contains the text *awk*.
NR==5	Matches the fifth record.
$3 ~ /[0-9]+/	Matches any record with a digit in the third field.
/[A-Z]+/,NR==10	Matches from the first line containing a capital letter up to line ten.

STATEMENTS

In the following, square brackets surround optional elements of each statement.

ASSIGNMENT   var = expression
An assignment statement assigns the value of an expression to a variable. Ordinary numeric assignments work as you might expect. When you are dealing with text, literals must be enclosed in double quotes, and two adjacent strings are automatically concatenated.

IF   if (condition) statement [else statement]
The if conditional executes the first statement if the condition is true. When the optional else clause is present, it will be executed if the condition is false.

WHILE   while (condition) statement
The while conditional executes the statement while the condition is true.

FOR   for (expression; condition; expression)
          statement
awk contains two separate types of for loops. The conventional for loop executes the statement while the condition is true. The first expression will be executed before the loop starts, and the second expression will be executed after the statement on every loop repetition.

FOR   for (var in array) statement
This form of the for loop courses through the indices of the array. On each iteration, the variable will have the value of one of the array indices. (Note that the order in which the array indices are assigned to the variable is undefined.)

BREAK   break
The enclosing while or for loop will be terminated.

CONTINUE   continue

The remainder of the enclosing while or for loop body will be skipped and the next iteration will begin.

BLOCK   { statement [; statement . . .] }

A group of statements can syntactically replace a single statement when they are surrounded by curly braces. awk's statement separator is either a semicolon (shown above) or a newline.

NEXT   next

The next record will be read in, and control flows to the top of the script.

EXIT   exit

Processing stops.

PRINT
```
print expression [, expression] [ > file ]
print expression [, expression] [ >> file ]
print expression [, expression] [ | cmd ]
```
The print statement outputs the value of its expressions. Numeric expressions are printed (by default) using the %g format. (See the OFMT variable.) Remember that adjacent values are concatenated, so you must separate the expressions with commas if you want them printed separately. Ordinarily the output from the print statement is directed to the standard output. However, the output can be directed into a named file using the > file notation, appended to a file using the >> file notation, or piped into a UNIX command using the | cmd notation. The statement print hello > "tmp" will output the word hello into the file named 'tmp'. Output files are only opened once.

PRINTF
```
printf format [, expression] [ > file ]
printf format [, expression] [ >> file ]
printf format [, expression] [ | cmd ]
```
The printf statement offers you more control over the output format. Its use is similar to the C language printf, except that the arguments aren't enclosed in parentheses. The format string specifies the form of the output.

COMMENT   # comments

A sharp introduces a comment, which is terminated by the end of the line.

OPERATORS

ARITHMETIC   + - * / %

Addition, subtraction, multiplication, division, and remainder.

ASSIGNMENT   += -= *= /= %=

The var op= expr shorthand stands for var = var op (expr).

INC/DEC   ++ --

The increment and decrement operators can be applied before or after a variable. In either case, the value of the variable will be incremented or decremented.

When the operator precedes the variable, the value used will be the new value; when the operator follows the variable, the value used will be the old. Thus, x=5;y=++x will set both x and y to six, while x=5;y=x++ will set x to six and y to five.

RELATIONAL   < <= == != >= >

The usual relational operators: less than, less than or equal, equal, not equal, greater than or equal, greater than. Numeric comparisons are performed if both operands are numeric; otherwise, string comparisons are performed.

MATCHING   ~ !~

The regular expression matching operators take a string on the left and a regular expression, enclosed in / characters, on the right. The ~ operator succeeds when the string matches the regular expression; the !~ succeeds when the string doesn't match the regular expression.

BOOLEAN   && | | !

Boolean and, or, and not. Parentheses are often used for grouping.

BUILT-IN VARIABLES

FILENAME
> The name of the current file.

NF The total number of fields in the current input record.

NR The number of input records that have been encountered. This total is cumulative across multiple files. You can reset NR each time a new file is encountered using the following awk code.

```
FILENAME != prev {
        NR = 1
        prev= FILENAME
        }
```

FS The input field separator character. The default is a space and a tab. Other common choices are commas, colons, and semicolons. You can assign a value to FS to change the field separator in your awk script, or you can use the -Fc command line argument to set FS to c. If you change FS, you can only set the separator to a single character.

RS The input record separator. The default is a newline. You can assign any single character to RS in an awk script, although it cannot be set with a command line option. As a special dispensation, if RS is empty, a blank line will be used as the record separator.

OFS
> The output field separator. The default is a space. The output field separator is placed after each field printed by the print statement. For

example, print a, b will print the value of a followed by the OFS character followed by the value of b. If the input is simply echoed, or printed by print $0, then the original FS will be preserved.

ORS

The output record separator. The default is a newline. It works the same as OFS.

OFMT

The output format for numbers. The default is %g, which will print most numbers reasonably. You can change OFMT to any of the numeric format specifications recognized by the standard UNIX system printf subroutine. OFMT applies to numbers printed by the print statement, not to numbers printed by the printf statement.

BUILT-IN FUNCTIONS

awk contains *functions* for performing arithmetic and for managing text strings. These functions can be used in expressions, almost as if they were variables. In the following descriptions, s is a string-valued argument, and n is a numeric argument. The function arguments can be constants, variables, or functions.

exp(n) The exp function calculates the exponential of its argument.

getline

The getline function reads in the next line in the input. Its return value is 0 for end of file and 1 for success. Following a successful getline, the built-in variables NR and NF reflect the latest line of input, and the execution resumes at the statement following getline.

index(s1,s2)

The index function is used to search the s1 string for an occurrence of the s2 string. If s2 is found, its location is returned. If it is not found, the value 0 is returned.

int(n) The int function returns the integer part of its argument.

length(s)

The length function returns the length of string s.

log(n) The log function returns the natural logarithm of its argument.

split(s,array,sep)

The split function divides the string s into fields. Each field will be placed into elements of the array, using the indices 1, 2, etc. If the sep parameter is supplied, it is used as the input field separator, instead of using the default FS. This function is useful when you want to separate an input into fields based upon several different criteria or when you want to access subfields.

```
sprintf(f,arg1,arg2,...)
```
> The sprintf function returns a string formatted according to its arguments. The format string f follows the conventions of the C language printf statement.

```
sqrt(n)
```
> The sqrt function returns the square root of its argument.

```
substr(s,n1,n2)
```
> The substr function is used to extract a string from s. The extraction starts at position n1, and continues to position n2. If n2 isn't given, then the extraction continues to the end of s.

ASSOCIATIVE ARRAYS

An awk array can be indexed by any value. Thus, you can have familiar numeric subscripts: x[0], x[1], or you can use any arbitrary text as the array indices: x["red"], x["blue"]. Array elements are created as you use them. The second form of the for statement is often used to cycle through the elements of an array by assigning each of the array indices to a variable.

The following example tallies the number of lines with a given number of words. It uses the 'lincoln' file from the first part of this manual page.

```
$ cat lengths
awk '   {len[NF]++}
END     {
        for(i=0;i<20;i++)
            if (len[i])
                print len[i], " lines with ", i, " words"
        }' "$@"
$ lengths lincoln
2  lines with  3  words
1  lines with  4  words
1  lines with  5  words
$ _
```

The ordinary for loop in this example could be replaced by the alternate form for loop, but the order of the output would be unpredictable.

EXAMPLES

Here is an awk script that prints a small table of the powers of *e*.

```
$ cat exp.awk
awk 'BEGIN {
        print "i e**i"
        for(i=0;i<10;i++)
                print i, exp(i)
        exit
        }'
$ exp.awk
i e**i
0 1
1 2.71828
2 7.38906
3 20.0855
4 54.5981
5 148.413
6 403.429
7 1096.63
8 2980.96
9 8103.08
$ _
```

Here is a simple example of the split function:

```
$ cat split.awk
awk 'BEGIN {
        v = "This:is:a split demo"
        n = split(v,words,":")
        for(i=1; i<=n; i++)
                print i, words[i]
        exit
        }'
$ split.awk
1 This
2 is
3 a split demo
$ _
```

The following script prints yesterday's day.

```
$ cat yesterday
date | awk 'BEGIN {
            day[0]="Sun";day[1]="Mon";day[2]="Tue"
            day[3]="Wed";day[4]="Thu";day[5]="Fri"
            day[6]="Sat";day[7]="Sun"
    }
    {

            for(i=1;i<=7;i++) {
                if (day[i] == $1) {
                    print day[i-1]
                    exit
                }
            }
            print "Day ", $1, " not in list"
    }'
$ date
Sun Mar 22 12:44:53 EST 1987
$ yesterday
Sat
$ _
```

Print the line that follows any line that contains the text pattern *G5*:

```
$ cat after.awk
awk '/G5/        { prline = NR + 1 }
NR == prline     { print FILENAME, $0 }' "$@"
$ after.awk ../awk.t
../awk.t PATTERNS
../awk.t STATEMENTS
../awk.t OPERATORS
../awk.t BUILT-IN VARIABLES
../awk.t BUILT-IN FUNCTIONS
../awk.t ASSOCIATIVE ARRAYS
../awk.t EXAMPLES
$ _
```

CAT

NAME

cat — concatenate and print files

SYNOPSIS

cat [options] [file ...]

DESCRIPTION

The cat program is used for at least three purposes: printing files on your terminal, combining (concatenating) several files into one using output redirection, and capturing the standard input and placing it into a file.

Back in Version 7, cat's only option was -u. The proliferation of options on commands became symbolized by cat's -v option. The motto *Cat -v Considered Harmful* has become an oft-heard lament in UNIX circles.

-u Suppresses the normal block buffering performed by cat.

-v Displays nonprintable characters using the ^X notation. Two suboptions of -v are available. The -t suboption displays tabs as ^I, and the -e suboption displays a $ at the end of each line. -t and -e are ignored when -v is not present.

-s cat won't complain about any I/O errors. Enabling this option disables complaints about missing files, complaints that an output file is the same as an input file, or complaints about output errors. (System V only.)

-s Squeeze adjacent blank lines into a single blank line. (Berkeley only.)

-n Number output lines. Adding the -b option to -n makes cat refrain from numbering blank lines. (Berkeley only. System V has the nl program for numbering lines in files.)

When you use cat to concatenate files, it is not acceptable for the output file to be the same as an input file. That is, the commands

    $ cat a b > a

and

    $ cat a b > b

will not work as you would like. One of the earliest chores performed by the shell is creating output files. Thus, the first step will be to truncate either 'a' or 'b'. In the first case, cat will copy (an empty) 'a' over itself and will then copy 'b' on top of 'a'. In the second case, cat will copy 'a' onto (empty) 'b', and will then read from 'b' and copy to 'b'. This process might continue until the filesystem fills up, or until you stop the program. Some versions of cat are able to detect and avoid this problem.

The correct way to tack one file onto the end of another is to use appending output redirection. Thus, to copy 'b' onto the end of 'a', you should execute the following command.

```
$ cat b >> a
$ _
```

EXAMPLES

Print the 'ch3' file on your terminal:

```
$ cat ch3
— ch3 appears on the screen —
$ _
```

Print several files on your terminal:

```
$ cat ch1 ch2 ch3 ch4
— ch1, ch2, ch3, and ch4 appear on the screen —
$ _
```

Combine several files into the file 'ch1-4.t':

```
$ wc chintro.t chvione.t chvitwo.t chvithree.t
    547    4246    27128 chintro.t
    987    6426    36565 chvione.t
   1099    7384    42582 chvitwo.t
    431    3266    19313 chvithree.t
   3064   21322   125588 total
$ cat chintro.t chvione.t chvitwo.t chvithree.t > ch1-4.t
$ wc ch1-4.t
   3064   21322   125588 ch1-4.t
$ _
```

Create an empty file named 'file.new':

```
$ ls file.new
file.new: not found
$ cat /dev/null > file.new
$ ls file.new
file.new
$ _
```

Create a file from the standard input:

```
$ cat > remember
Ralph needs help moving
tomorrow morning. Try to
be there by nine.
^D
$ cat remember
Ralph needs help moving
tomorrow morning. Try to
be there by nine.
$ _
```

TEXT FILE
UTILITIES

CRYPT

NAME

crypt — encrypt and decrypt files

SYNOPSIS

crypt [password]

DESCRIPTION

The crypt program encrypts files to ensure privacy. Protecting files with the file access privilege system (see chmod) ensures a degree of privacy in the UNIX system. However, encrypted files are considerably more secure than access-protected files. The encryption mechanism is governed by a password. The same password is used to encrypt a file or to decrypt an already encrypted file. If the password is not supplied on the command line, then crypt will prompt you for the password and turn off echoing while you enter the password. crypt reads from the standard input and writes the encrypted (or decrypted) result to the standard output. crypt doesn't accept filename arguments on the command line. Although crypt makes files hard to decipher for an amateur, there are several well-known methods of attack that could be employed by professionals. There are also UNIX security holes that impose limits on the amount of protection that crypt can provide. crypt is adequate for many purposes, but it should not be relied upon for protecting highly valuable or sensitive information.

EXAMPLES

Look at a few lines from 'salaryhist', encrypt that file using the password ''abracadid'', place the encoded version in 'salh.enc', and then use od to look at the last few bytes of the encrypted file:

```
$ tail -3 salaryhist
wilson   32,500    president
xavier   29,300    senior v.p.
arno     29,300    senior v.p.
$ crypt abracadid < salaryhist > salh.enc
$ od -c salh.enc | tail -3
9000     Y 252 251 362 376 020 035 354   U 352 327   _   i 375 206 30(
9020   240 204   E 265 375   2   ~   H   )   v 365 354 020   j 213
9040   032 022   g 254 276 274   +   Z 016   <   w 272 033 022 341
$ _
```

It is good practice to use crypt to display an encoded file before removing the original. This precaution guards against typos in the password. Print the original form (the clear version) of 'salh.enc' on the terminal, and then remove the original:

```
$ crypt abracadid < salh.enc | tail -3
wilson   32,500   president
xavier   29,300   senior v.p.
arno     29,300   senior v.p.
$ rm salaryhist
$ _
```

Recover the clear form of 'salh.enc' and place it in the file 'salary_hist':

```
$ ls sal*
salh.enc
$ crypt < salh.enc > salaryhist
Enter Key:
$ ls sal*
salaryhist    salh.enc
$ _
```

When the key is entered interactively, as shown above, it is not echoed to the terminal. Type carefully.

NOTES

crypt currently cannot be exported from the United States. Do not mail encrypted files to people outside of the United States because they probably will not have access to crypt.

It is best to avoid supplying the password on the command line. One reason is that the password will be temporarily available to programs such as ps that display command line arguments. Another reason is the increasing use of shells with history mechanisms, such as the Korn shell or the C shell, because they store past commands in ordinary files.

CUT

NAME

cut — cut a column from a file

SYNOPSIS

cut -c*list* [file . . .]
cut -f*list* [-d*x*] [-s] [file . . .]

DISTRIBUTION

Always available on System V, and often available elsewhere.

DESCRIPTION

cut is a System V program that extracts columns from files. cut is the vertical analog of grep, which extracts horizontal slices from files. The inverse of cut is paste, which glues together columns to form wider files.

cut identifies columns by two totally different methods. The simplest is by character position. Column one is the first character on each line, etc. The alternative way to identify columns is by column delimiters. A special character, which is a tab by default, separates the columns (which are sometimes called *fields*). Column one is everything up to the delimiter, column two is everything between the first and second delimiter, and so on. The SYNOPSIS shows that cut always requires a list of columns to cut, either a character list or a field list.

The following option is used when you want to specify which character positions should be extracted from the input. When this option is present, it should be the only option.

-c*list*   The character positions mentioned in *list* are extracted from the input. The *list* is a comma-separated list of numbers or hyphen-separated pairs of numbers. The list -c2,4,6 means extract characters two, four, and six; -c-4 means characters one through four; -c2,5-10 means characters two and five through ten; and -c8- means characters eight through the end. The columns in the output will have the same order as the input, even if your *list* is in a different order.

The following options are available when you extract delimited columns.

-f*list*   The specified columns will be extracted from the input. The format of the list is the same as for a character position list, which was explained above.

-d*x*   The character *x* will be used as the column delimiter. The tab is the default column delimiter. *x* may need to be quoted if it has a special meaning to the shell.

-s   Lines that do not contain a delimiter will be stripped from the output. Ordinarily such lines would be present. Note that when this option is used, the number of lines in cut's output may not match the number of lines in the input.

EXAMPLES

Extract columns of characters or colon-delimited fields from the '/etc/passwd' file:

```
$ tail -5 /etc/passwd | cut -c1-20
arturo:PYvZ2WFKsg6Ng
pms:YcCsQ/w/8gZUY:96
sonia:.2hEDA4d5hW5c:
jah:5Gv4GsiwURMy2:98
susana:maQjFs2iS/dL.
$ tail -5 /etc/passwd | cut -f1 -d:
arturo
pms
sonia
jah
susana
$ _
```

Extract the year from the date message and store it in a shell variable:

```
$ echo 123456789012345678901234567890
123456789012345678901234567890
$ date
Tue Dec  2 21:50:05 EST 1986
$ year=`date | cut -c25-`
$ echo $year
1986
$ _
```

Extract the fourth column from a table embedded in a document:

```
$ sed -n -e '/^.TS$/,/^.TE$/p' od.t
.TS
center;
cfUU l 4 cfUU l 4 cfUU l.
\e0      null    \eb      backspace        \ef    formfeed
\en      newline \er      carriage return \et    tab
.TE
$ sed -n -e '/^.TS$/,/^.TE$/p' od.t | cut -f4 -s
backspace
carriage return
$ _
```

DIFF

NAME

diff — report differences between text files

SYNOPSIS

diff [-efbh] file1 file2

DESCRIPTION

The diff program is used to compare two files. diff can be used in a pipeline by using the special name "-" in place of one of the filenames. If the two files are different, then diff usually prints a line that resembles an editor command (to indicate which lines are different) followed by the different lines from both files.

The following three types of editor pseudo commands are printed by diff:

n1 a n3, n4
> File1 is missing some of the lines that exist in file2. The difference will vanish if lines n3 through n4 from file2 are placed in file1 after line n1 of file1.

n1, n2 d n3
> File1 has some lines that are missing from file2. The difference will vanish if lines n1 through n2 are deleted from file1. (Alternatively, lines n1 through n2 from file1 can be added after line n3 of file2.)

n1, n2, c n3, n4
> File1 and file2 have a region that is different. The difference will vanish if lines n1 through n2 of file1 are changed to lines n3 through n4 of file2 (or vice versa).

For all three types of pseudo command, if n1 equals n2 (or if n3 equals n4), then only one number will be printed. Following the pseudo command the different lines from the files are printed. Lines from file1 are flagged by placing a < at the beginning of each line while lines from file2 are flagged with a >.

diff accepts four options:

-e Produce an editor script for the ed editor that will recreate file2 from file1. Differences are cataloged in reverse order (from end to beginning) so that the script will execute correctly.

-f Produce a similar script, but in the forward order. The script produced by this option *cannot* be used to recreate file2. The reverse order script produced by the -e option changes the end of the file before changing the beginning, thereby preserving the line numbers of not-yet-edited lines. Starting at the beginning and working toward the end might change the line numbers of lines at the end of the file. Most people find this script is more readable than the one produced by the -e option.

-h Perform the comparison quickly and on files of unlimited size. diff is not as good at resynchronizing using the -h option, and options -e and -f are not available.

-b Ignore differences between lines caused by different white space. When this option is invoked, any white space sequence (a sequence of spaces and tabs) will be equivalent to any other.

Berkeley diff accepts several additional options, the most useful of which is -c, to provide some context surrounding the different lines. The -c option allows a trailing numeric parameter that specifies how many lines of context. Context makes it much easier to locate and comprehend the differences between files.

TEXT FILE
UTILITIES

EXAMPLES

Compare the files 'notes.a' and 'notes.old':

```
$ diff notes.a notes.old
17c17
< a Caribbean island or even a
---
> a sleek yacht or even a
30,31d29
< The fumes are actually Mustard
< gas, of WWI fame.
$ _
```

Print an editor script so that 'notes.old' can be recreated from 'notes.a':

```
$ diff -e notes.a notes.old
30,31d
17c
a sleek yacht or even a
.
$ _
```

Create a file that is identical to 'notes.old' from 'notes.a' using ed:

```
$ ( diff -e notes.a notes.old
> echo w notes.c
> echo q ) | ed notes.a
10109
10055
$ diff notes.old notes.c
$ _
```

At some point in the past, a file named 'lsfile' was created by executing the command "ls > lsfile". To determine if the directory still has the same contents as when 'lsfile' was created, we want to compare 'lsfile' with the current contents of the working directory:

```
$ ls | diff - lsfile
$ _
```

The lack of output indicates that the directory contents are the same as when 'lsfile' was created. Note that the contents of individual files might have been altered.

NOTE

Berkeley diff accepts additional options, which direct it to compare all of the files in a pair of directories. On System V, directory contents can be compared using the dircmp program.

GREP

NAME

grep — search for text patterns in text files

SYNOPSIS

grep [options] expression [file ...]

DESCRIPTION

The grep program searches for text patterns in the named files or in the standard input if no files are mentioned. The text patterns are indicated by the expression argument, which is a regular expression constructed similarly to regular expressions in the ed or ex editor. (See the Regular Expressions section of the ex manual page.)

Without options, the grep program prints each line in the input that contains a text pattern that matches the expression. The options can be used to slightly alter this behavior:

-c   Produce a count of lines rather than the lines themselves.

-l   List the names of the files that contain text patterns that match the expression.

-s   Indicate the existence of matches using the exit status of grep. No output is produced. This option is useful for shell programs (Berkeley only).

-s   Don't complain about inaccessible files (System V only).

-n   Print the line number (from the input file) for each match.

-v   Print lines that don't contain text that matches the expression rather than lines that do contain matching text.

-b   The block offset in the file of each match is reported.

-i   Case distinction is ignored.

-w   The expression is constrained to match a whole word of the input (Berkeley only).

-e expression
    The -e option explicitly states that the next argument is the text expression, rather than another option. The advantage of using the -e option is that it lets you have a hyphen as the first character of the expression. Expressions that aren't introduced by the -e option must start with a

character other than hyphen (Berkeley only).

grep returns a true exit code when the search is successful, and false otherwise.

EXAMPLES

Print all of the occurrences of the string *troff* in a set of files:

```
$ grep troff chapt*
chapt2: However, the troff utility is an
chapt6: such as nroff and troff
chapt6: Neither program (nroff, troff) is able to
$ _
```

List the number of lines that contain the string *troff* in a set of files:

```
$ grep -c troff chapt*
chapt1: 0
chapt2: 1
chapt5: 0
chapt6: 2
chapt9a: 0
$ _
```

List all of the files that contain the string *artifact* in the current directory:

```
$ grep -l artifact *
chap7
appendix
query
brian
$ _
```

grep normally doesn't output the filename when only one file is examined. You can use the file '/dev/null' to force grep to output a filename.

```
$ grep normal grep.t
normally doesn't output the filename
$ grep normal grep.t /dev/null
grep.t:normally doesn't output the filename
$ _
```

Print and number all of the lines containing the word *bcount* in the file 'rgb.c' or the file 'hsv.c':

```
$ grep -n bcount rgb.c hsv.c
hsv.c: 181: factors in bcount. The other
hsv.c: 182: use of bcount relates to hue
hsv.c: 199: bcount or blocking factor.
$ _
```

Determine whether any user is logged in on tty30:

```
$ who | grep tty30
kc    tty30    Apr 28 20:20
$ _
```

Print all lines in a group of files that contain the word "super" but that don't contain a hyphen.

```
$ grep super *.t | grep -v -e -
csh.t:shell compatibility, superior performance, and
eqn.t:subscripts and superscripts are reduced
eqn.t:make \f2y\fP a subscript or superscript of \f2x\fP.
mail.t:superior if you use
$ _
```

If you want to use grep's exit status in a shell script, the best method is probably to discard grep's output into the universally available '/dev/null' rather than use the Berkeley -s option.

```
$ grep null grep.t
available `/dev/null´ rather than
$ grep -l null grep.t > /dev/null && echo found null
found null
$ grep empty grep.t
$ grep -l empty grep.t > /dev/null && echo found empty
$ _
```

In the example above, the -l speeds things up because it allows grep to abandon a file as soon as a match occurs.

NOTE

grep has two close relatives, fgrep, which can search for multiple strings at once, and egrep, which accepts an expanded regular expression language.

HEAD

NAME

head — print the beginning part of a text file

SYNOPSIS

head [-n] [file . . .]

DISTRIBUTION

Berkeley UNIX systems only.

DESCRIPTION

head prints the first few lines of a file. The argument n can override the default number of lines, which is ten. On System V, you can produce the same result using sed, as shown below. If several files are mentioned on the command line, head will print a header followed by the first few lines of each.

EXAMPLES

Print the first five lines of the '/usr/dict/words' dictionary:

```
$ head -5 /usr/dict/words
10th
1st
2nd
3rd
4th
$ _
```

Use sed as a substitute for head to print the first five lines of '/usr/dict/words':

```
$ sed 5q /usr/dict/words
10th
1st
2nd
3rd
4th
$ _
```

NOTE

Although head will print only the first few lines of a file, it will probably read more than it prints. Thus, you can't use head to skip the first few lines of the standard input in a pipeline.

```
$ head -4 /usr/dict/words
10th
1st
2nd
3rd
$ cat /usr/dict/words | (head -1 ; head -1)
10th
ate
$ grep -n ^ate$ /usr/dict/words
1478:ate
$ _
```

LP

NAME

lp — print a file on system printer
lpstat — print lp status information
cancel — cancel print requests

SYNOPSIS

lp [option] [file ...]
lpstat [options]
cancel [id] [printer]

DISTRIBUTION

System V only. The lpr command is used on Berkeley systems.

DESCRIPTION

The lp program is used to print files on a lineprinter. Since a lineprinter cannot be used simultaneously by several users, the lp program queues the print requests and arranges for one file to be printed at a time. If there are no files mentioned on the command line, then lp reads the text to be printed from the standard input. Thus, lp can be used as the final stage in a pipeline. lp prints a job id number for possible later use.

lp does not alter the text to be printed in any way; if you want a file to be paginated or titled, you should use pr to process the text before handing it to lp. Ordinarily lp does not copy your files to a spool directory, so the printed output will reflect any changes that you make to a file *after* issuing an lp request but *before* it is printed.

-c Copy the files to the spool directory.

-d*printer*

-d*class*

    Use the named *printer* or printer *class* to print the job. When the -d option isn't used, the output will go to the printer specified in the $LPDEST environment variable, or to the system default printer.

-m Send mail when the printing has been completed.

-n*n*

    Print *n* copies.

-o*ops*

Ops are printer or class dependent options. This option may be used more than once if you must specify several options.

-s   Make lp less verbose.

-t*title*

Use *title* as the title on the banner page.

-w   Print a message on the terminal when the printing is complete (if the user is still logged in) or send mail (if the user is not still logged in).

cancel is used to cancel print requests. You can specify a job *id* to cancel to cancel a particular print job, or you can specify a *printer* to cancel the job that is currently printing on that printer. You can only cancel your own print jobs, unless you are the super-user.

The lpstat program describes the status of the lp printing system. By default, lpstat prints the status of your current print jobs. Various options make lpstat display other information. The following lpstat options are often used by ordinary users; the options often used by system managers are omitted. In the options that accept lists, the list is either comma-separated without intervening spaces, or quoted, comma-separated, and possibly containing spaces.

-c[*classes*]

Print a list of the members of the listed printer classes, or a list of all the members of all the printer classes if *classes* is omitted.

-d   Print the name of the default printer.

-o[*list*]

Print the status of the jobs described by *list*, which may contain printer names, printer classes, or print job id numbers.

-p[*printers*]

Print the status of the listed *printers*.

-s   Print the printer and class names known by lp. This option is how you learn about what is available on a given system.

EXAMPLES

```
$ lpstat -d
system default destination: mx80
$ lp figs.1
request id is mx80-12 (1 file)
$ lpstat
mx80-11          root          105    Jan 28 22:58
mx80-12          kc            9901   Jan 28 23:01
mx80-13          ronw          2185   Jan 28 23:04
```

```
$ cancel mx80-12
request "mx80-12" cancelled
$ lpstat
mx80-11          root          105    Jan 28 22:58
mx80-13          ronw         2185    Jan 28 23:04
$ _
```

LPR

NAME

lpr — print a file on system printer
lpq — examine print queue
lprm — remove job from the print queue

SYNOPSIS

lpr [-P*printer*] [-printopt] [-filteropt] [file ...]
lpq [-P*printer*] [+ [secs]] [-l] [jobnum ...] [user ...]
lprm [-P*printer*] [jobnum ...] [user ...]
lpc

DISTRIBUTION

Berkeley only. The lp program performs the same function on System V. Version 7 UNIX prints files using a program named lpr but its usage is very different from the program described here.

DESCRIPTION

The lpr program is used to print files on the lineprinter. Since the lineprinter cannot be used simultaneously by several users, the lpr program queues the print requests and arranges for one job to be printed at a time. If there are no files mentioned in the command line, then lpr reads the text to be printed from the standard input. Thus, lpr can be used as the final stage in a pipeline.

There are two types of options that lpr recognizes: *printopts*, which manage lpr, and *filteropts*, which specify what output filter should be used. A filter is a program that lpr runs to print a particular type of data on a particular printer. The following table lists the standard *filteropts*, many of which may not be implemented on your machine:

-p Print text files with pr	-l Pass file through unchanged.
-t Print troff file	-n Print ditroff file
-d Print T$_E$X DVI file	-v Print raster image file
-g Print plot file	-c Print cifplot file
-f Print fortran output	

The *filteropts* are often provided automatically by local scripts. For example, on most systems you typeset documents with troff using a command script that automatically sends troff's output to lpr with the correct options. You needn't memorize the -t (or -n) option because it is wired into the troff script.

The following *printopts* are available:

-P*printer*
> Use the named printer instead of the default. Printer names are known by your system manager. Alternatively you can specify a printer in the $PRINTER environmental variable.

-#*n*
> Print *n* copies.

-s Use symbolic links instead of copying the files to the spool directory.

-r Remove the file after it has been printed.

-m Send mail when the file has been printed.

-i [*n*]
> Indent *n* (or eight, if *n* is omitted) spaces.

-w *n*
> Pass *n* to pr to use as the page width.

-T *title*
> Pass *title* to pr to use as the banner page title. This option and the previous are only effective if the -p *filteropt* is specified.

-h Don't print the customary header page.

-C *class*
> Print *class* on the header page as the job classification. The default classification is your system name.

-J *name*
> Print *name* on the header page as the job name, instead of the name of your first file.

You can display the print queue using the lpq program. The -P*printer* will direct lpq to print a particular printer's queue, the -l option will produce a long format listing, and mentioning user names or job numbers will restrict the output to those users or jobs. The + option, which may be followed by a number, will continuously print the queue until it is exhausted, every *n* (default is 30) seconds.

You can remove one of your jobs from the queue with the lprm command. You can specify a *jobnum* to remove a particular print job, *username* to remove all jobs for that user, or - to remove all jobs that you are allowed to remove. Only the super-user can remove others' jobs.

The lpc command is used by system administrators to manage the print spooler system. lpc lets you disable certain printers or restart inoperable spoolers.

TEXT FILE UTILITIES

EXAMPLES

The following dialogue shows lpr, lpq, and lprm in action. In the beginning of the dialogue, a command script named qtroff automatically places a print job into the queue. You can see the result using lpq. Next lpr is used to place a print job into the queue, then lprm removes that print job, and, in the final steps, the lpq program is executed repeatedly to wait for the queue to drain.

```
$ qtroff resume
$ lpq -Pqms
qms is ready and printing
Rank   Owner   Job  Files                  Total Size
1st    kc      633  (standard input)       9955 bytes
$ lpr -Pqms cat.t pr.t lpr.t
$ lpq -Pqms
qms is ready and printing
Rank   Owner   Job  Files                  Total Size
1st    kc      633  (standard input)       9955 bytes
2nd    kc      634  cat.t, pr.t, lpr.t     10124 bytes
$ lprm -Pqms 634
dfA634rna dequeued
dfB634rna dequeued
dfC634rna dequeued
cfA634rna dequeued
$ lpq -Pqms
qms is ready and printing
Rank   Owner   Job  Files                  Total Size
1st    kc      633  (standard input)       9955 bytes
$ lpq -Pqms
no entries
$ _
```

TEXT FILE
UTILITIES

The first print request in the example dialogue is made using the qtroff script, which internally sends troff output to lpr. The result is visible on the output queue using lpq. The explicit lpr request sends three files to the print queue, awaiting the completion of the original (job 633) print request. Toward the end of the dialogue, the lprm command is used to remove the second print request from the queue, and the lpq program is used repeatedly to wait for completion of the original request. In all of these commands the printer argument is supplied explicitly, which would be unnecessary if the qms printer were the default.

MORE

NAME

more — view a file using a terminal

SYNOPSIS

more [options] [file . . .]

DISTRIBUTION

Berkeley UNIX systems only. The System V analog is pg.

DESCRIPTION

more is the Berkeley file pager. It ordinarily displays files (or its standard input) on the screen one screenful at a time. After each screenful is displayed, more pauses to let you view the text. You can then enter simple commands to tell more to display another screenful, skip several screenfuls, search for a pattern in the text, and so on.

The following command line options let you customize more's behavior or start somewhere past the beginning of the file.

+*n* The first line displayed will be line *n*.

+*/pattern*
    The first displayed line will be two lines before the given pattern. The full regular expression language of ed may be used, although many special characters must be escaped from the shell.

-*n* The number *n* will be used as the window size, instead of the default of 22 for most 24-line terminals.

-c more will draw each screenful starting from the top, rather than by scrolling up from the bottom. Some prefer this approach. (Only valid on terminals with a clear to end of line capability.)

-f Long lines aren't folded. This option is often used when the input contains escape sequences, such as nroff output, that confuse more's line length calculations.

-s Multiple blank lines are displayed as a single blank line. This is useful so that paginated input, such as that produced by nroff or pr, doesn't display sparsely.

TEXT FILE UTILITIES

-l Ordinarily more interprets a form feed as the end of a page and automatically pauses at that point. This option makes more treat form feeds as just another character.

-u Ordinarily more interprets nroff underline requests appropriately for the output terminal. When this option is given, more outputs underline requests without change.

-d The prompt at the end of each screenful is more verbose.

Multiple files may be mentioned on the command line. more pauses at the end of each file before advancing to the next. more input may come from a pipeline, although the :p, :n, and ´ commands mentioned below won't operate because more is unable to back up while reading a pipe.

You can permanently engage your favorite more options by placing them in an exported shell variable named $MORE. For example, the following Bourne shell commands will engage the -s command line option of more for the remainder of the current login session.

```
$ MORE=-s
$ export MORE
$ _
```

Ordinarily the commands shown above would be placed in the file '.profile' in your home directory so that they would be executed at the beginning of each login session. (Or the analogous C shell commands could be placed into the '.login' file.)

After each screenful is displayed, more prints the message "--More--" at the bottom of the screen and waits for you to enter a command. The commands consist of single characters and you don't need to enter a carriage return after typing each command. Most commands may be preceded by a number, which has an interpretation that is given in the following list. Note the numeric prefix is not echoed to the screen. If you make a typo while entering a numeric prefix, delete the whole line by entering your system's line kill character and start again.

The most common commands are <space> to advance one more screenful, <CR> to advance one line, and q to quit. (And b on Berkeley 4.3 more, to go back one page.) Although rarely used by most users, the full set of more commands is listed below.

    <space>

        Display the next screenful. A numeric prefix means display that many more lines.

    <CR>

        Scroll one line. A numeric prefix means scroll that many lines.

z   Same as the <space> command except that the numeric prefix, if given, permanently becomes the new window size.

<^D> Scroll through the file. By default, the amount to scroll each time is one half screenful. You can specify a numeric prefix, which will set the scroll amount to that many lines.

s   Skip one line and then display a screenful. A numeric prefix means skip that many lines before the display.

f   Skip one screenful and then display a screenful. A numeric prefix means skip that many screens before the display.

=   Print the current line number.

h   Print a brief help message.

/*pattern*
     Search for the next occurrence of *pattern*. A numeric prefix means find the *n*-th occurrence of the pattern.

n   Search for the next occurrence of the previously entered pattern. A numeric prefix means search for the *n*-th occurrence of the pattern.

     Return to the starting point of the previous search, or return to the beginning of the file if no searches have been performed.

!command
     Execute the given shell command. In the command text the character % will be replaced with the current file name if the input is from a file. Also the character ! in the command text will be replaced with the previous command, if there was one. Leading backslashes can suppress the % and ! special meanings.

v   Invoke the vi text editor at the current point of the current file. When vi exits, you will return to more.

:n   Skip to the next file mentioned on the command line. A numeric prefix means skip to the *n*-th next file.

:p   Skip to the previous file mentioned on the command line. When you are in the middle of a file, this command will return you to its beginning. A numeric prefix means skip to the *n*-th previous file.

:f   Display the current file name and number.

q   Quit from more and return to the shell.

.   Repeat the previous command.

If the output of more isn't a terminal, it behaves similarly to cat, with the exception that three identification lines are output in front of each file. This more feature can be used to label files being sent to lpr's standard input. If the input of more is a terminal, it complains and exits.

NOTES

Starting in BSD 4.3, more contains a b command to back up.

more is used by the Berkeley programs man and msgs, and it is often a part of locally developed shell scripts. Any options engaged in the $MORE shell variable will alter the behavior of these programs.

PASTE

NAME

paste — combine columns (files) or subsequent lines of a single file

SYNOPSIS

paste [-d*list*] [file . . .]
paste -s [-d*list*] [file . . .]

DISTRIBUTION

Always available on System V, and often available elsewhere.

DESCRIPTION

paste is a System V program that can perform two similar, but distinct functions, depending on the -s option. When the -s option is absent, paste combines several input files into one wider output file, taking one input line from each of the input files in turn. This is called a *parallel* merge. However, when the -s option is present, paste combines subsequent lines of the input into a wider output file, which is called a *serial* merge.

These two separate functions are present in a single program for historical reasons, and they are discussed separately below.

PARALLEL MERGES

In most parallel merges the files specified on the command line are combined into one wider file. paste cycles through the input files, taking one line from each. The output will usually have as many lines as the longest input file, and it will usually have as many columns as there are input files. You can use a - in place of a filename to specify the standard input. (Multiple hyphens are allowed; one line from the standard input will be used each time a "hyphen" column is encountered.) Each line is terminated with a newline.

The -d option specifies the column separator character(s). If the list contains more than one character, they are used in turn, with the list being re-used as many times as necessary. The notation \n means a newline, \t means a tab, \\ means a backslash, and \0 means a null. The list may need to be escaped from the shell; in particular you will need to type two backslashes to get one through the shell. The default column separator is a tab.

When the -d list contains a newline character, the output might not have as many columns as input files, and it might not have as many lines as the longest input file.

SERIAL MERGES

A serial merge is performed when the -s command line option is present. In a serial merge the lines of the input are taken in turn and placed next to each other, separated by column separators. If the single default column separator is used, then the output is a single line long, consisting of all the input lines separated by tabs. Therefore, almost all serial merges use the -d*list* command line option, and the end of the *list* is usually a newline so that the output is divided into lines. paste makes sure that the last line ends with a newline.

The delimiter list for a serial merge is similar to that for a parallel merge. The two-character escapes described above are used to represent common control characters, and the list is used repeatedly as necessary. The principal difference is that the number of columns is always determined by the delimiter list, not by the number of input files. Thus, the delimiter list for a four-column output would have three real column delimiters, e.g., tabs, and then a newline as the fourth delimiter.

EXAMPLES

Simple parallel merges:

```
$ cat grk_let
alpha
beta
gamma
delta
$ cat grk_codes
\(*a
\(*b
\(*g
\(*d
$ paste grk_let grk_codes
alpha    \(*a
beta     \(*b
gamma    \(*g
delta    \(*d
$ paste -d: grk_codes grk_let
\(*a:alpha
\(*b:beta
\(*g:gamma
\(*d:delta
$ _
```

Serial merge using the default delimiter:

```
$ paste -s grk_let
alpha    beta    gamma    delta
$ _
```

Turn a single-column file into a two-column file using either a serial merge or a parallel merge:

```
$ paste -s -d´\t\n´ grk_let > grk_let1
$ cat grk_let1
alpha    beta
gamma    delta
$ cat grk_codes | paste - - > grk_codes1
$ cat grk_codes1
\(*a    \(*b
\(*g    \(*d
$ _
```

Two ways to merge the two-column files:

```
$ paste grk_let1 grk_codes1
alpha    beta    \(*a    \(*b
gamma    delta   \(*g    \(*d
$ paste -d´\n´ grk_let1 grk_codes1
alpha    beta
\(*a    \(*b
gamma    delta
\(*g    \(*d
$ _
```

Two methods of double spacing:

```
$ paste grk_let grk_codes | paste -d´\n´ - /dev/null
alpha    \(*a

beta     \(*b

gamma    \(*g

delta    \(*d
```

```
$ paste -d'\t\n' grk_let grk_codes /dev/null
alpha    \(*a

beta     \(*b

gamma    \(*g

delta    \(*d

$ _
```

PG

NAME

pg — view a file using a terminal

SYNOPSIS

pg [options] [file . . .]

DISTRIBUTION

System V only. See the more manual page for a description of the Berkeley file pager.

DESCRIPTION

pg is the System V file pager. It was developed subsequent to Berkeley's more pager, and it has similar options and commands. The major advantage of pg over more is that pg has a more flexible forwards/backwards capability. more moves forward, or back to the beginning of the file, whereas pg can move backwards incrementally.

pg ordinarily displays files (or its standard input) on the screen one screenful at a time. After each screenful is displayed, pg pauses to let you view the text. You can then enter simple commands to tell pg to display another screenful, skip several screenfuls, search for a pattern in the text, and so on. Three common pg commands are <CR> to advance one more screenful, 1 (letter *ell*) to advance one line, and q to quit. Each command character must be followed by a <CR> unless the -n option is given.

The following command line options let you customize pg's behavior or start somewhere past the beginning of the file.

+*n* The first line displayed will be line *n*.

+*/pattern/*
  The first displayed line will contain the given pattern. The full regular expression language of ed may be used, although many special characters must be escaped from the shell.

-*n* The number *n* will be used as the window size, instead of the default of 23 for most 24-line terminals.

-n When this option is specified, pg will execute each command as soon as the command character is entered, instead of waiting for a carriage return.

-c pg will draw each screenful starting from the top, rather than by scrolling up from the bottom. Some prefer this approach. (Only valid on terminals with a clear to end of screen capability.)

-f Long lines aren't folded. This option is often used when the input contains escape sequences, such as nroff output, that confuse pg's line length calculations.

-p *string*
    The given *string* is used as the prompt. A %d in the prompt will be replaced by the current page number. The default prompt is a colon.

-s Messages are displayed in inverse video, if possible.

-e pg won't pause at the end of each file.

Multiple files may be mentioned on the command line. pg pauses at the end of each file before advancing to the next unless the -e option has been specified. pg input may come from a pipeline.

After each screenful is displayed, pg prints a colon at the bottom of the screen and waits for you to enter a command. Most commands may be preceded by a number, which has an interpretation that is given in the following list. pg interprets signed numbers (leading + or -) relative to the current point in the file, and unsigned numbers as absolute locations in the file.

<space> or <CR>
    Display the next screenful. A negative numeric prefix displays that many screens in back of the current location, a signed positive prefix moves forward that many screens from the current position, and an unsigned prefix displays that many screenfuls from the beginning of the file.

l The screen is scrolled the given number of lines forward or back. If a numeric prefix isn't given, the screen scrolls one line forward.

<^D> Scroll a half screenful. Numeric prefixes have the meanings described in the <CR> command above, except that distance is measured in half screenfuls.

. or <Ctrl-L>
    Redisplay the current screen.

$ Display the last screenful of the input.

h Print a brief help message.

/pattern/

?pattern?

*^pattern^*

Search forward (/) or backward (? or ^) for the next occurrence of *pattern*. A numeric prefix means find the *n*-th occurrence of the pattern. There is no wraparound at the end of the file. If the given pattern is found, it is displayed at the top of the screen, unless the suffix m is used to cause display in mid-screen, or the suffix b is used to cause display at the bottom of the screen. The m and b suffixes stick; use the t suffix to revert to placing the matched text on the top line.

n   Switch to the next file mentioned on the command line. An unsigned numeric prefix *n* means examine the *n*-th next file.

p   Switch to the previous file mentioned on the command line. An unsigned numeric prefix *n* means examine the *n*-th previous file.

w   Display another screenful of text. This option is similar to <CR>, except the numeric prefix has a different meaning. The numeric prefix, if present, changes the display size to *n*.

s *file* Save the current input file in *file*.

!command

Execute the given shell command. This command must always be completed with a <CR> character.

q   Quit from pg and return to the shell.

NOTE

Scrolling backward is more awkward than in vi, and repeating searches is much more awkward than in vi, but familiarity with vi or more will help you to learn pg.

PR

NAME

pr — paginate and title files

SYNOPSIS

pr [option] [file ...]

DESCRIPTION

The pr command is usually used to prepare files for printing. pr paginates files, supplies headings, partitions a file into columns, and adjusts for varying page lengths or widths. If none of the options is specified, then pr produces single-column output with 66 lines per page and a short header and a short trailer. The output is either of the named files or the standard input when no files are named. The standard header contains the date, the name of the file, and the page number. If the output of pr is a terminal, then messages are suspended during output.

The following options can be used to adjust the format of the output.

-h   Use the following argument in the header in place of the file name.

-l*n*   Produce pages that are n lines long. The default is 66 lines.

-m   Print all files simultaneously, one file in each column.

-*n*   Produce *n* column output. pr will fill the first column on a page, then fill the second, and so on up to *n* columns, and then it will repeat the process on successive pages. The default is single-column output.

+*n*   Begin output starting at page *n*. The default is to start at page 1.

-s*c*   In multiple-column output, separate the columns with the character c (usually a tab character) rather than with the appropriate amount of white space. If c is missing, a tab is assumed.

-t   Do not produce the header or the trailer.

-w*n*   During multiple-column output, use the number n for the page width rather than the default of 72.

-f   Use a form feed character to separate pages rather than multiple newlines.

The following options are only available on System V.

-a   For multicolumn output, print successive lines from left to right, instead of filling one column before starting the next. This option may only be used with the *-n*, and not with the -m option.

-o*n*   Offset each line by n blanks. Lines are usually flush left.

-n*ck* Number each line. The width of the number is **k**, and the number is separated by the character **c** from the following text. The default for **k** is 5, and the default for **c** is a tab.

-i*ck* Replace white space in the input with tabs in the output. **k** is the width of the tab stops, and **c** is the character used as the tab. The default for **k** is 8, and the default for **c** is a tab.

-e*ck* Expand tabs in the input. **k** is the width of the tab stops and **c** is the input tab character. The default for **k** is 8, and the default for **c** is a tab.

-d   Double space the output.

-p   Pause at the end of every page.

-r   Don't complain about missing input files.

EXAMPLES

Print a file in the conventional format on the lineprinter:

```
$ pr myfile | lp
$ _
```

Columnate the output of the wc program:

```
$ wc * | pr -l1 -t -2
      7    27    79 ave.awk         9   49  134 ave2.awk
     14    37   147 aveline.awk     5   18   90 col.awk
     30    61   230 dark.awk        6   11   76 exp.awk
     11    26   134 fact.awk        2    3   26 grep.awk
      6    20   162 index.awk       7   20   99 nlogins.awk
     73   176   680 reduce.awk     17   49  208 rmdups.awk
      7    17   114 split.awk      10   31  154 tri.awk
     12    35   168 triangle.awk   14   38  202 twod.awk
    230   618  2703 total
$ _
```

The -l1 (letter *ell*, numeral *one*) option tells pr that pages are one line long, fooling it into thinking that it only needs one line of input before switching to the other column. Otherwise, it would attempt to collect over fifty lines of input before starting column two. The -t omits the headers and trailers, and the -2 tells pr to produce two-column output. The same result could be produced using the -a (System V only) option.

Print 'myfile' starting at page 10 and place the output in the file 'myfile.end':

```
$ pr +10 myfile > myfile.end
$ _
```

SED

NAME

sed — script-directed text editor

SYNOPSIS

sed [-n] [-e script] [-f scriptfile] [files]

DESCRIPTION

sed is a non-interactive text editor. It is similar to ed, but designed to work through a file one line at a time, from start to finish. Whereas ed may browse through the edit buffer each time a command is entered, sed browses through the command script each time a new line is read from the text input.

There are a few simple concepts that must be mastered to use sed. sed operates *cyclically*. A cycle usually consists of 1) sed reads a line of input into the pattern space, 2) sed executes the edit script, which may possibly alter the contents of the pattern space, and 3) sed copies the pattern space to the output and clears it. Note that this is simply the usual cycle; some of the commands in the edit script may produce alternate cycles.

sed, like ed, has an *edit* buffer to hold the text that is being edited. The difference is that the sed edit buffer, called the *pattern space*, typically contains just one line of text, whereas the ed edit buffer contains the entire file. Although there are sed commands that let you stuff more than a single line into the pattern space, conceptually it is a single-line buffer that can hold lines containing embedded newlines.

Besides the pattern space, sed contains a *hold* buffer. Several commands exist to swap text back and forth between the pattern space and the hold buffer.

sed accepts the following command line options:

-n Don't output the pattern space at the end of each cycle. When -n is given, output is only produced when one of the PRINT commands is encountered.

-e *script*
The -e argument specifies that the following argument is an editing script. Multiple editing scripts may be specified on a single command line. You can omit the -e flag if there is just a single script specified on the command line, and no scripts in auxiliary files.

-f *scriptfile*
>   The **-f** argument specifies the name of a file that contains the editing script.

sed addresses lines in the style of **ed**. An address may be

n   An absolute line number *n*. The line counter is not reset each time a new file is processed. Thus, if the first file has twenty lines, line twenty-one is the first line of the second file.

$ The last line of the input.

/pat/
>   A context address matches any line containing the *pat* regular expression. **ed** style regular expressions are allowed: . will match any single character except a newline, ^ will match the beginning of the pattern space, $ will match the end of the pattern space, [*abc*] will match any one of the enclosed characters, * will match 0 or more repetitions of the previous single character regular expression, and anything else will match itself. In **sed**, \n will match a newline embedded in the pattern space.

ed-style relative addresses, such as +++ or /sam/-- are not allowed.

Most **sed** commands accept zero, one, or two addresses. Zero addresses means perform the command on every line, one address means perform the command on all lines that match that address, and two addresses means perform the command on that range of lines. If the second address is less than the first, then the command is performed only on the line that matches the first address.

Any command may be preceded by a ! so that the command will be executed on lines that don't match the given address. You can surround a group of commands with {} to make them executed as a group. The syntax is one or two addresses followed by the { command, then commands on the following lines, and then a final } to delimit the end of the group.

TEXT MODIFICATION

>   *addr* a\
>
>   *text*\
>
>   *text*
>>   The append command places *text* on the output before the next input line is read. All but the last line of text must have a \ at the end to escape the following newline.

TEXT FILE
UTILITIES

addr1,addr2 c\

text

text

> The change command deletes each addressed pattern space, then outputs the *text*, and then starts a new cycle. All but the last line of text must have a \ at the end to escape the following newline.

addr1,addr2 d

> The delete command deletes the pattern space, and then starts a new cycle.

addr1,addr2 D

> The variant delete command deletes the initial segment of the pattern space, which extends from the beginning of the pattern space to the first newline, and then starts a new cycle. D is equivalent to d if the pattern space contains just one line.

addr i\

text

text

> The insert command immediately places *text* on the output. All but the last line of text must have a \ at the end of the line to escape the newline.

addr1,addr2 s/*expr*/*repl*/*f*

> Substitute *repl* for *expr* on all of the addressed lines. The text of *expr* may contain regular expression characters as explained under /*pat* above. The flags *f* may be: g to make all possible substitutions on the line (rather than just the leftmost); p to print the pattern space if a substitution is made; and w *wfile* to append the pattern space to the named file.

addr1,addr2 y/*string1*/*string2*/

> Change each occurrence of a character in *string1* into the corresponding character from *string2*. *string1* and *string2* must be the same length.

CONTROL FLOW

: *label*

> Make *label* a symbolic name for this location in the script.

addr1,addr2 b *label*

> Branch to the given label, or to the end of the script if *label* is absent.

addr1,addr2 n

> Write the pattern space to the output and then read in the next line of input. Note that the next line of the script to be executed will be the following line, not the first line of the script (which would be executed if a new cycle were executed).

addr1,addr2 N

Append the next line of input to the pattern space. The boundary between the previous end of the pattern space and the start of the newly added line will be marked with an embedded newline.

addr q

Quit writes the pattern space to the output, and then halts processing.

addr1,addr2 t *label*

Branch to the given *label* if any substitutions have been made since the last t or since the last line input. If *label* is missing, the branch will go to the end of the script.

INPUT AND OUTPUT

addr1,addr2 p

Print the addressed lines. An explicit print command isn't suppressed by the -n command line flag, which only stops the default output at the end of each cycle.

addr1,addr2 P

Print the initial segment of the pattern space. (The initial segment is from the beginning to the first embedded newline.)

addr1,addr2 r *file*

Read the named *file* and place its contents on the output before reading the next input line. The entire file will be copied to the output each time this command is encountered.

addr1,addr2 w *file*

Append the pattern space to the named file. Each file mentioned in a w command is created before the script starts to execute, and there can only be ten output files.

addr =

Print the line number on the standard output.

HOLD SPACE

addr1,addr2 g

Load the pattern space with the contents of the hold space. The original contents of the pattern space are lost.

addr1,addr2 G

Append the hold space to the end of the pattern space.

addr1,addr2 h

Load the hold space with the contents of the pattern space. The original contents of the hold space are lost.

addr1,addr2 H
>   Append the pattern space to the end of the hold space.

addr1,addr2 x
>   Exchange the pattern space and the hold space.

EXAMPLES

Two ways to double space a file:

```
$ cat lines
10
20
30
$ sed -n -e ´p
> g
> p´ lines
10

20

30

$ cat lines | sed -e ´a\
> ´
10

20

30

$ _
```

Print all lines in the input that have three or more adjacent capital letters:

```
$ date | deroff -w
Sun
Nov
EST
$ date | deroff -w | sed -n -e ´/[A-Z][A-Z][A-Z]/p´
EST
$ _
```

Replace symbolic chapter and section names with actual chapter and section numbers:

```
$ cat script
s/CUXBASIC/3/g
s/SCMDARGS/CSHONE.2/g
s/SMETA/CSHONE.8/g
s/CSHONE/4/g
$ cat doc
Chapter CUXBASIC covers the fundamental
features of the UX language. However, two
important features -- arguments and meta-
arguments -- aren't discussed until
Section SCMDARGS and Section SMETA.
$ sed -f script doc
Chapter 3 covers the fundamental
features of the UX language. However, two
important features -- arguments and meta-
arguments -- aren't discussed until
Section 4.2 and Section 4.8.
$ _
```

A script to print the *n*-th line of the input:

```
$ cat line_n
if [ $# -eq 0 ]
then
    echo usage: $0 n [ files ]
    exit -1
fi
n=$1
shift
case $n in
    [0-9] ) ;;
    [0-9][0-9]  ) ;;
    [0-9][0-9][0-9]  ) ;;
    [0-9][0-9][0-9][0-9] ) ;;
    [0-9][0-9][0-9][0-9][0-9] ) ;;
    *)  echo usage: $0 n [ files ]
        echo n must be a number
        exit -1
        ;;
esac
sed -n -e ${n}p "$@"
$ line_n 3 line_n
        echo usage: $0 n [ files ]
$ _
```

The sed command in this script will completely read all of its input, which might be undesirable when you print an early line of a long file. The script could be updated to make sed exit immediately after printing the desired line.

SORT

NAME

sort — sort and/or merge files

SYNOPSIS

sort [-cmu] [-tc] [-bdfinr] [+pos1 [-pos2]] ...
    [-o outfile] [file ...]

DESCRIPTION

The sort program sorts the input files. The output is sent to the standard output by default, or to a named output file if the -o option is used.

The rearrangement of the input is based on a sort *key*, which is the part of each line that sort examines to determine which line goes first. By default, the sort key is the entire line. However, if the position options are used, then the sort key is restricted to the indicated fields of the line. There can be several position options to indicate several sort keys; later keys are used only when the earlier keys compare as equal. As a last resort, lines that otherwise compare equal are ordered with all positions significant.

The following five options are used to control the general behavior of the sort program. (The ordering options will be discussed shortly.)

-c Check the input file to verify that it is sorted according to the rules. No output is produced unless the file is not properly sorted.

-m Merge the input files. Presumably the input files are already sorted, because sort will only examine one line of each input at a time.

-o *outfile*
    The output is written to the named file rather than to the standard output. sort doesn't start writing to the output until the input is completely read. This allows you to specify an output file that is the same as one of the input files. You cannot achieve this same result using output redirection, and you cannot count on this capability in other commands that have a -o outfile option.

-t*c*
    The character *c* is taken as the field separator. Blanks (spaces and tabs) are ordinarily used as the field separator.

-u Suppress all but one in a set of equal lines. (Each output line will be unique.) For the purposes of this option, equal lines are defined as lines

that compare as equal within all of the active sort keys. Fields outside of
the sort keys as well as ignored characters (see the -b and the -i options)
do not participate in the judgment of equality.

The position indicators are used to indicate the part of the line that controls the
sorting. Each line is constructed of *fields*, which are separated by field separator
characters. By default, the field separator is white space, but the -t option can
specify an alternate field separator. The syntax for the position indicators lets
you specify a particular field of the line, plus a character offset from the beginning of that field.

The position indicator +pos1 makes a sort key start at the indicated position. If
+pos1 is missing, then the sort key starts at the beginning of the line. The position indicator -pos2 makes a sort key stop just before the indicated position. If
-pos2 is missing, then the sort key stops at the end of the line.

The position indicators have the form m.n where m indicates the number of fields
to skip from the beginning of the line, and n indicates the number of characters
to skip further. The position indicator +5.2 indicates that a sort key starts after
skipping five fields and then the next two characters. The position indicator -0.2
indicates that a sort key ends after skipping zero fields and then two characters.
If the n part of a position indicator is missing, then zero is assumed.

The following options control the ordering of items. If these options appear
before any position indicators, then they apply to all of the fields. The ordering
options also can be placed following the position indicators in order to specify
the ordering for that particular field.

-b Ignore leading spaces and tabs when making a field comparison.

-d Enable dictionary-style ordering rather than the default ASCII collating
sequence. Only letters, digits, and blanks are significant in field
comparisons.

-f Fold upper-case letters into lower-case letters for the purpose of field comparisons. In the output, the original case is retained.

-i Ignore characters outside of the ASCII range 040 − 0176 in non-numeric
comparisons.

-n Perform numeric comparisons. A number may have leading blanks, an
optional minus sign, and zero or more digits with an optional decimal
point. The ordering is according to the numeric value, not the dictionary
ordering or the ASCII collating sequence.

-r Order the items in decreasing order. (Normally items are put into increasing order.)

-M Order the items according to the order of months in a year. Only the first
three non-blank characters in the field are important, and they are

assumed to be the first three letters of a month name. This option makes "Jan" less than "Aug". Case is ignored. (System V only.)

The following System V features are useful for optimizing large sorts. Most users can safely ignore these features.

-y*n*

Start with *n* kilobytes of memory for the sort. For sorting small files you might try the **-y**0 option, which will start with a minimal amount of memory. For large files, the **-y** (with no *n* specification) option may be best; it will start the sort with the maximum amount of memory.

-z*n*

Assume a maximum record size of *n* characters. This option is only needed when **sort** is merging already sorted files that contain large records.

EXAMPLES

The first few examples refer to the file 'tdata'.

```
$ cat tdata
apple
Balloon
apple
Apple
$ _
```

I am using an example with duplicates because handling duplicates is one of the major problems in controlling the sorting process.

Sort 'tdata' and place the output in 'tdata.1':

```
$ sort -o tdata.1 tdata
$ cat tdata.1
Apple
Balloon
apple
apple
$ _
```

The ordering occurs because in the ASCII sequence upper-case letters precede lower-case letters.

Sort 'tdata' without regard to capitalization:

```
$ sort -f tdata
Apple
apple
apple
Balloon
$ _
```

The three apple words are ordered by the last resort rule: when lines compare as equal, order them with every position on the line significant.

Sort 'tdata' and discard equal lines:

```
$ sort -u tdata
Apple
Balloon
apple
$ _
```

Sort 'tdata' without regard to capitalization and discard equal lines, producing the upper-case line if both cases are present. You might think first of this command:

```
$ sort -fu tdata
```

The problem is that the -u option will discard either the upper-case or the lower-case line. The -f option prevents sort's seeing the difference. The reliable solution is to perform two sorts: the first orders the lines and the second removes the duplicates.

```
$ sort -f tdata | sort -muf
Apple
Balloon
$ _
```

The first sort in the pipeline orders the lines, while ignoring case. However, upper-case lines will always precede lower-case lines because of the "last resort" rule. The second sort in the pipeline merges the already sorted data, discarding the trailing duplicate lines. Ordinarily the -m option is used when there are several input files, and sort's job is to pick the next line from among the choices. However, on a more fundamental level the -m option guarantees that the order in the input will be preserved. Hence, merging a single file allows one to predict which items will be discarded (the subsequent items) when the -u option is present.

Sort 'tdata' to produce all of the unique words. When a word is present in both the capitalized form and the lower-case form, the capitalized word should follow the lower-case word in the final list:

```
$ sort -u +0f +0r tdata
apple
Apple
Balloon
$ _
```

This is essentially a two-pass sort. Each +0 sort key specifies the entire line. The ordering in the second key (r—reverse) is used only to resolve entries that compare as equal under the ordering of the first key (f—ignore case distinction). In our example, the three apple words will compare as equal because of the f option. The second key specifies a reverse sort that will place the capitalized "Apple" following the lower-case "apple". The -u option discards the duplicate lower-case "apple".

The following few examples refer to the file 'numbs'.

```
$ cat numbs
ab: 40
cd:-20
ab:.30
$ _
```

Sort 'numbs' in dictionary order:

```
$ sort -d numbs
ab: 40
ab:.30
cd:-20
$ _
```

The colon, hyphen, and period are ignored in dictionary ordering. The space is not ignored, and, since a space precedes a digit, the two lines that start *ab* have the order shown above.

Sort 'numbs' by the second field (fields are separated by colons):

```
$ sort -t: +1 numbs
ab: 40
cd:-20
ab:.30
$ _
```

The ordering occurs because in the ASCII sequence space precedes the hyphen, which precedes the period.

Sort 'numbs' according to the numerical ordering of the second field:

```
$ sort -t: +1n numbs
cd:-20
ab:.30
ab: 40
$ _
```

Sort 'numbs' primarily according to the first field and, secondarily, according to the reverse numerical ordering of the second field:

```
$ sort -t: +0 -1 +1rn numbs
ab: 40
ab:.30
cd:-20
$ _
```

The +0 and -1 option specifies the first field as a sort key. The +1rn option specifies the second field as a sort key, and the rn part specifies that the order should be reversed and the comparisons should be numerical.

SPELL

NAME

spell — check spelling in text files

SYNOPSIS

spell [options] [file ...]

DESCRIPTION

The spell program extracts all of the words from the named files (or from the standard input if no files are named) and looks them up in a dictionary. All of the words that are not in the dictionary and cannot be derived from the dictionary words by applying standard inflections, prefixes, and suffixes are listed on the standard output as possible misspellings. Some of the words flagged by spell are correct, while certain errors in the text are not detected. However, even though spell is not perfect, it is a valuable aid for locating most spelling errors. spell ignores nroff/troff commands in files.

spell supports three options, which are seldom used by most users.

-b Check British spelling.

-v Print all words that aren't in the dictionary along with possible derivations.

-x Print every possible stem for each word.

When you check the spelling of a short file, it is often convenient to display spell's output on the terminal. However, for longer files it is useful to redirect spell's list of possible misspellings to a file, or to pipe spell's output to a file pager (more or pg). It is also often useful to use pr or paste to turn spell's single-column output into a multicolumn format.

The System V version of spell includes a feature that makes it easy to specify a list of correctly spelled words that spell doesn't have in its main dictionary. This lets you customize spell so that fewer correct words are spuriously reported in the output. Your local dictionary file should contain correctly spelled words, one per line, and the file must be sorted. You can use any text editor to create the file, but it is your responsibility to make sure that the file is sorted. When you run spell, you should use the command line option +localdict to tell spell to use your dictionary of correctly spelled words in addition to the standard dictionary.

TEXT FILE
UTILITIES

EXAMPLES

Check a file for misspelled words:

```
$ cat words
Words that i ofen mispell: precede (not preceede)
business (not buisness) occurrence (not occurence)
$ spell words
buisness
mispell
occurence
ofen
preceede
$ spell -v words
buisness
mispell
occurence
ofen
preceede
-t+ce occurrence
+s Words
$ _
```

The first five words in the -v output are words that spell can't find in its dictionary. The word "occurrence" isn't literally in the dictionary, but it can be derived from "occurrent" (which is in the dictionary) by deleting the final *t*, as indicated by the *-t* notation, and then adding the *ce* suffix, as indicated by the *+ce* notation. The word "Words" also isn't in the dictionary, but it can be derived from "word" by adding an *s*, as indicated by the "*+s*" notation.

Check the spelling of a few words:

```
$ echo remunerate | spell
$ echo repetoire | spell
repetoire
$ spell
proceed
precede
^D
$ _
```

Berkeley contains the look program that will print words from '/usr/dict/words' that start with the given letters:

```
$ look repet
repetition
repetitious
repetitive
$ look rep | grep oir
repertoire
$ _
```

TAIL

NAME

tail — print the end of a text file

SYNOPSIS

tail [offset] [option] [file]

DESCRIPTION

The tail program prints the last part of the named file or the last part of the standard input if no file is mentioned.

The offset argument is used to control how much of the end of the file is printed. When the offset argument is introduced by a hyphen, the offset is relative to the end of the file; when the offset is introduced by a plus sign, the offset specifies an amount to skip from the beginning of the file. The offset can be specified in units of lines, blocks, or characters by using the suffixes l (the default), b, and c, respectively. If no offset is mentioned, then tail prints the last ten lines of the file.

The -f option tells tail to wait when the end of file is reached, expecting the file to grow. This option is useful to observe the growth of a file that is being written by a running program.

Berkeley tail accepts the -r option, which causes the lines to be printed in the reverse order.

EXAMPLES

Print the last ten lines of the file '/usr/dict/words':

```
$ tail /usr/dict/words
zombie
zone
zoo
zoology
zoroaster
zoroastrian
zounds
z's
Zurich
$ _
```

Print the last twenty characters of '/usr/dict/words':

```
$ tail -20c /usr/dict/words
n
zounds
z's
Zurich
$ _
```

Print the last line of a long format listing of the '/bin' directory:

```
$ ls -l /bin | tail -1
-rwxr-xr-x 1 root   11264   Sep27 1983 write
$ _
```

NOTE

There is a limit to how far tail can back up from the end of a file.

```
$ wc /usr/dict/words
   24474    24474   201039 /usr/dict/words
$ tail -1000 /usr/dict/words | wc
    1000     1000     7442
$ tail -10000 /usr/dict/words | wc
    8054     8054    65536
$ _
```

TEE

NAME

tee — duplicate the standard input

SYNOPSIS

tee [-i] [-a] [file ...]

DESCRIPTION

The tee program duplicates the standard input by sending one copy to the named files and one copy to the standard output. tee in a UNIX pipeline is the equivalent of a tee fitting in a plumber's pipeline. tee usually is used when you want to place the output of a program in a file and see it too, although tee also can be used in pipelines to save intermediate stages of processing that would normally be invisible.

The -i option instructs tee to ignore interrupts and the -a option instructs tee to append its output to the output files rather than overwrite the output files.

EXAMPLES

Save the output of the spell program in a file and simultaneously view the output on the screen:

```
$ spell ch1.doc | tee ch1.errs
regiseter
simlar
Toklas
typcially
uou
$ wc ch1.errs
    5    5    38
$ _
```

Save the output of the wc program in the 'ch1.size' file, simultaneously append the output to the 'ch1.log' file, and also see the output on the terminal:

```
$ wc ch1.doc | tee -a ch1.log | tee ch1.size
   728   6228   38755   ch1.doc
$ cat ch1.size
   728   6228   38755   ch1.doc
```

```
$ cat ch1.log
    353    6228    17705    ch1.doc
    570    6228    28559    ch1.doc
    638    6228    30425    ch1.doc
    729    6229    38758    ch1.doc
    728    6228    38755    ch1.doc
$ _
```

Use tee to display an intermediate stage of a pipeline on the terminal:

```
$ ls
ac          script
$ ls -l | tee /dev/tty | lpr
total 1
-rwxr-xr-x  1 kc        898 Mar 25 00:47 ac
-rw-r--r--  1 kc         90 Mar 25 01:03 tscript
$ _
```

WC

NAME

wc — count words, lines, and characters in files

SYNOPSIS

wc [-lwc] [file ...]

DESCRIPTION

The word count program is used to count units of text in text files. The usual case is for wc to report the number of lines, words, and characters in its input files, or in the standard input if no files are mentioned in the command line. The options can be used to direct wc's attention to count just words (-w), lines (-l), or characters (-c).

EXAMPLES

Count the lines, words, and characters in 'mydoc':

```
$ wc mydoc
    72   622    3875    mydoc
$ _
```

Equivalently, one could use the command:

```
$ wc -lwc mydoc
    72   622    3875    mydoc
$ _
```

Count the number of words in 'mydoc':

```
$ wc -w mydoc
    622    mydoc
$ _
```

Count the number of words in 'mydoc' without displaying its name:

```
$ wc -w < mydoc
    622
$ _
```

Count the number of files in the current directory:

```
$ ls | wc -l
   61
$ _
```

Count the lines, words, and characters in several files. Note that a cumulative total appears at the end:

```
$ wc p*.t
      47     235    1446 passwd.t
     156     739    4768 paste.t
     141     904    5481 pg.t
     118     658    4412 pr.t
     136     613    3994 ps.t
     144     535    4384 psV.t
      25      60     334 pwd.t
     767    3744   24819 total
$ _
```

SECTION IV

PROCESS MANAGEMENT COMMANDS

A *process* is an executing program. The UNIX system has several programs that let you control and monitor your own processes. The most important is probably ps, which summarizes the status of your current processes. Berkeley and System V have slightly different ps programs, so be sure to read the appropriate manual page.

When processes are running in the foreground, you can stop them using keyboard signals (or keyboard commands during interactive programs), but you need the kill program to manage your background processes.

The other commands in this part of the book let you alter the environment of your processes. The nice command will run processes at reduced priority so that other more important tasks will get more attention. The nohup program will run processes that are immune to the hangup signal, so that you can start background processes that continue to execute while you are logged off. The time program times your process, so that you can see the total elapsed time, the time spent running ordinary user code, and the time spent by the system for the process.

PROCESS
MANAGEMENT

AT

NAME

at — run shell programs later

SYSTEM V SYNOPSIS

```
at time [ date ] [ +incr ]
at -r jobnum ...
at -l [ jobnum ... ]
batch
```

BERKELEY SYNOPSIS

```
at time [ date ] [ file ]
atq
atrm
```

DESCRIPTION

The at program is used to execute shell programs some time in the future. at makes a copy of commands read from the standard input (or a file on a Berkeley system) and then arranges to have those commands executed when the time occurs. When the commands are executed, they will be executed in your current directory with all of the environment variables set to the same values they had when you ran the at command. Thus, when the commands are actually executed, the environment will be the same as your environment when you execute the at command. If the commands in the shell script write to the standard output, you should use output redirection to save the results in a file.

The *time* argument to the at command consists of one to four digits optionally followed by an a for AM, a p for PM, an n for noon, or an m for midnight. If the time argument is either one or two digits, then the number is assumed to represent hours; if there are three or four digits, then hours and minutes are assumed. If no letters follow the digits, then the 24 hour clock is assumed.

The optional *date* argument takes one of two forms: either a month name followed by a day number or else a day of the week. A day of the week may be followed by the word week, in which case the command will be run a week later than the mentioned day. You can abbreviate the month names or the day names.

The System V version of at has a slightly more flexible time format. In addition to the *time* format described above, System V understands the times noon, midnight, now, and next. In addition to the *date* keywords mentioned above, System V also recognizes today and tomorrow. The +incr argument of System V lets you specify a time increment. It is formed from a number followed by minutes, hours, weeks, months, or years. For example, now +5 minutes means five minutes from now.

You can make a job run periodically by including another at command in the shell script. For example, the following skeleton shell script will run a job every morning at 2 AM.

```
$ cat $HOME/bin/periodic.sh
# put commands here to do something
# each morning
at 3a < $HOME/bin/periodic.sh
$ _
```

Of course this script must be started once manually, but once started it will continue to run daily.

The System V version of at supports two command line options that allow you to look at your queue of scheduled jobs, or to remove jobs from your queue.

-l [*jobnum*]
    List your jobs in the at or batch queue.

-r *jobnum*
    Remove a job from the at or batch queue.

System V contains two additional programs for executing shell programs at a later date. The batch program will run a job when system load is low, and the cron program will periodically run a job.

On Berkeley 4.3 the standard at program has been augmented by atq to examine your jobs on the queue and atrm to remove your jobs from the queue.

EXAMPLES

Run the shell program 'nroffbk.sh' at 2AM on Tuesday:

```
$ at 2 tues < nroffbk.sh
$ _
```

Run the shell program 'cmds.sh' on January 2 at 3PM:

```
$ at 3p jan 2 < cmds.sh
$ _
```

or equivalently

```
$ at 15 jan 2 < cmds.sh
$ _
```

Run the shell program 'cmds.sh' a week from Friday at midnight:

```
$ at 12m fri week < cmds.sh
$ _
```

NOTE

If you want to reduce system load, it is better to use at to run large programs during the wee hours of the morning rather than using nice during peak periods to run the programs at reduced priority.

KILL

NAME

kill — send a signal to a process

SYSTEM V SYNOPSIS

kill [-signalnumber] processid

BERKELEY SYNOPSIS

kill [-signalnumber] processid
kill [-signalname] processid
kill [-signalnumber] %jobnum
kill [-signalname] %jobnum
kill -l

DESCRIPTION

The kill command usually is used to terminate background processes or processes running on another terminal. In order to terminate a process you need to know its process id number and you must either own the process or be the super-user. You can acquire the process id number for a process using the ps command, or you can remember the number that is printed by the shell when you run a process in the background.

Most signals may be caught by a process, and handled as they deem fit. Thus, a process may receive a signal, but not react in the ordinary manner. For example, a process can receive the terminate signal without terminating. It is up to each process to arrange to catch any signal that it wants to handle. A few signals, such as the kill signal, cannot be caught by a process.

kill usually sends signal number 15, the terminate signal, to the target process. Other signal numbers can be sent by supplying the signal number on the command line. One very useful signal number is 9, the kill signal, which is a form of the terminate signal that cannot be caught or ignored.

If the special process id number 0 is specified, kill will send the signal to every job in the current process group—that is, all jobs resulting from the current login session. This is an easy way to send a signal to all of your processes. Beware that kill -9 0 will log you out by killing your shell. The C shell's built-in kill command omits the pid 0 convention.

Signals are sent from an active process to an inactive process. When the target process resumes execution, the first chore for the kernel is to examine the list of signals to see if any new signals have arrived. If there are new signals, the appropriate actions will be taken. A consequence of this strategy is that processes that are stuck in some non-executable state, often as a result of a hardware error or an error in a device driver, will never respond to their signals.

The Berkeley version of `kill` lets you specify signals by name, although you can still use numbers if you prefer. A list of signal names is produced using the `-l` option. See the example below. Another Berkeley feature is the ability to specify job numbers instead of process id numbers. The job number must be preceded by a % symbol.

Here is a list of the most common signals.

HUP	1	Sent when the phone line drops carrier.
INT	2	Sent when the user strikes the interrupt character.
QUIT	3	Sent when you type the quit character. The process will usually create a debugging file called 'core'.
KILL	9	The surest way to terminate a process because it cannot be caught or ignored. Only use as a last resort.
TERM	15	Sent to terminate a process, but it can be caught or ignored.

A complete list of signals can be gleaned from the '/usr/include/signal.h' file. The `signal(2)` or `sigvec(2)` manual page in most UNIX manuals can also provide more information on signals.

EXAMPLES

Kill process 1103:

```
$ cc -c corrsubs.c &
1103
$ kill 1103
$ ps
  PID TT STAT   TIME COMMAND
 1109 h0 R     0:01 ps
1103 killed
$ _
```

Note that the shell notifies you that the process was killed at the conclusion of the following command, just before printing the prompt.

On a Berkeley system, print a list of the signal names, and then send a KILL signal to a print request:

```
$ man -t sh &
[1]     28521
$ kill -l
EXIT HUP INT QUIT ILL TRAP IOT EMT FPE KILL BUS SEGV
SYS PIPE ALR MTERM URG STOP TSTP CONT CHLD TTIN IO
TINT XCPU VTALRM
$ kill -KILL 28521
$ ps
  PID TT STAT  TIME COMMAND
28537 h3 R     0:01 ps
[1] + Killed                     man -t sh &
$ _
```

Notice that the Korn shell (shown above) and the C shell print job number as well as the process id number when a process is placed into the background. The kill command in this example could have been kill -KILL %1.

NOTES

If kill is built into your shell, you can execute the '/bin/kill' command to run the command described here.

The C shell and the Korn shell let you use the notation %*jobnum* in place of a process id number to send a signal to a background job.

Sending the KILL (9) signal to a process is often not in your best interest. Since processes cannot catch or ignore KILL, it is the surest kill. But that also means that programs, such as vi, that do their best to preserve your data even in the worst of times, will not be able to perform their usual exit preserve and cleanup. Use the KILL signal only as a last resort.

You cannot kill a background setuid process with the kill command. On systems with job control, you can use the job control to bring the background process to the fore and then kill it using normal keyboard signals. Without job control your only recourse is to convince a system administrator to log in as root and kill the process for you.

NICE

NAME

nice — run a process at reduced priority

SYNOPSIS

nice [-n] command [arguments]

DESCRIPTION

The nice command is used to reduce the priority of a process, thereby reducing the demands that the process places on the system. nice typically is applied to time consuming background processes to prevent them from degrading system performance.

The optional numeric increment *n* is used to specify the priority reduction. The lowest priority attainable in the UNIX system is achieved with a value of 19. A barely perceptible decrease in priority is achieved with a value of 1. If no value is specified, then a default of 10 is assumed.

While ordinary users can only decrease the priority of their process, the super-user can run jobs at increased priority by specifying a negative value.

EXAMPLES

Run a process called 'bigjob' in the background at low priority:

```
$ nice bigjob &
1273
$ _
```

Run 'bigjob' at the minimum priority:

```
$ nice -19 bigjob
$
```

Run a process called 'importjob' at maximum priority:

```
$ nice --19 importjob
$ _
```

Note that you must be super-user to specify a negative value (− 19 in this case).

PROCESS
MANAGEMENT

NOTES

All active processes compete for resources, even when they are scheduled at low priority. Running processes at slack periods (see the at command) is a more effective way to reduce system load than running processes at low priority during peak periods. nice is also a C shell built-in function, whose argument takes the opposite sign. Thus, nice +10 cmd should be used by C shell users to reduce the priority by ten. C shell users can run the version of nice described here using the /bin/nice command.

Berkeley has a renice program that lets you reduce the priority of already executing background jobs.

NOHUP

NAME

nohup — run a program that is immune to hangups

SYNOPSIS

nohup command [arguments]

DESCRIPTION

Normally any commands that you have started in the background will be sent the hangup signal when you log off the system. Most programs exit when they receive the hangup signal. The nohup command is used to initialize processes so that they ignore the hangup and quit signals. Thus, any commands you run in the background using nohup will not die when you log off the system.

nohup will direct the standard output and the standard error output to the file 'nohup.out' unless you use output redirection to specify some other disk file.

EXAMPLES

nroff a file in the background using nohup so that you can log off while the processing is being performed:

```
$ nohup nroff -ms chapt?.n > chaps.nr &
18941
$ _
```

PROCESS
MANAGEMENT

PS (Berkeley)

NAME

ps — print process status

SYNOPSIS

ps [options] [namelist]

DISTRIBUTION

Berkeley only. A different program of the same name is used in System V. Berkeley's version of ps is a descendent of the Version 7 ps.

DESCRIPTION

The ps command is used to print information about the active processes. ps does for processes what ls does for files. Without options the ps command prints the following information for all your personal processes: the process id number, the name of the controlling tty, the process state, the cumulative execution time, and an approximation of the command line.

The state field is coded as four letters:

	First Letter — Run Status		Second Letter — Swap Status
		W	Swapped
R	Running	*blank*	Not Swapped
T	Stopped	>	Exceeding soft core limit
P	Page Wait		Third Letter — Priority
D	Disk/Short Wait		
S	Sleeping (less than 20 sec.)	N	Reduced Priority
I	Idle (more than 20 sec.)	*blank*	Normal Priority
		<	Raised Priority

The fourth letter details virtual memory usage and is not useful to most users.

The following options can be used to modify the action of the ps command:

-a   Print information about all processes with a controlling tty, not just your personal processes.

-g   Print information for additional processes, such as children of init, sleeping processes, and zombies. The -g option must be combined with the -a option to examine processes other than your own. The number of processes listed by the -g option is less than or equal to the number listed by the -x option.

-x   Print information for additional processes such as children of init, sleepers, and zombies, even if they don't have a controlling tty. The -x option combined with -a prints every process in the system.

-t*name*

Print information for the named tty. *Name* has the same form as in the ps output: co is the console, 30 is '/dev/tty30', etc.

-l   Produce a long format listing. Most of the information presented in a long format ps listing is too technical to be of much use for ordinary users—see the -u option.

-u   Print more useful information about each process. The most active processes are listed first. The USER field is the login name of the user, the %CPU and %MEM fields detail what percent of the machine's cpu time and real memory are dedicated to the process, the SZ and RSS fields list the program size in kilobytes and the amount (the resident set) actually in core, and the other fields are as discussed above. This option is more useful to most users than the traditional -l option.

-v   Print virtual memory statistics.

pid   If a process id number is mentioned, then the information for that process is produced. This option must be last.

EXAMPLES

Produce a list of the current processes:

```
$ ps
 PID TT STAT  TIME COMMAND
2262 h3 R     0:02 ps
$ _
```

Produce a user format list of the information for your active processes:

```
$ ps -u
USER    PID %CPU %MEM   SZ  RSS TT STAT  TIME COMMAND
kc     2285 54.8  9.1  173  111 h3 R     0:02 ps -u
$ _
```

Produce a user format list of all of your processes:

```
$ ps -gu
USER      PID %CPU %MEM   SZ  RSS TT STAT  TIME COMMAND
kc       2309 49.2 10.1  187  124 h3 R     0:07 ps -gu
kc      28868 0.3  3.6   107   41 h3 S     0:14 -sh
$ _
```

Print some information about process 1930:

```
$ ps 1930
  PID TT STAT   TIME COMMAND
 1930 h3 S      1:02 vi /usr1/julie/unixbook/man.t
$ _
```

The -t option is useful when something gets fouled up on one terminal and you go to another terminal to fix (kill the offenders) the problem.

```
$ ps -uti3
USER      PID %CPU %MEM   SZ  RSS TT STAT TIME COMMAND
kc      28466 52.8 2.5   63   27 i3 R     0:54 tip mpc
kc      18767 0.1  2.9  107   32 i3 I     0:04 -sh
kc      28465 0.0  2.5   63   27 i3 I     0:00 tip mpc
$ _
```

The -ax option will list information about every process in the system. It is often useful to filter the ps output with grep to look at a subset of the system's processes:

```
$ ps ax | grep tu
20347 h6 S    0:00 grep tu
   64 i5 IW   0:00 /usr/local/tu/tu58 -s9600 /dev/ttyi5
23859 ic IW   0:11 /usr/local/tu/tu58 -s9600 /dev/tty12
$ _
```

NOTE

The Version 7 ps command is closer to this version than to the System V ps.

PS (System V)

NAME

ps — print process status

SYNOPSIS

ps [options]

DISTRIBUTION

System V only. Version 7 users should use the Berkeley ps manual page.

DESCRIPTION

The System V ps command lists information about processes. By default, a brief summary of your own processes is listed. Options let you direct ps to look at additional processes, and to print additional information for each process. In addition, there are systems management options that are used for post-mortem systems debugging.

First let's discuss the options that control which processes are listed. The last four options refer to a *list* argument, which may be a comma-separated list of items that doesn't contain blanks, or a quoted list of items where the items are separated by either commas or blanks.

-a Print information about all processes, except for processes that are not attached to a terminal, or processes that are process group leaders.

-d Print information about all processes, except for process group leaders.

-e Print information about all processes, including those excluded from a -a listing.

-t *list*
   Print information about processes attached to any of the ttys in the list.

-p *list*
   Print information about processes whose PID numbers are in the list.

-u *list*
   Print information about processes owned by the users in the list. Users may be identified by user id number or by login names.

-g *list*
   Print information about processes in the given process groups.

PROCESS MANAGEMENT

Ordinarily the listing contains four fields: the process id number, the tty name, the cumulative execution time, and the name of the command. More information will be listed for each process when one of the following options is used.

-l   Print a long description of each process. Much of the information listed is too technical for most users.

-f   Print a full description of each process. A full description contains the login name of the process' owner, the process id number, the process id of the process' parents, the recent cpu usage of the process, the starting time of the process, the name of the process' tty, the cumulative execution time for the process, and the command string. Processes are free to obliterate their arguments, so the command string may be incorrect. Only the name (not the entire command string) will be printed for swapped out processes.

EXAMPLES

Display the status of your processes:

```
$ ps
  PID TTY TIME COMMAND
   36 co  0:02 sh
   61 co  0:04 ps
$ _
```

Display the status of all of the active processes:

```
$ ps -e
  PID TTY TIME COMMAND
    0  ? 73:16 swapper
    1  ?  0:01 init
   36 co  0:02 sh
   37 02  0:01 getty
   23  ?  0:00 update
   28  ?  0:00 lpsched
   32  ?  0:01 cron
   38 03  0:01 getty
   39 04  0:01 getty
   40 05  0:01 getty
   41 06  0:01 getty
   70 co  0:04 ps
$ _
```

PROCESS MANAGEMENT

Display a full listing of the current processes:

```
$ ps -f
   UID  PID PPID  C   STIME TTY  TIME COMMAND
   kc    36    1  0 17:45:10 co  0:02 -sh
   kc    73   36 79 18:58:08 co  0:04 ps -f
$ _
```

Display the status of the processes attached to '/dev/console' or to '/dev/tty02':

```
$ ps -t 02,console
 PID TTY TIME COMMAND
  36 co  0:03 sh
  37 02  0:02 sh
  95 02  0:01 eqn
  93 02  0:02 tbl
  94 02  0:06 nroff
 103 co  0:04 ps
$ _
```

Display a full format listing of process thirty-seven:

```
$ ps -fp 37
   UID  PID PPID  C   STIME TTY  TIME COMMAND
   kc    37    1  0 17:45:10 02  0:02 -sh
$ _
```

Display a full format list of the processes in the process group headed by process thirty-seven:

```
$ ps -fg 37
   UID  PID PPID  C   STIME TTY  TIME COMMAND
   kc    37    1  0 17:45:10 02  0:02 -sh
   kc    95   94  0 19:02:16 02  0:01 eqn
   kc    93   37  0 19:02:16 02  0:02 tbl /usr/dict/words
   kc    94   37  0 19:02:16 02  0:06 nroff -ms
$ _
```

PROCESS MANAGEMENT

TIME

NAME

time — time a process

SYNOPSIS

time command [arguments]

DESCRIPTION

The time command allows you to time a process. When the process is complete, the time program prints three indications (in seconds): the total elapsed time, the user execution time of the process, and the system time of the process. The times can depend on a variety of random factors; most notably, the total elapsed time is highly dependent on the system load.

(If you want to see what time it is, run the date program.)

EXAMPLES

Time the who process:

```
$ time who
gilbert    ttyh1    May 3 15:35
jurgen     ttyh3    May 8 21:17
dan        ttyi9    May 8 13:30
    0.6real   0.1user   0.2sys
$ _
```

Time the ls program producing a long format listing of the '/bin' directory:

```
$ time ls -l /bin > /dev/null
    2.8real   1.3user   1.3sys
$ _
```

NOTES

The Korn shell and the C shell contain a built-in time command. You may have to use the name '/bin/time' to access the command described here.

The command time a | b will only time a because the shell pipes the output of the time a command into the b command. However, shells that have a built-in time command may time both commands. The easiest way to time an entire pipeline is `time sh -c ´a | b´`. The shell's `-c` option is discussed on the shell manual page.

The output format of the time information varies widely.

`time`'s output goes to the standard error. This feature makes it easy to time a command whose output has been redirected, but it is difficult to capture `time`'s output in a pipeline.

The C shell contains an internal variable named `time`. When `$time` is set, any command that takes more than `$time` cpu seconds will automatically be timed.

SECTION V

UNIX SHELLS

.	:	eval	exec
exit	export	newgrp	read
readonly	shift	times	trap
ulimit	umask	unset	wait

In the early days of the UNIX system there was just one shell, the simple Version 6 shell. It demonstrated the concept of providing a powerful command interpreter combined with a programming language, and it demonstrated that an ordinary program could provide a flexible interface between users and the system.

The Version 6 shell was replaced by two separate shells, the Bourne shell, created by Steve Bourne, then of Bell Laboratories; and the C shell, created by William Joy, then of Berkeley. Since both shells were heavily influenced by the Version 6 shell, there are surprisingly large areas of similarity. Features like I/O redirection, pipelines, and filename generation, which are much of the most critical user interface code in the shell, are extremely similar. Where these two shells differ is in their programming language features. Treatment of variables is a little different; treatment of programming language control structures is very different.

The Bourne shell, which is universally available and has one or two technical features that are much admired, has become the standard shell for writing portable command scripts. The C shell also features a powerful command language, but its unavailability on System V makes it a poor choice for writing command scripts that may be used on many systems.

However, the C shell goes considerably farther in the development of an interactive user interface than the original Bourne shell. The C shell has a history mechanism, which lets you construct new commands out of your old commands. It also has job control, which is a flexible way to switch your attention between several simultaneous tasks. There are also a few less important user interface features, such as tilde substitution for naming people's home directories, aliases for creating new names for existing facilities, a directory stack to make it easier to move around the filesystem, and a few wrinkles in the filename generation process. These advantages have made the C shell a much used interactive command interpreter, and that is how it is described here. I have purposely omitted the programming language features of the C shell to more completely cover its very useful interactive features.

The Bourne shell, because it is commonly used both for interactive command entry and for writing command scripts, is covered more completely. The Bourne shell itself is covered in a (long) manual page, and its programming language control constructs—case, for, if, while, and until—are covered in their own manual pages. One of the Bourne shell's most important built-in commands, set, is also covered in its own manual page.

This part of the manual also covers a pair of programs that are often used in shell scripts. expr is a simple arithmetic and string-matching program. It is often used to perform arithmetic on shell variables. test evaluates conditions and checks to see if files exist. It is often used in if or while statements as the conditional statement.

For more casual users, the programming language features of the shells can be ignored. For C shell users, the first two sections of the C shell manual page, *Filename Generation* and *I/O Redirection, Pipelines, and Background Processes*, are probably most important. If you want to get the most out of the C shell, you should read the entire manual page. For Bourne shell users, the most important sections are probably *Pipelines, I/O Redirection, and Background Processes* and *Argument List Generation and Quoting*. If you want to be proficient in interactive use of the Bourne shell (but not in writing shell scripts), you should probably read the entire manual page, although the separate pages on the programming language control structures, plus `set`, `test`, and `expr`, can be omitted.

CASE

NAME

case — Bourne shell conditional to execute one of a group of lists

SYNOPSIS

case *name* in [*pattern* [| *pattern*] ...) *list* ;;] ... esac

DESCRIPTION

The case command is the Bourne shell conditional that performs a One-of-N-way branch. The body of a case statement consists of a group of lists, each identified by one or more patterns. The value of the shell variable *name* is compared in turn with the patterns. When a match occurs, the given list is executed, thereby completing the execution of the case statement. The order of the patterns is important because when there are several patterns that match *name*, only the list following the topmost match will be executed. Notice that the end of each command list is marked by a pair of semicolons. The end of the entire case statement is marked by the word *esac*, which is case spelled backwards.

The patterns may contain the usual shell metacharacters (*, ?, and [) for filename generation. An additional metacharacter, |, is available as shown in the SYNOPSIS. In the context of a case statement the | loses its meaning as a pipeline indicator and is instead used to specify multiple patterns for a given command list. The list will be executed if the variable *name* matches any of the | separated patterns. There isn't a built-in alternative that is executed if all of the other options fail (such as the *default* clause in the C language), but one can be created using the pattern * to identify the last list.

UNIX SHELLS

EXAMPLES

The following shell program chooses a text preprocessor for a file based on the filename's suffix. Files whose names end in '.t' are processed by tbl, those whose names end in '.e' are processed by eqn, those whose names end in '.p' are processed by pic, and all others are sent (unmodified) to the mmt text formatter by cat.

```
$ cat roffem
PREPROC=""
case "$1" in
    *.t) PREPROC=tbl ;;
    *.e) PREPROC=eqn ;;
    *.p) PREPROC=pic ;;
    *) PREPROC=cat ;;
esac
$PREPROC $1 | mmt
$ _
```

Note that this simple example handles only a single argument, and no option arguments are allowed.

The case construct is often used inside a for loop to process command line arguments. For example, consider a shell script that accepts the options -a and -b, and then one or more file names. In the following fragment of a shell program, a case statement is used inside a for loop to process the arguments. If either of the allowed options is present, a variable is set to the value *y*; any disallowed option argument generates an error message, and the supplied filenames are accumulated into a variable called FILES.

```
$ cat examplcase
AFLAG="n"
BFLAG="n"
FILES=""
for i
do
    case $i in
        -a) AFLAG="y" ;;
        -b) BFLAG="y" ;;
        -*) echo Invalid option argument: $i ; exit ;;
        *) FILES="$FILES $i"
    esac
done
echo Aflag $AFLAG Bflag $BFLAG Files $FILES
$ examplcase -x y z
Invalid option argument: -x
$ examplcase -a a b c
Aflag y Bflag n Files a b c
$ _
```

CSH

NAME

csh — C shell command interpreter   .

SYNOPSIS

csh [options] files

DISTRIBUTION

All Berkeley systems. The C shell is also available on many hybrid systems, such as the XENIX System.

DESCRIPTION

The C shell is a command interpreter developed by William Joy at the University of California at Berkeley. The C shell, like the Bourne shell, is both an interactive interface to the UNIX system and a complete programming language that allows you to develop command scripts that execute UNIX system commands. The name C shell is a reminder that its syntax was designed to resemble the syntax of the C language.

The C shell was developed at about the same time as the Bourne shell, and, like the Bourne shell, it was developed to overcome the shortcomings of the Version 6 UNIX shell. Many people prefer the C shell for interactive use, although most UNIX users today recommend the universally available Bourne shell for writing command scripts. However, the emergence of the Korn shell (AT&T's extension of the Bourne shell, developed by Dave Korn) is luring many C shell devotees back to the AT&T fold. The Korn shell offers Bourne shell compatibility, superior performance, and extensions that provide the interactive features demanded by C shell users. Unfortunately the Korn shell is not yet universally available, so a viable niche for the C shell remains.

This manual page concentrates on the most important interactive features of the C shell. No attempt is made to be complete; rather the attempt is to highlight the most important and productive features for interactive use. Covered features include ordinary commands, pipelines, I/O redirection, aliases, the directory stack, job control, and history.

If you want the C shell to be your standard command interpreter, you should have your system administrator change the shell field of the '/etc/passwd' file for your account to */bin/csh*, or, on Berkeley systems, you can use the chsh command to change your default login shell. However, if you prefer to keep the Bourne (or some other) shell as your default login shell, you can still use the C shell at any time by entering the csh command. After entering C shell commands, you can return to your original shell by entering the exit command.

For simple commands, the C shell is very similar to both the Bourne shell and the primeval Version 6 shell. The most visible difference is the prompt, which is a % by default on the C shell. (The C shell prompt can be changed to whatever you want by assigning a value to the prompt variable; see the *Variables* section of this manual page.)

When the C shell prints its prompt, this indicates that it is ready to accept a command. Type in the command name and any arguments. When you strike the return key, the C shell will execute the command. When the command is complete, the C shell will print another prompt.

Each time a C shell starts to run, it executes the commands in '.cshrc' in your home directory. You typically place commands in '.cshrc' that should be executed each time you run a fresh C shell. Typical '.cshrc' controls features such as history and aliases, which are not inherited by child shells. You typically do not set terminal modes or environment variables in '.cshrc'.

Once '.cshrc' has been executed, the C shell determines if it is a login shell. If it is, it executes the commands in '.login'. You typically place commands in .login that you want executed once, at the beginning of every session. '.login' is a good place to set your favorite stty options, to assign values to environmental variables, and to do other once-only chores.

The last chore of a login shell before it exits is to execute the commands in '.logout'. Some users place commands in '.logout' to clean up temporary files and update personal log files.

FILENAME GENERATION

The C shell may make several kinds of textual changes to the text of your commands. These changes are provided to make it easier for you to enter commands, but they are discouraging when they occur unexpectedly. If the text of your commands consists simply of letters and numbers, you are safe from every substitution except aliases. (Enter the aliases command to see a list of the current aliases.)

Here is a list of the textual substitutions that may modify your commands. The column on the left shows what characters will trigger the substitution.

* ? [] {}
   If the text of your commands contains these characters, the C shell may expand them into corresponding lists of files (filename generation).

~   Words that start with a tilde may have the tilde replaced by the pathname of someone's home directory.

! Words that contain an exclamation point may by altered by the C shell's history mechanism.

$ Words that contain a currency symbol may be interpreted as references to C shell's variables.

Filename generation and tilde substitution are discussed in the following paragraphs; the other textual substitutions will be discussed in more detail in the appropriate sections of this manual page.

The purpose of filename generation is to save keystrokes. It allows you to specify groups of files without having to type each name, or to specify the name of a single file without having to type it exactly. Filename generation is easy to avoid: simply type filenames exactly. On those rare occasions when a filename literally contains one of the filename generation special characters (*, ?, [], {}, or ˜) you can type the special character with a leading \ to restore its literal meaning. Obviously it is best if you don't create filenames that contain these characters. The other way to avoid filename generation is to set the C shell variable named noglob. (*Globbing* is an alternate term for filename generation.)

The two easiest filename generation characters are * and ?. An asterisk will match any sequence of characters, while a question mark will match any single character. Thus, the pattern x* will match any name that starts with an *x*, while the pattern x? will match any two-character name that starts with an *x*. You can use * and ? repeatedly. For example, the pattern x*y*z? will match any filename that starts with *x*, has a *y* in the middle, and a *z* as the next-to-last character. Filename generation works most productively when you name your files consistently.

```
% ls
readme      typescript  x.c      xy.c      y.c
% echo ?.c
x.c y.c
% echo *.c
x.c xy.c y.c
% echo x?.c
xy.c
% echo x*.c
x.c xy.c
% _
```

A single character in a filename may be matched by one of a specified set of characters. This is indicated by enclosing the set of candidate characters inside square brackets. For example, the pattern jones[01234] will match any filename that starts *jones* and ends in one of the digits zero through four. You can also indicate a range of characters; for example [a-z] is any lower-case letter, or [N-Z] is an upper-case letter from the last half of the alphabet.

```
% ls
readme      typescript  x.c        xy.c        y.c
% echo *[aeiou]*
readme typescript
% echo [0-9]
echo: No match.
% _
```

An error is generated if you use the *, ?, or [] filename generation characters without getting some match (unless the $nonomatch variable is set). This is different behavior than the Bourne shell, which simply passes along patterns that don't match filenames. For example, in the C shell, if the current directory doesn't contain any files whose name starts with *x*, the pattern x* will cause an error message. Another fact to keep in mind is that filenames that start with a period are treated specially: the period must be matched explicitly. Another fact is that patterns can't match the / that separates elements in a pathname. For example, the pattern a?b won't be expanded into a/b, even if the current directory has a subdirectory called 'a' that contains a file named 'b'.

```
% ls -l
total 2
drwxr-xr-x  2 kc        512 Nov 10 21:55 a
-rw-r--r--  1 kc         51 Nov  6 21:46 letter
-rw-r--r--  1 kc          0 Nov 10 22:48 typescript
% ls -l a/b
-rw-r--r--  1 kc          3 Nov 10 21:55 a/b
% ls a?b
No match.
% _
```

The {} symbols are a different sort of filename generation operator. Unlike the operators mentioned above, which match typed patterns against lists of files in the UNIX filesystem, the {} operators simply generate text strings, without regard for the existence of files by the same name. The curly brackets surround comma-separated alternates that are expanded. For example, the pattern jones{0,1,2,3,4} will expand into five words, *jones0*, *jones1*, and so on. The difference between the square brackets and the curly braces is that the matching of the square brackets relies on the presence of the files. For example, in a directory whose sole occupant is the file 'jones4', the construct jones[01234] will expand into *jones4*, while the pattern jones{0,1,2,3,4} will always expand into the five words mentioned above.

```
% echo beatles-{john,paul,george,ringo}
beatles-john beatles-paul beatles-george beatles-ringo
% _
```

The C shell also contains a filename generation character that can be used to refer to someone's home directory. When a ~ occurs at the beginning of a word, it is expanded (if possible) into that user's home directory. For example, if your system has a user named joe whose home directory is '/usr1/joe', then ~joe will expand into */usr1/joe*. A ~ immediately followed by a / will expand into the name of your own home directory. This construct is very useful on systems where user home directories sometimes change, or on systems where there are several different places where user directories are stored.

```
% grep julie /etc/passwd
julie:.phC1FRCwdPMw:76:1:Julie Doll:/usr1/julie:/bin/csh
% echo ~julie/bin
/usr1/julie/bin
% _
```

I/O REDIRECTION, PIPELINES, BACKGROUND PROCESSES

Many UNIX commands are filters; they read data from their standard input and write results to the standard output. By default, the standard input and output are attached to the terminal, but they can be redirected (rerouted to files) using C shell I/O redirection syntax.

The <, >, and >> characters indicate I/O redirection. Most commands read from the standard input and write to the standard output. By default, both the standard output and the standard input are connected to your terminal. When a command contains the directive > filename, the shell creates the specified file and then routes the command's standard output to that file (instead of to your terminal). Any previous contents of the file will be overwritten. A variant is the directive >> filename, which means append the standard output to the specified file. The same idea applies to input redirection. When a command contains the notation < file, the shell will connect the command's standard input to the specified file, instead of to the terminal.

The C shell has a safety mechanism that lets you prevent accidental overwrites of files using output redirection. If you set the noclobber variable, then the C shell will refuse to redirect a command's output to an existing file. As an exception, the C shell will always allow you to redirect a command's output to a character special file, such as a communication line special file (e.g. '/dev/tty8') or the null device '/dev/null'. You can use the notation >! to override the noclobber setting.

```
% set noclobber
% echo Hiya Sammyboy > letter
% echo Hi There Sam > letter
letter: File exists.
```

UNIX
SHELLS

```
% cat letter
echo Hiya Sammyboy
% echo Hi Sam >! letter
% echo I am enjoying camp >> letter
% echo But I wish you were here >> letter
% cat letter
Hi Sam
I am enjoying camp
But I wish you were here
% mail sam < letter
% _
```

Besides the standard input and output, the UNIX system reserves an I/O connection for error messages, called the standard error. If you simply redirect the standard output of a command into a file, the error messages will still appear on the terminal. Using the notation >& you can force both the standard and the diagnostic output into a file.

```
% ls jjwilson > jj.list
jjwilson not found
% cat jj.list
% ls jjwilson >& jj.list
% cat jj.list
jjwilson not found
% _
```

A pipe connection routes the standard output of one command into the standard input of another. This simple facility lets UNIX programs work together without the necessity of intermediate files. The classic example is to count the files in a directory by piping the output of the ls command into the wc command. Pipelines have had a profound effect on the evolution of the UNIX system because pipes give you an incentive to remove programs' extraneous chatter.

The UNIX symbol for a pipe connection is the vertical bar. When two commands are separated by |, the output of the first is routed as input to the second.

```
% cat letter
Hi Sam
I am enjoying camp
But I wish you were here
% wc letter
      3      12      51
% cat letter | wc
      3      12      51
```

```
% who | awk -e ´ { print $2 }´
console
ttyh1
ttyh3
ttyi3
ttyp0
% _
```

When a program executes interactively or in a shell script, its input and output are attached by default to your terminal. This makes it easy to write shell scripts that accept input from the terminal, but it makes it more difficult to write shell scripts for unattended operations that use commands that read from the standard input. One classic example is a shell script that wants to mail a message upon completion of some task. The message could be placed in a separate file, but it is more convenient to place the message in the original script using a *here document*.

The syntax for here documents is built from the syntax for input redirection. Instead of one < symbol, a here document requires << and then a word that, when it appears alone on a line, will indicate the end of the here document. For example, the following shows a shell script that mails a message to a user named 'jpstj':

```
% cat hi_jp
echo about to ring jpstj
mail < < end_of_msg
Hey John,
I´m back in town and I´d love to see ya.
Call after work today or tomorrow morn.
See Ya.
jj
end_of_msg
echo sent.
% hi_jp
about to ring jpstj
sent.
% _
```

Here documents are usable interactively, but there isn't much point because commands that read from their standard input will read from the terminal by default. The reason for here documents is to let you embed the input for commands in a shell script.

You can run a program in the background by following the command with an & (ampersand). Once the background program has been started, the C shell will immediately prompt you to enter another command. You can continue to interact with the C shell (or other programs) while your background program runs unattended. A program running in the background will block if it attempts to read input from the keyboard, but it can still send output to your terminal unless the command `stty tostop` has been executed. The section on *Job Control* has more information about manipulating background processes.

```
% troff letter &
[1] 21355
% ps
  PID TT STAT  TIME COMMAND
21125 p0 S     0:03 -csh
21355 h3 I     0:32 troff letter
21359 p0 R     0:01 ps
% _
```

ALIASES

A C shell alias is a pseudonym, an alternate name for a familiar command. Although obscure uses abound, the most common use of aliases is to personalize the names of standard UNIX utility programs and to establish default options. For example, a person familiar with the MS-DOS operating system is accustomed to using a command named TYPE to display files on the screen. The analogous UNIX command is named `cat`. Making `type` an alias for `cat` preserves part of the user's MS-DOS understanding. Emulating the MS-DOS DIR command is a more complicated task. By default, the UNIX system displays short format directory listings, and MS-DOS displays long format directory listings. Making `dir` an alias for `ls -l` preserves even more of the MS-DOS user's environment.

Aliases are established with the `alias` command. The first argument is the name of the alias; the remaining arguments are the alias text. Entering the `alias` command without arguments prints a list of the current aliases; entering the command with a single argument prints the alias, if any, for that word.

```
% alias dir ls -l
% alias DIR ls -l
% alias dir/w ls
% alias DIR/W ls
% alias type cat
% alias TYPE cat
```

```
% alias
DIR      (ls -l)
DIR/W    ls
TYPE     cat
dir      (ls -l)
dir/w    ls
type     cat
% alias dir
(ls -l)
% dir
total 2
drwxr-xr-x  2 kc        512 Nov 10 21:55 a
-rw-r--r--  1 kc         51 Nov  6 21:46 letter
-rw-r--r--  1 kc          0 Nov 10 23:14 typescript
% dir/w
a          letter       typescript
% TYPE letter
Hi Sam
I am enjoying camp
But I wish you were here
% _
```

Most users place their favorite aliases in their '.cshrc' file so that they will be available every time they start the C shell. The **unalias** command can remove an alias.

VARIABLES

The C shell, like the Bourne shell, has variables. And like the Bourne shell, there are two separate groups of variables: shell variables and environment variables. Shell variables are internal to the shell, although their values may be passed as arguments to commands. Environment variables are made available as name/value pairs to executed commands.

Shell variables are given a value with the **set** command. The simplest form is the **set** command without arguments—this simply prints a list of the set variables and their values. To set a variable to a value, you issue the **set** *name* = *value* command. You can see the value of a specific variable using the **echo** command. To *use* the value of a variable you must place a $ (currency symbol) in front of the name. You must surround the name in curly braces if the variable is immediately followed by text. You can unset a variable with the **unset** command.

```
% set willis=/usr2/w/willis
% echo $willis is a directory
/usr2/w/willis is a directory
% echo ${willis}ton
/usr2/w/williston
% _
```

Besides simple variables, the C shell also contains variables that are analogous to arrays. You can set the value of an individual member of the array with the set *name[n]=value* command or you can set the entire array with the set *name=(wordlist)* command. The words in the *wordlist* are separated by white space, and variable substitution occurs within the list. The expression $name[*n*] will select the n-*th* element of the variable. Without the selector, you would get all of the words stored in the variable.

```
% set birds=(sparrow hawk humming owl)
% set birds[1]=robin
% echo $birds
robin hawk humming owl
% echo $birds[2]
hawk
% set favorite=1
% echo $birds[$favorite]
robin
% _
```

Environment variables can be set or displayed using the setenv command. The syntax differs slightly from the set command; you set an environment variable by entering the setenv name value command. You can reference the value of an environmental variable by placing a currency symbol in front of its name. Environment variables cannot consist of multiple words. You can delete an environmental variable using the unsetenv command.

```
% set int=Internal_value
% setenv ext External_value
% printenv
HOME=/usr1/kc
PATH=:/bin:/usr/bin:/usr/local/bin:/usr/hosts:/usr1/kc/bin
SHELL=/bin/csh
TERM=adm31
USER=kc
ext=External_value
% echo $int $ext
Internal_value External_value
```

```
% cat sub_showenv
printenv
echo Ext $ext
echo Int $int
% /bin/csh sub_showenv
HOME=/usr1/kc
PATH=:/bin:/usr/bin:/usr/local/bin:/usr/hosts:/usr1/kc/bin
SHELL=/bin/csh
TERM=adm31
USER=kc
ext=External_value
Ext External_value
int: Undefined variable.
% _
```

Although `int` is a shell variable in the interactive C shell, it is not an environment variable. Thus, it doesn't get exported to the C shell that is created to interpret the commands in 'sub_showenv'. That's why the 'sub_showenv' C shell script complains that `int` is an undefined variable.

The standard environmental variables $USER, $TERM, $PATH, and $HOME are automatically mirrored in the ordinary variables $user, $term, $path, and $home. By changing the values of a shell variable, you can alter the values of the corresponding environment variable (but not vice versa).

The $PATH environment variable specifies where the C shell looks for commands. Each time you enter a command, the C shell looks in turn in each directory in $PATH, trying to find your command. You should make sure that $PATH lists just those directories that contain programs that you use. Almost all $PATH variables specify '/bin' and '/usr/bin'. Other directories are added to the list depending on your needs, often in the '.login' command script. The format of $PATH is a colon-separated list, as expected by most UNIX commands, but the format of $path is a wordlist, the standard format for C shell variables. Many people find it easier to manage the wordlist format of $path than the colon-separated format of $PATH.

```
% echo $PATH
/usr/ucb:/bin:/usr/bin:/usr/local/bin
% echo $path
/usr/ucb /bin /usr/bin /usr/local/bin
% set path=($path /usr/hosts)
% echo $PATH
/usr/ucb:/bin:/usr/bin:/usr/local/bin:/usr/hosts
% echo $path
/usr/ucb /bin /usr/bin /usr/local/bin /usr/hosts
% _
```

UNIX
SHELLS

The C shell contains a special command called @ that lets you perform arithmetic on shell variables. Superficially the @ command resembles the set command. One difference is that the values for the @ command may be numeric expressions. The expression may contain most of the syntax for numeric expressions in the C language, although the > (greater-than), < (less-than), & (bitwise and), and | (bitwise or) operators must be placed in parentheses to suppress their ordinary meaning to the C shell. You must separate the components of the expression into words using spaces.

```
% @ i = 50
% echo $i
50
% @ i = $i * $i - 30 ; echo $i
2470
% @ j = 64 * 1024 * 1024
% echo $j
67108864
% @ bits = ( 7 & 11 )
% echo $bits
3
% @ bits++
% echo $bits
4
% _
```

THE DIRECTORY STACK

Most people visit and re-visit several directories during the course of a UNIX session. If each directory were chosen at random, then the familiar cd command would be an optimal interface. However, most users visit only a few of the directories on their system, and most movements from directory to directory are eventually reversed. The C shell directory stack commands and the cdpath directory search path capitalize on these common usage patterns.

Although the C shell implements the familiar cd command for moving from directory to directory, many users rarely use it. Instead, you can move from directory to directory using the C shell commands pushd and popd. The pushd command is almost a direct replacement for cd. You can move to a given directory with the command cd *name*, but the advantage of pushd over cd is the directory stack. Each time you pushd to a directory, the C shell remembers where you were, so that you can conveniently return with the popd command. At any time, you can list the directory stack with the dirs command.

The pushd command has two variant forms. If you don't mention a directory name when you issue the pushd command, you will simply exchange the top two elements on the stack, and then move to the top directory in the stack. If instead of a directory name you supply the argument +*n* to pushd, then you will rotate the n-*th* element on the stack with the top, and then move to the top directory on the stack. The top directory is numbered 0, the next is 1, etc. Thus, the command pushd +1 is equivalent to pushd without an argument. Each time you enter the pushd command, the directory stack will be printed, with the top at the left.

The popd command pops the top directory off the stack, and then moves to the new top directory. You can also specify +*n* to remove the n-*th* entry from the stack (without moving anywhere).

```
% pwd
/
% pushd bin
/bin /
% pushd ../usr/local/bin
/usr/local/bin /bin /
% pushd ..
/usr/local /usr/local/bin /bin /
% pushd ../../etc
/etc /usr/local /usr/local/bin /bin /
% pushd
/usr/local /etc /usr/local/bin /bin /
% pwd
/usr/local
% dirs
/usr/local /etc /usr/local/bin /bin /
% pwd
/usr/local
% popd +2
/usr/local /etc /bin /
% pwd
/usr/local
% popd
/etc /bin /
% pwd
/etc
% _
```

The cdpath is a list of directories that may contain subdirectories that you want to visit. For example, if you commonly need to visit the directories that contain the troff formatter source code, you might put */src/titroff* (the root directory for troff source on my system) into your $cdpath variable. The $cdpath is to searching for directories as the $PATH variable is to searching for executable commands. One important difference is that $cdpath is unique to the C shell, whereas the $PATH feature has been built into both the C shell and the Bourne shell. The Bourne shell analog of the $cdpath C shell feature is its $CDPATH shell variable. The most important difference is that the C shell $cdpath feature implicitly searches in the current directory first, whereas the $CDPATH can be set up so that the Bourne shell looks only in the named directories.

The cdpath is a list of words, each of which names a directory that will be searched each time you enter a cd or pushd command to a directory whose name doesn't start with a / (slash). Each time a directory is located in one of the cdpath directories, the full path name is printed so that you can keep track of where you are.

```
% set cdpath=(~/unixbook /src/titroff /src2/newqms)
% echo $cdpath
/usr1/kc/unixbook /src/titroff /src2/newqms
% ls $cdpath
/src/titroff:
eqn          qms          tbl.new        troff
burble       ideal        refer          titroff.new
docs         pic          tbl            tmac
/src2/newqms:
READ_ME.ms  lg1200.rom  makefile    misc       src
lg1200       lg1200_old  man         qfontinfo  test
/usr1/kc/unixbook:
jan          man          originals  rev1        text
% pushd man
~/unixbook/man ~
% pushd refer
/src/titroff/refer ~/unixbook/man ~
% popd
~/unixbook/man ~
% _
```

Notice that the pushd man command switched to the 'man' subdirectory of the '~/unixbook' directory rather than the 'man' subdirectory of the '/src2/newqms' directory because the order of the $cdpath directories matters.

JOB CONTROL

Traditionally the UNIX system enables you to run a program in the background by following the command with the & character. However, the C shell, in conjunction with an improved terminal driver, allows for more control of jobs running in the background. This feature may not be available everywhere the C shell is available because it relies on kernel features (the improved terminal driver) that are not universally available.

The major advantage of C shell style job control is that it allows you to move jobs between three possible states: running in the foreground, running in the background, or suspended. Thus, if you start a program in the foreground but decide to temporarily switch your attention to another chore, you can immediately suspend the original program and run another program in the foreground. When the interruption is complete, you can return the original program to the foreground and resume where you left off.

Some interactive programs, such as vi, have a command that suspends them. For example, you can enter the :stop<CR> command to suspend vi. However, most programs don't have a built-in suspend command because striking ^Z (the default susp character) will usually suspend the current job. (The ^Z character won't always suspend the current job because processes can catch the suspend signal.) You will immediately get a new shell prompt, allowing you to enter shell commands in the foreground. One option at this point would be to enter the bg command to start running the program in the background. This would be appropriate for a non-interactive job, such as a text formatting job, but inappropriate for an interactive job, such as an editor, because it would block if it attempted to read from the keyboard while running in the background. When you are ready to resume your original job, you can enter the fg command to bring the command back to the foreground.

Up to this point the discussion has pretended that there is only a pair of jobs. Actually there can be numerous jobs, each identified by a job number, which is different from a process id number. The jobs command will print a list of the current jobs. By default, the fg and bg commands refer to the current job, but they can act on a specific job by mentioning the job number preceded by a %.

UNIX SHELLS

```
% nroff -ms csh.t
^Z
Stopped
% jobs
[1]  + Stopped              nroff -ms csh.t
% ps
  PID TT STAT  TIME COMMAND
 8246 h3 S     0:01 -h -i (csh)
 8247 h3 T     0:00 nroff /usr/bin/nroff -ms csh.t
 8248 h3 R     0:01 ps
% bg %1
[1]     nroff -ms csh.t &
% jobs
[1]     Running              nroff -ms csh.t
```

```
% ps
  PID TT STAT  TIME COMMAND
 8246 h3 S     0:01 -h -i (csh)
 8247 h3 R     0:01 nroff /usr/bin/nroff -ms csh.t
 8253 p1 R     0:01 ps
% mail charles
The problem with the laser printer
^Z
Stopped
% jobs
[1]  - Running              nroff -ms csh.t
[2]  + Stopped              mail charles
% fg %1
nroff -ms csh.t
^C
% jobs
[2]  + Stopped              mail charles
% fg %2
mail charles
(continue)
is random power outages.
kc
^D
% _
```

In the dialogue shown above, the nroff job is first suspended and then put in the background. Notice in the ps listing that the status changes from *T*, which means stopped, to *R*, which means running. Then the mail program is stopped, the nroff job is brought to the fore, and then killed with a ^C. The + and - symbols in the jobs listings indicate the current job and the previous job, respectively. Notice the brief messages that the C shell prints each time a job changes state.

HISTORY

If we were all perfect typists, and if subsequent commands were always unlike previous commands, there would be little need for a history mechanism. Unfortunately, few of us are perfect typists, and commands during a UNIX session often resemble each other. Thus, the C shell's history mechanism, which lets you construct new command lines out of previous ones, is one of its major enhancements.

Each time you enter a command, it may be saved on the history list. The size of the history list is controlled by the history variable. A history substitution pulls out some text from the history list and then uses that text in the current command. You can re-use either a full command or some words from a command.

UNIX
SHELLS

A history reference may appear anywhere in a command line, and there can be several history references in a single command line.

The most general form of a history reference has three parts: a command selection, a selection of words from that command, and then modification of the selected words. An exclamation point precedes the command selection, and the remaining parts, if present, are separated by colons. Thus, in general, a history reference looks like

. . . !*which_event*:*which_words*:*what_changes* . . .

The default for *which_event* is the previous command, the default for *which_words* is the entire selected command, and the default for *what_changes* is no change. Here is a more complete description of each of these three parts.

Which_event. There are three ways to select a previous event: by event number, by the text of its first word (the command name), or by some text that is present in the command. You can display event numbers with the `history` command, which lists the events together with their event numbers. For example, !38 refers to event number thirty-eight, or !-5 refers to the event fifth from the end of the list. If the ! is followed by plain text (instead of a number), then the most recent event whose name started with that text is selected. Thus !vi refers to the last `vi` command and !di refers to the last command whose name started with *di* (e.g., `diff`). If you want to refer to arbitrary text in a previous command, you must surround it with question marks. For example, !?dave? refers to the last command that contains the text *dave* in the name or arguments. For convenience, the previous command can always be recalled using the !! selector.

```
% set history=15
% set prompt="[\!] "
[3] pwd
/usr1/kc/unixbook/man
[4] ls -l csh.t
-rw-r--r--  1 kc          31575 Nov 12 23:28 csh.t
[5] history
     1  set history=15
     2  set prompt="[!] "
     3  pwd
     4  ls -l csh.t
     5  history
[6] !4
ls -l csh.t
-rw-r--r--  1 kc          31575 Nov 12 23:28 csh.t
[7] !p
pwd
/usr1/kc/unixbook/man
```

```
[8] !?csh?
ls -l csh.t
-rw-r--r--  1 kc              31575 Nov 12 23:28 csh.t
[9] _
```

This dialogue also shows that history substitions are printed by the csh before they are executed.

Which__word. You can select a particular word or words by number, or by using a notation that resembles the notation in the ed editor. By number is probably easiest. For example, :0 selects the first word (the command name), :3 selects the third argument (fourth word), :1-4 selects arguments one through four, :-4 selects the command name through to the fourth argument, and :1- selects all the arguments except (surprisingly) the last. The ed-like notation uses :^ to select the first argument, :* to select all of the arguments, and :$ to select the last argument. The final word selector is :%, which selects the word that matched *txt* in the immediately preceding !?*txt*? command selection.

n	Word *n* of the command. (0..nargs)	n-m	Words *n* through *m*.
-n	Words 0 through *n*.	n-	Words *n* through nargs-1.
^	Word 1 (the first argument).	$	The last word (nargs).
*	The command arguments.	n*	Words *n* through nargs.
%	Word matched by previous !?*txt*?		

Here are some examples of word selections.

```
[4] ls -l csh.t
-rw-r--r--  1 kc              33439 Nov 13 00:20 csh.t
[5] wc !ls:2
wc csh.t
     793     4873     33439 csh.t
[6] wc !ls:*
wc -l csh.t
     793 csh.t
[7] !ls:0- ex.t
ls -l ex.t
-rw-r--r--  1 kc              33421 Nov  2 21:13 ex.t
[8] !7 !4:2
ls -l ex.t csh.t
-rw-r--r--  1 kc              33439 Nov 13 00:20 csh.t
-rw-r--r--  1 kc              33421 Nov  2 21:13 ex.t
[9] _
```

What__changes. Once you have selected text from the history list, you can modify it several ways. Usually these modifications alter just the first modifiable word, although the g modifier can lead to a global (all of the selected words) change. You can apply several modifications, although each separate command must be preceded by a colon. The :h and :t modifiers select the head or tail of a pathname. The head is everything up to the final /, while the tail is everything after the last / in the pathname. The :r and :e modifiers select the root or extension of the filename. The root is everything up to the last period, while the extension is everything after the last period. The :s/*old*/*new*/ modifier is similar to the ed substitute command. It changes *old* into *new*, but *old* is taken literally—regular expression matching is not available. Thus, :s/dff/diff/ will insert the *i* to fix the spelling of a diff command. The modifiers discussed above and several others are described in the following table.

h	Select head of a pathname.	t	Select tail of a pathname.
r	Select root of a filename	e	Select extension of a filename.
s/l/r/	Change *l* into *r*.	p	Print instead of execute.
&	Repeat previous change.	g	Make changes globally.
q	Quote the words.	x	Quote words individually.

Here are some examples.

```
[2] ls ~/unixbook/rev1/chawk.t
/usr1/kc/unixbook/rev1/chawk.t
[3] echo !:$:h !:$:t !:$:r
echo ~/unixbook/rev1 chawk.t ~/unixbook/rev1/chawk
/usr1/kc/unixbook/rev1 chawk.t /usr1/kc/unixbook/rev1/chawk
[4] echo !2:$:s/awk/intro/
echo ~/unixbook/rev1/chintro.t
/usr1/kc/unixbook/rev1/chintro.t
[5] !4:s/echo/ls/:p
ls ~/unixbook/rev1/chintro.t
[6] !!
ls ~/unixbook/rev1/chintro.t
/usr1/kc/unixbook/rev1/chintro.t
[7] !!:0 -i :*
ls -i ~/unixbook/rev1/chintro.t
15091 /usr1/kc/unixbook/rev1/chintro.t
[8] _
```

EXPR

NAME

expr — evaluate simple command line expressions

SYNOPSIS

expr arg . . .

DESCRIPTION

expr evaluates expressions that are specified on the command line. It contains the *or* and *and* operators, relational operators, and simple arithmetical operators. The *or, and,* and relational operators work on either integers or strings, while the arithmetic operators work only on integers. expr also contains a string-comparison operator. Remember that expr doesn't understand numbers that contain decimal points (e.g., 1.5) or exponents (e.g., $10e-2$). In expr, both of those "numbers" will be treated simply as text.

Many of the expr operators are special characters to the shell. They must be quoted, either with a leading backslash or by surrounding that argument with single or double quotes. You cannot surround the entire expression with quotes because each element in the expression must be a separate command line argument. Numbers may be preceded with a unary minus, which is expr's only unary operator. All other operators are binary operators.

The following list details expr's operators, in order of increasing precedence. The syntax for all binary operators is

   expr op expr

where *expr* is an arbitrarily complicated expression, and *op* is one of the operators listed below. Parentheses may be used to force evaluation order, but be careful to make each parenthesis a separate argument.

| The *or* operator returns the left expression if it is neither null or zero, otherwise it returns the right expression.

& The *and* operator returns the first expression if both expressions are non-null and non-zero, otherwise it returns zero. Notice that *or* and *and* don't perform either a boolean (always returns true or false) or bitwise operation.

= > >= <= < !=
The comparison operators return a true (one) or false (zero) value

depending upon whether the comparison succeeds or fails. If both the left and right expressions evaluate to integers, a numeric comparison is performed; otherwise a text comparison is performed.

+ -

The addition and subtraction operators perform the given operations on numeric expressions.

* / %

The multiplication, division, and remainder operators work on integers.

: The text matching operator compares a fixed string on the left with a regular expression on the right. It normally returns the length of the match, or zero when there is no match. The regular expression may contain all of the ed metacharacters, which are . to match any single character, $ to anchor a pattern to the end of the fixed string, [*list*] to match any one of the characters in the list, and * to match zero or more occurrences of the previous single-character expression. Unlike ed, the regular expressions in expr are always anchored on the left. Thus, the ^ isn't a metacharacter. If you bracket part of the regular expression with \(and \), then that part of the expression will be printed if there is a match.

EXAMPLES

Repeatedly add two to a shell variable:

```
$ i=0
$ while :
> do
> i=`expr $i + 2`
> echo $i
> done
2
4
6
^C
$ _
```

Simple calculations:

```
$ expr 50 % 8
2
$ expr 19 \* 3 + 33 - 14 \* 3
48
$ expr 12865 - 7734
5131
$ _
```

Simple logical expressions:

```
$ expr 3 \| 8
3
$ expr 3 \& 0
0
$ expr yes \| 4
yes
$ expr 50 \< 10
0
$ expr 50 \> 10
1
$ expr yes \< YES
0
$ expr 4 != 4
0
$ expr 4 != four
1
$ _
```

Read and respond to a Yes/No input:

```
$ cat rd
read ans
if      expr X$ans : ´X[yY]$´ ´|´ X$ans : ´X[yY][Ee][sS]$´ >/dev/null
then    echo Yes
else    echo No
fi
$ rd
y
Yes
$ rd
nono
No
$ rd
yEs
Yes
$ rd

No
$ _
```

Separate pathnames into heads (the directories) and tails (the final name):

```
$ cat pathsep
while [ $# -gt 0 ]
do
        echo Name: $1
        echo Head: `expr $1 : '\(.*\)/.*' \| .`
        echo Tail: `expr $1 : '.*/\(.*\)' \| $1`
        shift
done
$ pathsep . .. joe ../joe/sam /usr1/kc/xcdir
Name: .
Head: .
Tail: .
Name: ..
Head: .
Tail: ..
Name: joe
Head: .
Tail: joe
Name: ../joe/sam
Head: ../joe
Tail: sam
Name: /usr1/kc/xcdir
Head: /usr1/kc
Tail: xcdir
$ _
```

The or operator in this script is necessary for simple filenames, which are pathnames that don't have a / character. When the / is absent, the pattern match returns a null string, so the | (or) operator swings into action, substituting its right hand argument. The script is written so that the head of a simple filename is . (the name of the current directory), and the tail of a simple filename is the filename. (Both System V and Berkeley have the basename program, which will deliver the last part of a pathname, and System V has the dirname program, which will output everything but the last part of a pathname.

FOR

NAME

for — Bourne shell command to repeat a list of commands
break — Break out of a for loop
continue — Start next iteration of a for loop

SYNOPSIS

for *var* [in *words*] do *list* done

break [*n*]

continue [*n*]

DESCRIPTION

The for command is used to execute repeatedly a list of UNIX commands. In a for loop, the shell variable *var* is assigned a sequence of values, and the list of commands is executed once for each value. If the list of *words* is present, they are the values for *var*. Otherwise the values are obtained from the arguments supplied to the shell program, and the loop won't execute if the argument list is empty. The for command can be used interactively or in a shell program, but when used interactively the list of words is usually supplied in the command. The words in the list are expanded as usual, so the standard metacharacters (such as *, ?, $, and `) have the usual meanings.

The break and continue commands are used inside for (and while) loops to alter the normal flow of execution. When break is encountered, the processing of the for loop is terminated, and control flows to the first statement following the loop. When a continue statement is encountered, the next iteration of the loop starts immediately, without executing any of the remaining statements in the loop. break and continue are most often executed conditionally, either in an if or in a case statement. Both break and continue accept an optional numeric argument that specifies the number of levels. *n* equal to 1 means the immediately enclosing loop, *n* equal to 2 means the second enclosing loop, and so forth.

EXAMPLES

Echo the command line arguments, one per line:

```
$ cat lecho
for i
do
    echo $i
done
$ lecho where is max smart
where
is
max
smart
$ lecho home
home
$ lecho
$ _
```

A *for* loop similar to that shown above is usually used when a shell program must process its arguments individually.

The following shell program uses a *for* loop to generate a list of the setuid or setgroupid programs in a group of directories. Notice that it is possible to have false hits because of the simple pattern used in the **grep** command.

```
$ cat findsetuid
for dir in /bin /usr/bin /usr/local/bin
do
    cd $dir
    echo $dir:
    ls -l | grep [w-]s
done
$ findsetuid
/bin:
-rwsr-xr-x   1 root       10240 Sep 27   1983 chgrp
-rwsr-xr-x   1 root       12288 Sep 27   1983 df
-rwsr-xr-x   1 root       21504 Sep 27   1983 login
-rwsr-xr-x   1 root       29696 Feb 14   1984 mail
-rwsr-xr-x   1 root       14336 Sep 27   1983 passwd

        – more output is generated –

$ _
```

The following shell program shows how `break` and `continue` are used to modify the behavior of a `for` loop.

```
$ cat stopgo
for i
do
    case $i in
        cont) continue ;;
        brk) break ;;
    esac
    echo $i
done
$ stopgo a b c
a
b
c
$ stopgo a b cont c d
a
b
c
d
$ stopgo a b brk c d
a
b
$ _
```

`for` loops are often used during interactive command entry to automate simple repetitive tasks. For example, the following dialogue shows how you could find each occurrence of the word *system* in a group of files, all of whose names end in the suffix '.t'. The results for a file named 'filex.t' should be stored in a file called 'filex.t.s'.

```
$ for srch in *.t
> do
>     echo $srch
>     grep -i system $srch > $srch.s
> done
ch1.t
ch2.t
ch3.t
$ ls *.s
ch1.t.s    ch2.t.s    ch3.t.s
$ _
```

Notice the secondary prompts (>) that prompt you to enter the trailing lines of the `for` command. (The -i option tells `grep` to ignore case distinction.)

NOTE

On many versions of the Bourne shell, the `do` and `done` keywords can be replaced by { and }. This simplifies text editing of complex shell scripts.

IF

NAME

if — Bourne shell command to conditionally execute command lists

SYNOPSIS

if *list* then *list* [elif *list* then *list*] ... [else *list*] fi

DESCRIPTION

The if conditional is a Bourne shell command that lets you conditionally execute a list of commands. The condition that is tested is the success or failure of a UNIX command. Perhaps the most commonly used command is test although any command that properly controls its exit status can be used. UNIX programs are supposed to exit with a zero status to indicate success, and with a non-zero status to indicate failure. (Unfortunately, some programs ignore this convention.)

The if command in the Bourne shell resembles the if statement of most structured programming languages. Each condition list is executed in turn until one of them succeeds. After one succeeds, then the associated action list is executed, and the if statement is complete. If none of the condition lists succeeds, the action list for the else clause (if it exists) is executed.

EXAMPLES

Many shell programs contain sections similar to the following:

```
$ if test -d /usr/local/robots
> then
>    cd /usr/local/robots
> else
>    echo /usr/local/robots: no such directory 1>&2
> fi
/usr/local/robots: no such directory
$ _
```

The -d option of test examines the following argument to see if it is a directory. The output from echo is redirected to the standard error output because that is the conventional destination for error messages in the UNIX system.

Two close relatives of the if statement are the && (and) and || (or) operators. When two lists of commands are separated by a &&, then the second list is executed only if the first succeeds. Similarly, when two lists are separated by | |, the second list is executed only if the first fails. Here is a series of commands that achieves the same result as the previous example.

```
$ robo=/usr/local/robots
$ test -d $robo && cd $robo
$ test -d $robo || echo ${robo}: No such directory
/usr/local/robots: No such directory
$ _
```

In many programming languages, the if statement and the case statement are closely related. The relationship is less close for these two statements in the Bourne shell than in some other programming languages because the case statement contains regular expression pattern matching capabilities that aren't duplicated in the if statement. However, when a Bourne shell case statement uses fixed strings (instead of regular expressions), it can always be recoded as an if statement. Here is the *stopgo* example (from the for manual page) recoded to perform its testing using an if statement instead of a case statement.

```
$ cat stopgo1
for i
do
    if test "$i" = cont
    then
        :
    elif test "$i" = brk
    then
        break
    else
        echo $i
    fi
done
$ stopgo1 xx yyy cont zzzz brk wwwww
xx
yyy
zzzz
$ _
```

The : command shown above is a Bourne shell built-in that does nothing. In this example, it could have been replaced by the continue command.

NOTE

Some of the shell's built-in commands don't work well with the if statement. For example, the following if statement doesn't work on many systems because cd is a shell built-in command:

```
if cd /usr/local/robots
then
    echo ok
else
    echo /usr/local/robots: no such directory
fi
```

SET

NAME

set — set the Bourne shell's options and positional parameters

SYNOPSIS

set [-ekntuvx] [arg . . .]

DESCRIPTION

The set command is called each time a Bourne shell is invoked to process its command line options. The options described here may be activated when you start a shell, or they may be controlled interactively or within a Bourne shell script. For example, you can run a shell script with the -x flag set either by entering the command

```
$ sh -x cmdfile
```

or by placing the command set -x at the beginning of 'cmdfile'.

You should note that the shell accepts four options— -c, -s, -r, and -i—whose action cannot be duplicated using set. See the sh manual page for information on these four options.

Once the options have been attended to, set takes the remaining arguments and assigns them to the positional parameters $1, $2, and so on. If this feature of set is used (i.e., the *args* are present) in a shell script, then the original values of the positional parameters will be lost; otherwise set can be used to change the flags without affecting the positional parameters.

If set isn't supplied with either options or arguments, it will print the names and values of all the variables. This feature is often useful interactively to see what variables are present.

set accepts the following option flags. The flags are set when preceded by a - ; they will be unset when preceded by a + .

-e is used in shell scripts to cause an immediate exit if a command fails. This option must be used with extreme caution because many UNIX programs don't properly set their exit status, and thus may appear to fail when everything is fine.

-k causes all keyword arguments (i.e., arguments that look like an assignment) to be placed into the environment of the given command. When this option is set, it is hard to pass an argument to a program that

UNIX
SHELLS

contains an embedded equals sign, but this option does make the notation for passing environmental variables more attractive. This option is most often set in an interactive shell to make it easier to run shell scripts that make heavy use of environmental variables.

-n tells the shell to read commands without executing them. It is useful when you want to test the syntax of a shell script without actually running it. -n is often used together with -v for syntactic debugging of shell scripts. Setting -n in an interactive shell is disastrous—all you can do is exit by creating an end of file (striking <Ctrl-D>).

-t makes the shell exit after executing one command.

-u makes it an error to reference an unset variable. Ordinarily an unset variable expands to nothing.

-v tells the shell to print its input as it is read. Note that the shell reads structured commands (loops, conditionals) in a single gulp. This option is useful as a debugging tool to trace shell scripts.

-x tells the shell to print each command, preceded by a +, as it is executed. This option is probably the most commonly used shell script debugging tool.

-   tells the shell to disable the -v and -x debugging flags.

-- is an option no-op. None of the flag options will be changed. It is useful when some of the arguments may have leading hyphens. If arguments with leading hyphens aren't preceded with the -- option, the set command will interpret those arguments as its own options, and havoc will ensue.

Keep in mind that set is commonly used for three distinct purposes: it automatically manages the options and arguments when the shell is invoked, it lets you change the shell options as needed, and it lets you take a multiword line and place those words into the positional parameters. The second two uses will be demonstrated below.

EXAMPLES

If set isn't given any options or arguments, it prints a list of the current variables.

```
$ set
EDITOR=/bin/ed
HOME=/usr1/kc
IFS=

PATH=:/usr/ucb:/bin:/usr/bin:/usr/local/bin:/usr/hosts
```

```
PS1=$
PS2=>
PS3=#?
PWD=/usr1/kc/unixbook/man
TERM=adm31
USER=kc
WWBLEV=s
$ _
```

The blank line following the $IFS variable results from the newline that is part of its value.

```
$ echo "$IFS" | od -bc
0000000   040 011 012 012
            \t  \n  \n
0000004
$ _
```

Many shell scripts have debugging facilities that are activated by command line options. Here is the prototype for such a script. Its command line options, -U, -V, and -X, control the shell's corresponding options.

```
$ cat opts
#
# skeleton script
#   to set sh debugging options from command line flags
#
while test $# -gt 0
do
    case $1 in
    -U)
        set -u
        shift
        ;;
    -V)
        set -v
        shift
        ;;
    -X)
        set -x
        shift
        ;;
    #
    # other option handling goes here
    #
```

UNIX
SHELLS

```
        esac
done

echo The body of the shell script goes here.
```

```
$ opts
The body of the shell script goes here.
$ opts -X
+ shift
+ test 0 -gt 0
+ echo The body of the shell script goes here.
The body of the shell script goes here.
$ _
```

The preceding script could be written more compactly as follows:

```
$ cat opts
#
# skeleton script
#    to set sh debugging options from command line flags
#
while test $# -gt 0
do
    case $1 in
    -U| -V| -X)
        set `echo $1 | tr UVX uvx`
        shift
        ;;
    #
    # other option handling goes here
    #
    esac
done

echo The body of the shell script goes here.

$ _
```

set is a flexible way to separate a line of input into separate words:

```
$ date
Mon Aug 11 22:40:08 EDT 1986
$ set -- `date`
$ year=$6
$ echo $year
1986
```

```
$ ls -l /etc/motd
-rw-r--r--  1  root   staff   270 Aug 11 00:00 /etc/motd
$ set -- `ls -l /etc/motd`
$ echo $9 : $5 $1
/etc/motd : 270 -rw-r--r--
$ _
```

Once you have used **set** to parse a line into individual words, the original arguments are unavailable. In a shell script, this technique is only possible following the argument processing section.

In case you don't understand the necessity of the -- option of **set**, here is the last part of the previous example repeated without using the -- option.

```
$ ls -l /etc/motd
-rw-r--r--  1  root   staff   270 Aug 11 00:00 /etc/motd
$ set `ls -l /etc/motd`
sh: -rw-r--r--: bad option(s)
$ _
```

Some shell scripts use the following technique to duplicate the facility provided by the -- option.

```
$ set X `ls -l /etc/motd`
$ shift  #moves args to their usual position
$ echo $9 : $5 $1
/etc/motd : 270 -rw-r--r--
$ _
```

When **set** divides a line of input into words, it uses the field separators in the **$IFS** variable. If you want to use different field separators, you can set $IFS differently.

```
$ date
Wed Mar 25 21:07:20 EST 1987
$ set -- `date`
$ hms=$4 ; echo $hms
21:07:21
$ saveifs="$IFS"
$ IFS=:
$ set -- $hms
$ IFS="$saveifs"
$ hrs=$1 ; mins=$2 ; sec=$3
$ echo $hrs $mins $sec
21 07 21
$ _
```

Variable assignments that are made before the command name are automatically exported into the environment of that command. This feature can be extended to variable assignments that occur following the command name by setting the -k flag.

```
$ cat myname
echo My name is $name and my argument is $1
$ echo $-
sim
$ name=george myname john
My name is george and my argument is john
$ myname name=george john
My name is and my argument is name=george
$ set -k
$ echo $-
sikm
$ name=george myname john
My name is george and my argument is john
$ myname name=george john
My name is george and my argument is john
$ _
```

NOTE

This manual page describes the set program that is built into the Bourne shell. The C shell also contains an internal command called set, but its operation differs sharply from that of the command described here.

UNIX
SHELLS

SH

NAME

sh — Bourne shell command interpreter

SYNOPSIS

sh [-ceiknrstuvx] [arg] . . .

DESCRIPTION

The Bourne shell is the standard UNIX command interpreter. It reads commands either from a stored script or from a user engaged in a login session and then arranges to have those commands executed. Some commands, such as cd, are built into the shell although most major applications programs are separate programs. From a user's perspective it is possible to run a shell built-in program or an external program (either a shell script or a binary executable program) using the same syntax.

The UNIX system allows command interpreters to be assigned to each user based on preference and needs. Many users choose to use one of the alternative shells, such as the Berkeley C shell, the Korn shell, or one of several menu-oriented shells. The Berkeley C shell has some advantages over the Bourne shell as an interactive interface. However, the Korn shell, a newer version of the Bourne shell, shares most of the interactive improvements of the Berkeley C shell in a Bourne-shell-compatible package. The menu shells may be preferable interfaces to UNIX for many users, but most sophisticated users need to have a thorough understanding of the Bourne shell.

The shell is much more than a program that simply lets you enter the name of a command to be executed. Because it is designed to execute command scripts, the shell contains a full repertoire of programming language features such as loops, conditionals, and variables. To make it easy to combine simple programs to form new tools, the shell has a rich selection of operators for redirecting a program's input and output to files or to other programs. The shell also does extensive processing of the text of each command so that you can select groups of files using a pattern-matching language. Each of these features is discussed in the remainder of this manual page.

Many of the shell's built-in commands warrant a manual page of their own. In this book, the following shell built-in commands are discussed in their own manual page. Some of these commands are mentioned in the remainder of this manual entry, but the full descriptions must be found elsewhere in this section of the manual.

UNIX
SHELLS

break
: Break out of a `while` or `for` loop. (Discussed on the `while` and `for` manual pages.)

case   Execute one of a group of lists.

cd   Move from one directory to another.

continue
: Skip to the next iteration of a `while` or `for` loop. (Discussed on the `while` and `for` manual pages.)

for   Repeat a list of commands for each word in a list of words.

if   Conditionally execute command lists.

until
: Repeatedly execute a command until a condition is satisfied. (Discussed on the `while` manual page.)

while
: Repeatedly execute a command list while a condition is satisfied.

In the simplest case, the shell reads a line of input. The first word on the line is called the command name, and the subsequent words are arguments. The shell finds the executable file for the named command and tells the UNIX kernel to run that program. The arguments are passed to the program. Most programs accept two kinds of arguments: *option* arguments, which control the behavior of the program, and *filename* arguments that tell the program which files to use. Option arguments typically start with a hyphen, and filename arguments follow the UNIX conventions for naming files. It is up to each program to process and interpret their arguments; the shell merely generates the argument list and then hands it to the program.

PIPELINES, I/O REDIRECTION, BACKGROUND PROCESSES

To run one program at a time, you simply type the program name and the arguments on a line and then hit return. The shell will arrange to have that program executed. When the execution is complete, the shell will print another prompt and wait for you to enter another command. Other behavior can be controlled by placing one or more of the following special characters after the command.

\#
: A sharp at the beginning of a word starts a comment. Any remaining text on the line will be ignored. The end of the line is the terminus of the comment. Multiline comments need a sharp on each line. (Some older systems don't recognize the sharp as a comment indicator.)

&
: Placing an ampersand after a command tells the shell to run that program in the background. The shell will start the command, print the process id number of the command, and then immediately prompt you to enter

another command. Noninteractive jobs, such as document formatting, make ideal background jobs; interactive jobs, such as text editing, make poor background jobs.

;   The semicolon can be placed between commands, allowing you to enter more than one command on a line. The commands will be executed sequentially — the second won't start until the first has finished.

| The vertical bar is the shell's pipeline indicator. Placing a vertical bar between two commands tells the shell to arrange to have the output of the first command supplied as input to the second command.

&&   A double ampersand between two commands tells the shell to run the second command only if the first succeeds. If the first command fails, signified by its exit status, the second command won't run.

| | A double vertical bar between two commands tells the shell to run the second command only if the first fails.

'cmd args'
The standard output of a command surrounded by reverse single quotes is substituted for the command. When this construct is recognized by the shell, the command is executed. The command's standard output is collected and conceptually placed in the script in place of the command. Trailing newlines are removed.

(*list*)
A parenthesized list of commands is executed in a subshell. This is useful if you want to execute a group of commands with a slightly different state than that of the current shell. For example, if the *list* contains the cd command, you will still be in your original directory after the *list* has been executed.

{ *list* ; }
A list of commands surrounded by curly braces is executed as a group, but by the original shell, not by a subshell.

> *filename*
A right angle bracket followed by a filename indicates *output redirection*. It tells the shell to take the standard output of a command and place it in the named file. The file will be created, if necessary, and any previous contents will be lost.

>> *filename*
A double right angle bracket followed by a filename is an alternate form of output redirection. It tells the shell to take the standard output of a command and append it to the named file. The file will be created, if necessary, but the previous contents will not be lost.

< *filename*

A left angle bracket followed by a filename indicates *input redirection*. It tells the shell to take the standard input of the command from the named file.

<< *word*

A pair of left angle brackets followed by a word indicates the presence of a *here document*. The remaining input, up to the end or to a line consisting of *word*, is taken as the standard input of the command. This facility lets you place the input for a command within a shell script. If any part of *word* is quoted, the here document will be read literally. When *word* is unquoted, the following substitutions occur: command substitution, parameter substitution, escaped newlines are ignored, and backslash will quote \, $, and `.

<&*n*

>&*n* A left (or right) angle brace followed by an ampersand and a numeral indicates that the standard input (or output) should be duplicated from file descriptor *n*.

<&–

>&– A left (or right) angle brace followed by an ampersand and a dash indicates that the standard input (or output) should be closed.

Any of the input or output redirection, duplication, or closing symbols may be preceded by a numeral *n* to signify that the given file descriptor should be used instead of the default (zero for the standard input, one for the standard output).

Here are some examples of these features:

Comments:

```
$ echo this # but not that
this
$ _
```

Background tasks:

```
$ crunchdata &
15943
$ ps
  PID TT STAT  TIME COMMAND
15943 h3 R     0:02 crunchdata
15946 h3 R     0:01 ps
$ _
```

The number 15943 is the process id number of the crunchdata background job. The ps command lists your processes, verifying that crunchdata is running in the background even while the shell is prompting you to enter more commands.

Sequential command execution:

```
$ date ; who
Thu Jul 31 22:37:03 EDT 1986
gilbert   ttyh1    Jul 31 13:54
kc        ttyh3    Jul 31 21:36
kc        ttyi3    Jul 31 22:22
dan       ttyi9    Jul 31 15:22
$ _
```

Pipeline:

```
$ who | wc
      4      20     120
$ _
```

Conditional true:

```
$ test -r /binn && echo ok
$ test -r /bin && echo ok
ok
$ _
```

Conditional false:

```
$ test -r /binn || echo ok
ok
$ test -r /bin || echo ok
$ _
```

Command substitution:

```
$ echo `date`
Tue Aug  5 19:33:04 EDT 1986
$ echo 39 times 7 is `expr 39 \* 7`
39 times 7 is 273
$ _
```

In-line subshells:

```
$ pwd
/usa/kc
$ ( cd /usr/spool/uucp ; ls LCK* ; tail -5 LOG* )
LCK..cubsvax  LCK..cul0
uucp rnb (8/11-23:16-4397) OK (startup)
root esquire (8/11-23:16-4227) REQUEST (S D.rnaXBwb0 X.rnaXBwb0 ro
uucp rnb (8/11-23:16-4397) OK (conversation complete)
root esquire (8/11-23:16-4227) OK (conversation complete)
root esquire (8/11-23:17-4227) TIMEOUT (esquire)
$ pwd
/usa/kc
$ _
```

Output redirection:

```
$ who > names
$ cat names
gilbert  ttyh1   Jul 31 13:54
kc       ttyh3   Jul 31 21:36
kc       ttyi3   Jul 31 22:22
dan      ttyi9   Jul 31 15:22
$ _
```

Create an empty file using output redirection:

```
$ > newandempty
$ ls -l newand*
-rw-r--r--  1 kc        0 Mar 25 00:15 newandempty
$ _
```

Appending output redirection:

```
$ who > names
$ date >> names
$ cat names
gilbert  ttyh1   Jul 31 13:54
kc       ttyh3   Jul 31 21:36
kc       ttyi3   Jul 31 22:22
dan      ttyi9   Jul 31 15:22
Thu Jul 31 22:48:54 EDT 1986
$ _
```

Input redirection:

```
$ cat > msg
My number in Fla. next week
is 813-383-9027. kc
^D
$ cat msg
My number in Fla. next week
is 813-383-9027. kc
$ mail dan owen < msg
$ rm msg
$ _
```

Here document:

```
$ wc << heredoc
> This input has two lines, ten words,
> and sixty-four characters.
> heredoc
      2      10      64
$ _
```

Quoted and unquoted here documents:

```
$ cat << theend
> I am using a $TERM terminal
> It is now \
> `date`
> theend
I am using a cit500 terminal
It is now Fri Mar 13 00:58:32 EST 1987
$ cat << 'theend'
> I am using a $TERM terminal
> It is now \
> `date`
> theend
I am using a $TERM terminal
It is now \
`date`
$ _
```

I/O duplication and closing:

```
$ cd /bum
sh: /bum: bad directory
$ cd /bum | wc
sh: /bum: bad directory
        0       0       0
$ cd /bum 2>&1 | wc
        1       4      24
$ cd /bum 2>- | wc
        0       0       0
$ _
```

Because '/bum' doesn't exist, cd prints an error message on the standard error out, file descriptor two. When the standard error is duplicated to the standard output, the error message is sent to wc. When the standard error connection is closed, the error message is discarded.

VARIABLES AND THE ENVIRONMENT

Like most programming languages, the shell has variables that are used to store values. All shell variables store text strings, although the text can represent numbers. There are two basic things you need to know about shell variables:

1. The value of a variable is *set* using an assignment command. For example, you use the following command to set a variable named x to the value "hello":

    ```
    $ x=hello
    $ _
    ```

    Any spaces in the value must be quoted, and the name shouldn't contain any of the shell's special characters.

2. The value of a variable is *used* (referenced) by placing a currency symbol in front of the name. For example, the following dialogue shows how the echo command might use the value of x:

    ```
    $ echo $x sam
    hello sam
    $ _
    ```

If a variable's name is followed immediately by text that might look like part of the name, you must surround the name with curly braces, as in the following.

```
$ echo many ${x}s to you
many hellos to you
$ _
```

People are often surprised that the shell doesn't have any built-in arithmetic or comparison operations for variables. In many shell programs the two basic operations, assignment and referencing, are enough. Variables often take on values as a script executes, and then those values are used as arguments for commands. However, many scripts do need more facilities: arithmetic operations are provided by the `expr` command, and comparisons are provided by the `test` command. Both `expr` and `test` are described in their own manual pages. (`test` is a built-in command on modern versions of the shell.)

A shell program, like any program, can receive and process command line arguments. In a shell script, you refer to arguments by number: `$1` is the first argument, `$2` is the second, and so on. `$0` is the name of the shell script. The `shift` command is often used to process arguments to a shell script. `shift` moves the argument list one position to the left and reduces the argument count by one so that `$2` becomes `$1`, and `$3` becomes `$2`. Many shell scripts process `$1`, then `shift`, then process `$1`, and so on until they run out of arguments. `shift` accepts an optional numeric parameter that specifies how many positions to shift; the default is one.

The shell contains several built-in variables that contain status information. These variables are set automatically during the shell's execution, and their values may be used as necessary in shell scripts or interactively.

`$#` is the number of arguments passed to the shell. This variable isn't very useful interactively, but in shell scripts it is a key part of most argument-processing code. `$#` is reduced by one each time `shift` is executed.

`"$*"`
is equivalent to `"$1 $2 . . ."` Notice that `"$*"` is a single word. It is useful when you want to treat the argument list as a single word.

`"$@"`
is equivalent to `"$1" "$2" . . .` Notice that `"$@"` may be more than one word. If you want to take the arguments that a script has received and pass them intact to a program, use `"$@"`. Without the double quotes the argument count will change if any of the arguments contain spaces, tabs, or newlines (the `$IFS` characters). (Older shells had a bug that incorrectly handled `"$@"` when there weren't any arguments. On those shells a

workaround is ${1+"$@"}, which substitutes nothing when the first argument is null, or "$@" otherwise.)

$- is a list of the shell options that are currently active.

$? is the exit status of the last command. The value zero conventionally indicates success and other values are error codes. Some programs don't reliably provide an exit code.

$$ is the process id number of the shell itself. This value is often used to generate unique filenames because each process has a unique pid.

$! is the process id number of the last background process. This value is useful if you want to kill (send a signal to) a background process.

There are several variables that you can alter to control the operation of the shell.

$CDPATH

is a colon-separated list of directories that specify where cd should search for subdirectories. In the traditional shell, cd looked for directories in the current directory, unless the directory name started with a '/', which means start the search in the root directory. The $CDPATH is a list of your frequently visited directories; it makes navigation easier in large filesystems. Directory names in the $CDPATH list are separated by colons, and a leading or trailing colon or a pair of internal colons means the current directory. For example, if your $CDPATH is /:/usr: then cd will search for subdirectories first in the root directory, second in the '/usr' directory, and finally in the current directory. If you had the preceding $CDPATH and your current directory contains a directory named 'bin', then the command cd bin would move to the '/bin' directory, not to the 'bin' subdirectory (or to the '/usr/bin' directory) because the root directory would be searched first. To move to the 'bin' subdirectory you would enter the command cd ./bin. Alternatively, you could use the value :/:/usr for $CDPATH so that your home directory would always be searched first. $CDPATH must be set by you. If $CDPATH is unset, then cd will search only in your current directory, or in the root directory when you enter absolute pathnames. $CDPATH is present in System V shells; it is not available in the version of the Bourne shell distributed with Berkeley systems.

$HOME

is the name of your home directory. $HOME is your initial position in the filesystem, and it is the place where the shell's '.profile' startup script is located. Many programs besides the shell use the $HOME directory to locate files in your subtree. $HOME is not set by the shell; rather it is set by the login program near the conclusion of the login procedure.

$IFS is a list of the characters that the shell uses as field separators. (The field separators are the characters that separate words of a command.) The default list of field separators is the space, tab, and newline. $IFS is set by the shell and rarely needs to be changed.

$MAIL

is the name of a mailbox that the shell should check periodically to see if mail has arrived. If $MAIL is unset, the shell will only check for the arrival of mail at the beginning of a login session. On Berkeley systems your mailbox is usually '/usr/spool/mail/*username*', while on System V your mailbox is usually '/usr/mail/*username*'. You must set $MAIL if you want to be notified by the shell of the arrival of mail.

$PATH

is a list of directories that the shell searches for your commands. When you enter the name of a command, the shell goes to each directory in the $PATH trying to find the program. If a program is stored in a directory not mentioned in your $PATH, then you can't execute it simply by typing its name. Instead, you must type its full pathname.

On most systems, common commands are placed into the '/bin' and '/usr/bin' directories. Other commands are usually placed in more specialized directories. For example, a database subsystem, which could contain dozens of commands, might be placed in its own directory. Only those who use the database actually need to include its directory in their search path.

The $PATH variable has the same format as the $CDPATH variable. It contains a list of directories separated by colons. A leading or trailing colon, or a pair of colons in the middle of the list, means the current directory. The search path

```
/bin:/usr/bin:/usr/graph:
```

tells the shell to search for programs in the '/bin', '/usr/bin', '/usr/graph' directories, and then in the current directory. $PATH is set to a reasonable default by the shell, but it is commonly modified to meet individual needs.

The length of your search string has an effect on the quality of your interaction with UNIX. If you search too few directories, then oft-needed commands won't be readily available, but if you include every executable directory in your path, then the shell will spend too much time searching each time you enter a command. The order of your search string is also important. For example, if you spend most of your time entering graphics commands, then you should put the graphics directory first in your search string.

UNIX
SHELLS

$PS1   is the shell's primary prompt. The default is "$ " in the Bourne shell, but you can modify the prompt to suit your preference.

$PS2   is the shell's secondary prompt. The default is "> ". The secondary prompt is printed when the specification of a command is incomplete.

Another important variable is $TERM, which contains the name of the output terminal. It doesn't appear in the list above because it isn't used by the shell, but it is used by many programs that use cursor addressing and other terminal-dependent facilities. $TERM should be set correctly before you use the vi text editor.

Ordinarily, the shell's variables are its own business. The programs that the shell executes don't normally have access to the shell's variables. However, it is possible to *export* a variable. The value of an exported variable is made available in the *environment* of each program that the shell runs. The environment is very similar to a program's argument list because it is a set of values that are passed from a parent process to a child process. The difference is that the environment is a series of name/value pairs, whereas the argument list is a positional list of values.

A shell variable can be placed into the environment using the export command. The word *export* is followed by the name of the variable that you want to export. If you enter the export command without supplying the name of a variable, then all of the currently exported variables will be listed. A similar list of all shell variables is produced with the set command.

You can augment the environment for a single command by placing variable assignments before the command. For example, the command line

```
$ x=20 y=30 xplot xdat.1
$ _
```

will place the variables *x* and *y* with the given values into the environment of the xplot program. The environment is augmented for just the one command, and any values that *x* or *y* had before the command will be retained.

The readonly command operates similarly to export. Any variables may be marked as readonly by mentioning them in a readonly command. Once a variable has been marked as readonly, its value may not be changed within that shell's lifetime. A complete list of the readonly variables can be obtained by entering the command readonly without arguments.

Besides assignment and referencing, the shell has a handful of operations that let you handle the case of variables being unset, or set to null. In all of the following descriptions the name *x* will stand for any variable, and the value *w* will stand for any value that can be assigned to a variable.

${x-w}

is used to check that the variable x has been set (created). If it has been set, then its value will be used, but if it is unset, then the value w will be used. x isn't altered in any way—if it is unset at the outset, it will remain unset at the conclusion.

${x:-w}

is the same as **${x-w}**, except that x is checked to see if it is set and non-null. (Available on all System V and some Berkeley systems.)

${x=w}

is an alternate way to check that the variable x has been set. If x is unset, it will be assigned the value w. In any case, the value of x will be substituted.

${x:=w}

is the same as **${x=w}**, except that x is checked to see if it is set and non-null. (Available on all System V and some Berkeley systems.)

${x?w}

is a third way to check that the variable x has been set. If x has not been set, the message w will be output and then the shell will exit. If w is omitted, then the message "x null or not set" will be printed.

${x:?w}

is the same as **${x?w}** except that x is checked to see if it is set and non-null. (Available on all System V and some Berkeley systems.)

${x+w}

substitutes the value of w if x is set. Otherwise this produces nothing (the null string).

${x:+w}

is the same as **${x+w}**, except that x is checked to see if it is set and non-null. (Available on all System V and some Berkeley systems.)

Here are some examples of using shell variables:

Command substitution and variables:

```
$ n=`expr 9 \* 18`
$ echo $n
162
$ n=`expr $n - 1`
$ echo $n
161
$ _
```

UNIX
SHELLS

The argument list and the **$#** (argument count) built-in variable:

```
$ cat showargs
echo arg count and first three args
echo $# $1 $2 $3
shift
echo arg count and first three args after shift
echo $# $1 $2 $3
$ showargs a bb ccc
arg count and first three args
3 a bb ccc
arg count and first three args after shift
2 bb ccc
$ _
```

The difference between **"$*"**, **"$@"**, and **$@** :

```
$ set arg1 arg2
$ echo "$*"
arg1 arg2
$ echo "$@"
arg1 arg2
$ echo echo \$# > nargs
$ chmod +x nargs
$ cat nargs
echo $#
$ nargs "$*"
1
$ nargs "$@"
2
$ nargs $@
2
$ set A "B C D" E
$ nargs "$*"
1
$ nargs "$@"
3
$ nargs $@
5
$ _
```

The **$$** (pid) and **$!** (background pid) built-in variables:

```
$ sleep 5 &
3802
$ ps -x
  PID TT STAT   TIME COMMAND
 2165 h3 IW    0:04 -sh (sh)
 3802 h3 S     0:00 sleep 5
 3803 h3 R     0:01 ps -x
$ echo $$
2165
$ echo $!
3802
$ _
```

The **$?** (exit status) built-in variable:

```
$ test yes = no
$ echo $?
1
$ test yes = yes
$ echo $?
0
$ _
```

Local and exported variables:

```
$ cat review
$* is a $judgment film.
$ judgment=great
$ review Gone With the Wind
Gone With the Wind is a film.
$ judgment=fantastic review Gone With the Wind
Gone With the Wind is a fantastic film.
$ echo $judgment
great
$ export judgment
$ export
export HOME
export PATH
export TERM
export judgment
$ review Gone With the Wind
Gone With the Wind is a great film.
$ _
```

Handling unset variables:

```
$ echo ${x-hi} george
hi george
$ echo $x george
george
$ echo ${x=hi} george
hi george
$ echo $x george
hi george
$ cat isxset
echo ${x?"x is not set"} george
echo ${x+"x must be set"} today
$ isxset
isxset: x: x is not set
$ export x
$ isxset
hi george
x must be set today
$ _
```

Unset variables may also be detected without using the facilities shown above:

```
$ if test "x$name" = x
> then echo 'The $name variable is not set'
> fi
The $name variable is not set
$ name=sambeau
$ if test "x$name" = x
> then echo 'The $name variable is not set'
> else echo '$name' is $name
> fi
$name is sambeau
$ _
```

ARGUMENT LIST GENERATION AND QUOTING

One of the primary roles of the shell is to give you powerful facilities for generating arguments for commands. Two of these features, command substitution and variables, have been discussed above. In this section, I describe two other features of the process: blank interpretation and filename generation, and then I describe a related topic, quoting.

Each time you enter a command, the text of that command is scanned to see if you have used any of the shell's argument list generation facilities. The following actions are performed in the order given:

Parameter Substitution
   Shell variables are replaced by their values.

Command Substitution
   Commands surrounded by reverse single quotes are executed and then replaced by their output.

Blank Interpretation
   The command is separated into words. Quoted null arguments remain.

Filename Generation
   Each word is scanned for the filename generation metacharacters, *, ?, and [. When these occur, the shell attempts to expand the given word into a list of filenames.

Filename generation lets you specify a file or a group of files without typing each name individually. To make maximal use of filename generation, you should name your files consistently so that related files have some part of their name in common. Many of the common UNIX subsystems require this. For example, the C compiler makes you name all of your C language programs with the *.c* suffix.

There are three special characters that let you control the filename generation process.

? The question mark matches any single character. For example, the pattern ?.o matches any three-character filename ending in .o, the pattern ?? will match any filename that is exactly two characters long, and the pattern jones.? will match any file whose name starts with *jones.* and ends with any character.

* The asterisk matches any text pattern, including the null pattern. For example, the pattern * will match all of the files in the current directory, the pattern *.c will match all files whose names end in .c, and the pattern *ibm* will match all files that have the letters *ibm* anywhere in their name.

[...] The left square brace introduces a character set. A character set will match any one of the characters in the set. In a character set, a pair of characters separated by a hyphen indicates that range of characters. For example, [a-m]* matches any filename starting with the letters *a* through *m*. The pattern jones.[osm] will match any of these three filenames: 'jones.o', 'jones.s', or 'jones.m'. The pattern pie[0-9] will match any four-character filename starting with *pie* and ending with a digit. If the first character in the set is a !, then the set will match any character not mentioned. For example, the pattern pie[!0-9] will match any four-character filename starting with *pie* that does not end with a digit.

When the filename generation process yields a group of files, that group will be sorted alphabetically. For example, the pattern * will be replaced by an alphabetically sorted list of the files in the current directory. In the UNIX filesystem, the current directory is always named . and the name .. is used for the parent directory. Because of these conventions, the filename generation process requires you to explicitly match a period that occurs at the beginning of a file. For example, the pattern *rc won't match a file called '.exrc'; instead you must use the pattern .*rc. If there is no match between your pattern and the filenames, then the pattern is left alone and passed to the program.

Quoting removes the special meaning from a character. For example, when the shell encounters an unquoted $, it attempts to find a variable with the given name; but, when it encounters a quoted $, it simply treats it like any other character. The shell has three quoting mechanisms.

\   The backslash is used to quote the following character. The character sequence <backslash><newline> vanishes.

" "

Double quotes are a weak mechanism for quoting a string of characters. Within double quotes, parameter and command substitution occur. Thus, $ and ` are magic within double quotes, but the other special characters lose their meaning.

´ ´   Single quotes are a strong mechanism for quoting a string of characters. Within single quotes all special characters lose their meaning. Even newlines have no special meaning within single quotes; thus, single quotes allow you to pass a multiline parameter to a program.

Here are some examples of argument list generation and quoting.

Parameter substitution, command substitution, and filename generation:

```
$ n=3
$ ls *.`expr $n - 2`
ex.jan.1      semma.1
$ _
```

After the parameter substitution phase, the ls command is as if the user entered the command

```
ls *.`expr 3 - 2`
```

After command substitution, the command above is as if the user entered the command

```
ls *.1
```

After filename generation, the command above is as if the user entered the command

```
ls ex.jan.1 semma.1
```

Finally, the `ls` command executes, producing the short form listing of the two named files.

Quoting:

```
$ echo *.1
ex.jan.1 semma.1
$ echo \*.1
*.1
$ echo "*.1"
*.1
$ echo '*.1'
*.1
$ echo "$TERM"
vt100
$ echo '$TERM'
$TERM
$ _
```

Multiline arguments:

```
$ echo 'hi
> there
> sam' and bob
hi
there
sam and bob
$ _
```

In this example, `echo` is passed three arguments; its first argument contains two embedded newlines.

Escaped newlines:

```
$ echo hi\
> there
hithere
$ echo hi \
> there
hi there
$ _
```

An escaped newline vanishes. In the first example, echo receives a single argument, the seven characters *hithere*. In the second command, there is an explicit space before the escaped newline, thus echo gets two arguments: *hi* and *there*.

BUILT-IN COMMANDS

The shell contains about twenty-five built-in commands. These commands typically perform tasks that would be awkward to do outside the shell. Many of these commands change the state of the shell. The output of these commands (except exec) can't be redirected to a file or to a pipeline—a bug in many people's opinion.

. *file*

A period tells the shell to read its commands from *file*. This command is useful for executing shell scripts in the current shell, rather than in a subshell, which is the usual method. A shell script executed by the current shell can alter its variables and other aspects of its state (such as the current directory). One common use of this command is to re-execute the commands in '.profile' after they have been changed.

:

A colon command does nothing but return a true (zero) exit status. It can be used as the test condition in a while, until, or if statement. Another common use is as a placeholder statement, such as the statement in the then part of an if statement, or as the body of a while statement. Archaic shell programming used the colon as a comment—an extremely bad practice because the words to the right of the colon are evaluated as usual by the shell. Use # for comments on modern systems.

break [*n*]

The break statement breaks out of a while, until, or for loop. It is discussed on the while and for manual page.

case

The case statement executes one of a group of statements based upon pattern-matching successes. It is discussed on its own manual page.

cd [*dirname*]

The cd command moves from one directory to another. It is discussed on its own manual page.

continue [*n*]

The continue statement starts the next iteration of a while, until, or for loop. It is discussed on the while and for manual page.

eval [*arg . . .*]

The eval command makes the shell evaluate the given arguments. This gives the shell another chance to perform command and parameter substitution. This command is primarily required when a shell variable contains the name of another variable, or when the execution of a command forms new commands.

exec [*arg* . . .]

The exec command replaces the shell with the named process. Instead of the usual fork/exec operation, the named process is exec'd directly. After a successful shell exec, the original shell no longer exists. I/O redirection is allowed. The exec command is often used when you want to replace one command interpreter with another. If a login shell execs another process, then, when that process terminates, the init process will be notified, and the login procedure on that port will be started.

If exec is invoked without arguments, then any I/O redirection will redirect the current shell's input/output. This lets you do several interesting chores, such as reading from the terminal in the midst of a script whose input has been redirected.

exit [*n*]

The exit command causes a shell to terminate, either with status *n* or with the status of the most recently executed command. This command is used in command scripts and interactively. The shell will also exit when it encounters an end of file.

export [*name* . . .]

The export command marks the given list of variables for export. They will be passed to all processes as part of their name/value environment. If no arguments are mentioned, then the current list of exported variables will be printed. In an export command, the names of the variables should not be preceded by a currency symbol.

for

The for statement implements a loop where a control variable attains each value in a list of values. It is discussed on its own manual page.

if   The if statement is a conditional branch. It is discussed on its own manual page.

newgrp [*arg* . . .]

The newgrp command changes your group affiliation to the group named as an argument. Without an argument, the new group is the one mentioned in your entry in the 'passwd' file. (System V only.)

read [*name* . . .]

The read command lets you interactively direct the operation of a shell script. read reads a line of input from the standard input, assigning the first word of the input to the variable mentioned as the first argument, the second word to the second variable, and so on. The final variable swallows any extra words.

UNIX
SHELLS

readonly [*name* . . .]

The **readonly** command marks a list of variables as readonly. The shell will issue an error message if you try to alter the value of a readonly variable.

set [*option*] [*arg*]

The **set** command sets several of the shell's internal options, and it sets the positional parameters, such as $1. It is discussed on its own manual page.

shift [*n*]

The **shift** command shifts the argument list one position to the left. It is discussed in the previous section on shell variables.

test [*expr*]

The **test** program performs file existence tests, arithmetic comparisons, and string comparisons. Some shells have the **test** program built-in, and it is discussed on its own manual page.

times

The **times** program prints the accumulated user and system times for all the programs that have been run. It is especially useful on systems where you are charged for execution time.

trap [*arg*] [*n*]

The **trap** command is used in shell scripts to control what happens when a signal arrives. If there aren't any arguments, then a list of the current actions for various signals is printed. If there are signal numbers without an *arg*, then the default action for those signals will be restored. When both *arg* and *n* are present, *arg* is a command that will be executed when signal *n* arrives. The number 0, which doesn't correspond with any conventional signal, means that the given argument will be executed when the shell exits. The *arg* is usually one or more commands surrounded by single quotes so that it will be a single word. **trap** typically is used to remove temporary files and perform other housekeeping chores.

ulimit [*n*]

The **ulimit** command imposes a limit of *n* on the size of files that can be written by the shell or by child processes. Any size file can be read. Without arguments, the current limit is printed. Some systems have system-wide limits, and those limits can only be decreased using **ulimit**.

umask [*nnn*]

The **umask** command specifies an octal mask that affects the access mode for created files. The left digit applies to the owner's permissions, the middle digit to the group's privileges, and the right digit to the others' privileges. For a given digit, a value of one turns off execute privilege, a value of two turns off write privilege, and a value of four turns off read privilege. The values are additive; for example, 6 turns off both read and write privilege.

unset

 The unset command removes a variable. It is only present on newer shells.

until

 The until command executes a command list until a given condition is satisfied. It is discussed on the while manual page.

wait [*n*]

 The wait command waits for the given background process, identified by pid *n*, to terminate. The exit status of wait will be the exit status of the awaited process. Without a pid, the shell will wait for all of the background process.

while

 The while command executes a command list while a given condition is satisfied. It is discussed on its own manual page.

Here are some examples of built-in commands.

Sourcing commands:

```
$ cat doenv
echo setting preferences
TERM=vt100
ED=vi
PS1="hi-> "
export ED TERM
$ echo $TERM $ED $PS1
adm31 $
$ doenv
setting preferences
$ echo $TERM $ED $PS1
adm31 $
$ . doenv
setting preferences
hi-> echo $TERM $ED $PS1
vt100 vi hi->
hi-> _
```

Another example of sourcing commands:

```
$ cat chdir
cd $1
$ pwd
/usr1/kc/unixbook/man
$ chdir /bin
$ pwd
/usr1/kc/unixbook/man
$ . chdir /bin
$ pwd
/bin
$ _
```

Doing nothing:

```
$ if :
> then echo ': returns a true'
> else echo ': returns false'
> fi
: returns a true
$ _
```

Why : is a bad comment character:

```
$ echo in a command a : does not start a comment
in a command a : does not start a comment
$ echo in a command a # does start a comment
in a command a
$ : then ; causes problems
sh: causes:  not found
$ # then ; does not cause problems
$ _
```

The eval command:

```
$ sam=old
$ person=sam
$ echo $"$person"
$sam
$ eval echo $"$person"
old
$ _
```

The **exec** and **exit** command:

```
$ ps x
  PID TT STAT  TIME COMMAND
 2888 h3 S     0:00 -sh (sh)
 2891 h3 R     0:02 ps x
$ csh
% ps x
  PID TT STAT  TIME COMMAND
 2888 h3 S     0:00 -sh (sh)
 2894 h3 S     0:01 -sh (csh)
 2895 h3 R     0:03 ps x
% exit
% $ ps x
  PID TT STAT  TIME COMMAND
 2888 h3 S     0:00 -sh (sh)
 2900 h3 R     0:03 ps x
$ exec csh
% ps x
  PID TT STAT  TIME COMMAND
 2888 h3 S     0:03 -sh (csh)
 2903 h3 R     0:03 ps x
% exit
login: _
```

The read command:

```
$ read a b c
This is five words total
$ for i in a b c
> do
>       eval echo $i $"$i"
> done
a This
b is
c five words total
$ read a b c
Two words
$ for i in a b c
> do
>       eval echo $i $"$i"
> done
a Two
b words
c
$ _
```

read combined with **exec** can read from somewhere other than the script's standard input.

```
$ cat canals
echo How many martians did you observe?
read nmartians
echo $nmartians martians
$ canals < /dev/null
How many martians did you observe?
martians
$ cat canals2
exec 3<&0       # save stdin in file 3
echo How many martians did you observe?
exec 0< /dev/tty
read nmartians
exec 0<&3 3<&-  # restore stdin and close 3
echo $nmartians martians
$ canals2 < /dev/null
How many martians did you observe?
 50
50 martians
$ _
```

Note that the 'canals' script didn't work as expected because its input was redirected. 'canals2' shows how you can temporarily redirect a script's input. In 'canals2', the input was switched to the terminal for the read statement, and then switched back to the default.

Signal handling:

```
$ cat trapdemo
trap 'echo Exiting normally' 0
trap 'echo Got Signal 1;rm $TMPFILE;trap 0;exit' 1
trap 'echo Got Signal 2 or 3;rm $TMPFILE;trap 0;exit' 2 3
TMPFILE=/tmp/trapdemo$$
#
# A typical shell script goes below
#
echo $$ > $TMPFILE
n=0
while test $n -lt 50
do
    n=`expr $n + 1`
    sleep 2
done
$ trapdemo &
3715
$ kill -1 3715
Got Signal 1
$ trapdemo &
3723
$ kill -2 3723
Got Signal 2 or 3
$ date ; trapdemo ; date
Thu Aug  7 23:45:24 EDT 1986
Exiting normally
Thu Aug  7 23:47:37 EDT 1986
$ _
```

The umask command:

```
$ umask 000
$ echo > junk
$ ls -l junk ; rm junk
-rw-rw-rw-  1 kc     staff        1 Aug 12 23:57 junk
$ umask 022
$ umask
022
$ echo > junk
$ ls -l junk ; rm junk
-rw-r--r--  1 kc     staff        1 Aug 12 23:58 junk
$ umask 266
$ echo > junk
$ ls -l junk ; rm junk
-r--------  1 kc     staff        1 Aug 12 23:58 junk
rm: override protection 400 for junk? y
$ _
```

The wait command:

```
$ date
Thu Aug  7 23:55:16 EDT 1986
$ sleep 10 & sleep 100 &
3894
3895
$ wait 3894 ; ps
  PID TT STAT   TIME COMMAND
 3895 p0 S      0:00 sleep 100
 3896 p0 R      0:01 ps
$ wait ; date ; ps
Thu Aug  7 23:56:49 EDT 1986
  PID TT STAT   TIME COMMAND
 3924 p0 R      0:01 ps
$ _
```

SHELL FUNCTIONS

A shell function is a list of shell commands that are executed together, much like a function or procedure in a conventional programming language. The shell has always had this capability, provided that you placed the list of shell commands into a separate file. The advantage of the new shell function mechanism is that it allows the list of commands to appear within a script. Thus, you can have a single shell script that contains several shell functions.

Unfortunately, shell functions are a relatively new addition to the shell. They are available starting in System V release 2 from AT&T, but they are not currently available in the Version 7, or most Berkeley versions of the UNIX system. They are available in all versions of the Korn shell.

It is difficult to decide whether you should use shell functions when you are developing a shell script. You should certainly use them, if available, for strictly local (or once only) scripts. If your script is for wide distribution, the best advice at this time is probably to refrain from using shell functions because they aren't available in many UNIX systems.

The syntax for a shell function is its name, followed by a pair of parentheses, followed by a list of commands within a pair of curly braces. You can create shell functions interactively although they are more often found in scripts or in your '.profile' file. Here is a shell function that prints today's date in a numerical form.

```
$ today ()
> {
> day=`date | cut -c9,10`
> echo $day
> }
$ date
Sun Feb  1 21:57:26 EST 1987
$ today
1
$ expr `today` + 1
2
$ _
```

You can see if you have shell functions implemented in your system by trying to enter a shell function.

```
$ fns () { echo yes; }
$ fns
yes
$ PS1=osh- /bin/oldsh
osh- fns () { echo yes; }
syntax error: `(' unexpected
osh- fns
fns: not found
osh- exit
$ _
```

A shell function and the surrounding script share access to the same variables, except for the positional parameters. Inside a function, **$1** ... refers to the *function's* command line arguments; on the other hand, outside a function, $1 ... refers to the *script's* command line arguments.

```
$ cat fn
fn1 () { echo $* $EX ; local=3 ; }
echo $*
EX=one
fn1
echo local $local
fn1 These are args to fn1
$ fn arg1 arg2
arg1 arg2
one
local 3
These are args to fn1 one
$ _
```

Here is a much larger script that contains shell functions. The purpose of this script is to reformat the information provided by the date command. The output format contains five two-digit fields, one each for the year, month, day, hour, and minute. This format was chosen because it is similar to that needed when the **date** command is used to set the date. (Note: in System V, the operation performed by this shell script could alternatively be done using the format control options of the **date** command.)

```
$ cat fmtdate
mon () {            # return 2 digit month number
     case $2 in
          Jan) echo 01 ;;
          Feb) echo 02 ;;
          Mar) echo 03 ;;
          Apr) echo 04 ;;
          May) echo 05 ;;
          Jun) echo 06 ;;
          Jul) echo 07 ;;
          Aug) echo 08 ;;
          Sep) echo 09 ;;
          Oct) echo 10 ;;
          Nov) echo 11 ;;
          Dec) echo 12 ;;
          *) echo Bad month name 2>&1 ;;
     esac
}
day () {            # return 2 digit day of month
     echo $3 | sed -e 's/^.$/0&/'
}
hour() {            # return 2 digit hour
     echo $4 | cut -c1,2
}
minute() {          # return 2 digit minute
     echo $4 | cut -c4,5
}
year () {           # return 2 digit year
     echo $6 | sed -e 's/..//'
}
DATE=`date`
MO=`mon $DATE`
DA=`day $DATE`
HR=`hour $DATE`
MN=`minute $DATE`
YR=`year $DATE`
echo $DATE
echo $YR $MO $DA $HR $MN
$ fmtdate
Sun Feb 1 23:17:24 EST 1987
87 02 01 23 17
$ _
```

EXECUTING A SHELL SCRIPT AND INTERACTIVE SHELLS

There are several different ways to execute a shell script. While a script is being developed, or for a simple script that is used once or twice and then discarded, it is simplest to explicitly tell the shell to execute the script. When you mention the name of a file on the shell command line, the shell executes the commands in that file. Any words after the command name will be passed to the script as its arguments.

```
$ sh nuscript arg . . .
```

The advantage of this approach is that you can pass option flags to the shell that interprets the script to control its operation. For example, the -x option (see the set manual page) tells the shell to print each command as it is executed, which is a useful debugging aid.

```
$ sh -x nuscript arg . . .
```

The disadvantage of this approach is that you will have to supply the full pathname for the script if it is not in the current directory.

Sometimes it is necessary for your current shell, not a secondary shell, to execute a shell script. As described above, the . command will direct the current shell to read its commands temporarily from a named file, just as if you had typed them from the keyboard.

The UNIX system assumes that a text file whose file mode is executable is actually a shell script. You can make a shell script executable using the chmod command, and then the shell will automatically be called to execute the script when you type its name. This facility gives shell scripts the same command line interface as other UNIX software, and executable shell scripts in any of the 'bin' directories may be executed without specifying a full pathname.

```
$ echo echo hi > hiscript
$ cat hiscript
echo hi
$ hiscript
sh: hiscript: cannot execute
$ chmod a+x hiscript
$ hiscript
hi
$ mv hiscript /usr/local/bin
$ hiscript
hi
$
```

When you explicitly tell the shell to execute a command file, you can set certain options by placing them before the command name on the command line. Most of these shell options are discussed on the set manual page, because they can also be set or unset within a shell script by using the set command. However, there are four shell command line options that can't be controlled by the set command, so they are discussed here.

-s directs the shell to take its input from the standard input. Remaining words on the command line will be used as arguments. The shell will send its output to the standard error output.

-i tells the shell that it is an interactive shell. In an interactive shell, signals are handled differently: the interrupt signal (the signal that is generated when you hit the interrupt key, usually ^C or DEL) is caught and ignored, and the terminate signal (the standard signal sent by the kill command) is ignored. Any shell whose input and output are attached to a terminal will always be an interactive shell.

-r forces the shell to be a restrictive shell, which is more secure than the ordinary shell. (Not available on all systems.)

-c *string*

tells the shell to read its commands from the *string*. The *string* isn't the name of a command file, rather it is the command itself. This facility is most often used by interactive programs, such as vi, which provide a traditional UNIX command line interface within the program.

A *login* shell is one that is executed as your base command interpreter at the conclusion of the login process. Such a shell can identify itself because, as part of the login process, a hyphen is prepended to its name. That's why when you do a ps your login shell is called -sh, while other shells are simply called sh. Each time a shell starts executing, it checks its name to see if it is a login shell. If it is, then it reads the systemwide startup commands from '/etc/profile', and then it reads your personal startup commands from the file '.profile' in your home directory. Typically, you customize your own '.profile' so that your terminal is set correctly and the $PATH is set according to your needs. If you customarily use commands that rely on environmental variables, you should set those variables in '.profile'.

UNIX
SHELLS

The following example shows how the –s and –c flags may be used:

```
$ echo echo \$# \$1 \$2 \$3 > script
$ cat script
echo $# $1 $2 $3
$ sh script hi there
2 hi there
$ sh -s hello friends < script
2 hello friends
$ sh -c "echo echo is a useful command"
echo is a useful command
$ _
```

NOTE

This manual page describes most features of the System V Bourne shell. The version of the Bourne shell found on Berkeley systems is slightly different.

The Shell — Outline

Argument List Generation and Quoting

Built-in Commands

Shell Functions

Executing a Shell Script and Interactive Shells

† Discussed on its own manual page.

TEST

NAME

test — perform string and numeric comparisons, and file access tests

SYNOPSIS

test expression
[expression]

DESCRIPTION

The test program can test strings for equality, it can compare numbers, and it can determine several facts about files, such as whether they are readable or writable. test is usually used in a shell script conditional such as the if statement or the while statement. The *expression* determines test's exit status. test exits with a true if the tested condition is true, and false otherwise. If no arguments are on the command line, test returns a false exit status—a feature that can be used to check whether a shell variable has been set to some value.

The name [is a recognized pseudonym for test. Many people think that it looks better to write a condition as

> if ["$1" = run]

than as

> if test "$1" = run

When the name [is used (instead of test), you must include a] as the last argument.

File Access Tests

-*x file* tests a file for the given condition *x*, which must be one of the following:

f	Ordinary File	r	Readable	w	Writable
d	Directory File	s	Size > 0		

t [*n*] tests to see if file descriptor *n* (assumed to have the value one if *n* isn't supplied) refers to a terminal.

On System V the following tests are also available:

c	Character Special	b	Block Special	p	Pipe (fifo)
u	Set-user-id	g	Set-group-id	k	Sticky Bit
		x	Executable		

String Tests

-z *s1*	returns true if string *s1* has zero length.
-n *s1*	returns true if string *s1* has length greater than zero.
s1	returns true if string *s1* has length greater than zero.
s1 = *s2*	compares the two strings for equality.
s1 != *s2*	compares the two strings for inequality.

The -n s1 form of testing a string is better than simply supplying s1 on the command line. The second form will have problems if the string begins with a hyphen. In all cases, if the strings are variables they should be enclosed in quotes to protect against embedded spaces.

Numeric Comparisons

"n1 -op n2" compares two numbers. Most versions of test can only compare integers. *op* must be one of the following:

eq	Equal	gt	Greater Than	ge	Greater or Equal
ne	Not Equal	lt	Less Than	le	Less or Equal

Boolean Operators

test also allows you to combine tests using the following boolean operators.

!	NOT	-a AND	-o	OR

The precedence of OR is lower than AND. Parentheses (which must be escaped from the shell) may be used for grouping.

EXAMPLES

Simple file typing:

```
$ ls -l /bin/time
-rwxr-xr-x  1 root    staff   9216 Sep 27  1983 /bin/time
$ if test -d /bin/time
> then
> echo /bin/time is a directory
> else
> echo /bin/time is not a directory
> fi
/bin/time is not a directory
$ _
```

Waiting for a file to be created:

```
$ (sleep 25 ; echo > semafile) &
14507
$ while test ! -r semafile
> do
> echo semafile not present yet
> sleep 5
> done
semafile not present yet
semafile not present yet
semafile not present yet
$ _
```

Numeric comparison:

```
$ f1=/bin/test
$ f2=/bin/[
$ inum1=`ls -i $f1 | cut -c1-5`
$ inum2=`ls -i $f2 | cut -c1-5`
$ if [ $inum1 -eq $inum2 ]
> then
> echo $f1 and $f2 are links to the same file, inum $inum1
> fi
/bin/test and /bin/[ are links to the same file, inum 193
$ _
```

test's options and values must be passed as separate arguments. Combining several inputs into a single argument doesn't work because **test** will evaluate it as a string, not as a series of values and operators.

```
$ test 50 -lt -50 || echo must have failed
must have failed
$ test '50 -lt -50' && echo must have passed
must have passed
$ _
```

Notice that in the first command shown above, **test** gets the "correct" answer (false) because it performs a numeric comparison on its three arguments. In the second command shown above, however, **test** exits with a true status because its single argument is a non-null string.

NOTES

test is built into newer versions of the Bourne shell. You can always run the test program described here by using the full name /bin/test.

Since the test program is often used with shell variables, you should keep in mind that shell variables may contain blanks, and they might start with a hyphen or otherwise look like an option flag or operator. The following few examples address these problems, which occur in all shell programming.

It is easy to keep variables in one piece using quotes, as shown in the following example.

```
$ msg="hello there"
$ test $msg = hi && echo true
sh: there: unknown test operator
$ test "$msg" = hi && echo true
$ _
```

It is also easy to keep arguments from looking familiar by tacking something onto the front. The most common front-end protector is the letter *X*. For example, in the following command the first positional parameter's value has the value -f, which confuses test.

```
$ msg=-f
$ test $msg = hi && echo true
true
$ test X$msg = Xhi && echo true
$ test " $msg" = " hi" && echo true
$ _
```

The disadvantage of tacking an *X* onto the front of variables is that it precludes numeric comparisons, and you still must quote to keep variables with embedded spaces glued together. An explicitly quoted leading space, shown in the third test command above, will also protect against parameters that look like options, and it will work for either string or numeric comparisons.

WHILE and UNTIL

NAME

while — Bourne shell conditional to repeat a list while a condition is true
until — Bourne shell conditional to repeat a list until a condition is true
break — Bourne shell statement to break out of a while or until loop
continue — Bourne shell statement to start the next iteration of a while or until loop

SYNOPSIS

while *list* [do *list*] done

until *list* [do *list*] done

break [*n*]

continue [*n*]

DESCRIPTION

while and until are Bourne shell commands that repeatedly execute a list of commands while (or until) a condition is satisfied. The tested condition is the exit status of the first *list* in the SYNOPSES above. The test command is the most often used command to test various conditions, although any command that properly sets its exit status can be used.

break and continue can alter the normal processing of a while or until loop. When break is encountered, the processing of the enclosing loop is terminated and control moves to the first statement beyond the loop. When a continue statement is encountered, any remaining statements in the loop are skipped, and the next iteration of the loop is started. Both break and continue may have an optional numeric argument that specifies which outer loop. The default of one means to use the immediately enclosing loop, two means the loop enclosing the immediately enclosing loop, and so forth.

EXAMPLES

Wait for a file named 'sema' to be created.

```
$ cat waitforsema
while test ! -f sema
do
    sleep 5
done
$ _
```

Notice that the `test` program's test had to be negated by passing it a `!` argument. The following program behaves exactly the same as the previous; the only difference is that `while` is replaced by `until` and the sense of the test is reversed by omitting the `!` argument.

```
$ cat waitforsema1
until test -f sema
do
    sleep 5
done
$ _
```

Both `for` and `while` loops are used to process the arguments in a shell program. When a `while` is used to process arguments, the loop condition is usually that there are still some arguments to process, and the `shift` statement is used to discard already processed arguments. Each time `shift` is called, the argument count (in the `$#` variable) decreases by one. The general approach in all such programs is the following:

```
while test $# -gt 0
do
    process $1
    shift       # $2 becomes $1, $# decreases by one
done
```

In the `case` manual page I presented a short program that processes its arguments using a `case` statement inside a `for` loop. Here is the that program redone as a `case` statement inside a `while` loop.

```
$ cat exampwhile
AFLAG="n"
BFLAG="n"
FILES=""
while test $# -gt 0
do
    case $1 in
        -a) AFLAG="y" ; shift ;;
        -b) BFLAG="y" ; shift ;;
        -*) echo Invalid option argument: $1 ; exit ;;
        *) FILES="$FILES $1" ; shift ;;
    esac
done
echo Aflag $AFLAG Bflag $BFLAG Files $FILES
$ exampwhile -b  gen1 gen2
Aflag n Bflag y Files gen1 gen2
$ _
```

In many programs, certain options come in pairs. For example, many filters accept a *-o filename* pair of options that tells the program to place their output in *filename*. It is easy to handle a pair of options using a `while` loop simply by picking up both values when the flag is recognized, and then `shift`ing twice instead of once.

The example immediately above can be done with a `break` that halts the `while` loop as soon as the option arguments are exhausted.

```
$ cat exampwhile1
AFLAG="n"
BFLAG="n"
FILES=""
while test $# -gt 0
do
    case $1 in
        -a) AFLAG="y" ; shift ;;
        -b) BFLAG="y" ; shift ;;
        -*) echo Invalid option argument: $1 ; exit ;;
        *) break ;;
    esac
done
FILES="$@"    # Note $@ means the remaining arguments
echo Aflag $AFLAG Bflag $BFLAG Files $FILES
$ exampwhile1 -b -a  genx geny gena
Aflag y Bflag y Files genx geny gena
$ _
```

Infinite loops are often coded as

```
while true
do
    something
done
```

Although the `true` program reliably returns a true exit status, it is not built into the shell and it requires the overhead of starting an executable program. A slightly more efficient method is to use the : shell built-in command.

```
while :
do
    something
done
```

SECTION VI

THE EX/VI TEXT EDITOR

THE EX/VI
EDITOR

The UNIX system's original text editor was ed, a powerful and capable editor that was the standard for text editing on many early versions including Version 6, Version 7, PWB, and System III. ed was renowned for its power, but few admired its terse user interface or its command line style of operation.

William Joy, then of the University of California at Berkeley, enhanced ed to form ex and vi. ex is, like ed, a command line editor. It has additional features, but essentially ex is very similar to its forebear.

The more important member of the ex/vi family is vi. It features a visual interface that portrays on your screen a part of the file being edited. As changes are made to the file, your screen is immediately updated to reflect those changes. vi shows its heritage in three important ways—it is terse, it doesn't maintain a status display on screen, and it is powerful.

vi and ex are actually two faces of a single program, and each contains commands that let you switch from one to the other. Most people find vi easier to use than ex, so that is probably the best place to start.

The vi and ex manual pages are designed primarily as a reference. Both pages are organized topically so that you can easily find the information that you need.

The third manual page in this section describes the vi options. vi is a very configurable text editor, and you can customize several aspects of its behavior by using these options. The most important option setting is term, which tells vi what kind of a terminal you are using. vi must know about your terminal so that it can properly display your text on the screen. The value of vi's term option is usually taken from the $TERM environment variable.

Several other text editors are widely available for UNIX systems, including multiple versions of Emacs, and the widely used and admired Rand editor. Although these editors can be used for editing programs, or for creating nroff/troff documents, they are not covered here because none of them is part of the standard UNIX distributions of System V, Berkeley, or Xenix.

THE EX/VI
EDITOR

EX

NAME

ex — command line interface to the ex/vi editor

SYNOPSIS

ex [options] [files]

DESCRIPTION

ex is a line editing interface to the ex/vi family of text editors. ex is strongly reminiscent of the older ed editor because it was originally developed from ed's source code. Although ex does improve significantly upon ed, the major improvement is visual editing, which is described on the vi manual page. ex's command line options are identical to those of vi; thus they are described on the vi manual page. The ex/vi family of editors has various operational modes that can be controlled using the editor's set command; they are described on the vi *Options* manual page.

For most users the vi interface is more convenient. vi requires a terminal with an addressable cursor, but such terminals are commonplace. ex is best when you want more power and speed than the visual interface can provide, or when you want ex to perform commands stored in an editing script.

OVERVIEW

ex is a program that lets you modify text files. You can enter your editing commands interactively, or provide them in a supplied script. Commands are typically entered one per line. Most commands operate on a region of the text, which is specified as a line or a range of lines. For convenience, ex keeps track of the current line, which is the default region for many commands. For most other commands the default region is the entire text.

When you are editing a file with ex, you are actually working with a copy of that file, which is stored in an ex buffer. Changes made to the buffer don't alter the original file until you issue a write command. Once understood, this aspect of ex becomes a feature, because mistaken alterations of the buffer's contents needn't destroy the original file. However, novices sometimes have trouble with this concept, and forget to write out the buffer contents at the end of the edit session, thereby losing their work. (ex prints a warning and refuses to quit if the buffer has not been saved, but there is an alternate quit command that will always quit.)

ex is a multimode editor. This means that the interpretation of what you type depends on ex's mode. The two native ex modes are command line mode and text entry mode. In command line entry mode, ex prints a : prompt at the beginning of each line; each of your input lines is presumed to be ex commands. In text entry mode, there isn't an explicit prompt; each of your input lines is presumed to be text that is added to the file. ex has several commands that initiate text entry mode, and you can change from text entry mode to command line mode by entering a period alone on a line. ex also has commands that can lead to the vi side of the editor, where the vi specific modes (discussed on the vi manual page) apply. In my experience, ex's modes are its most difficult feature.

You can usually return to command line mode from within the ex portion of the editor by typing a line that consists of a single period. This code will return you to command line mode if you are in text entry mode, or it will print the current line if you are already in command line mode. Returning to a known mode (state) is somewhat harder if you wander into the visual or open line editing portion of the editor. To return to ex command line mode from visual or open line editing, you should press the escape key and type an upper-case Q.

LINE SPECIFIERS

ex contains multiple ways to identify lines in a file. You can mention a line number, but you can also refer to lines by their relative address, their content, or marks. The following paragraphs discuss each of these strategies in more detail.

Line Numbers are the easiest way to specify a line, and they are also the least ambiguous method. In ex you can always discover the line number of the current line by entering the command

        :.=

You can also determine line numbers by using the number command, which is an alternate form of the print command. (The number *option* applies only to vi.) The first line in the buffer is numbered 1, although line 0 can be mentioned to make it easier to place text in front of line 1.

Relative Line Numbers are used when you want to address lines in the immediate vicinity of the current line. For example, -3 is the line three in front of the current, and +5 is the fifth line past the current. You can also code relative line numbers with sequences of + and -. For example, --- is the line three in front of the current and +++++ is the fifth line past the current. +++--- is a wanton way to address the current line.

Marked Lines are referred to by 'x (apostrophe x) where *x* is any lower-case letter. Before you can reference a mark, you must set it using the mark command. Your location in the buffer previous to your last non-relative movement is named ' ' (two single quotes). You can add an offset to a mark; for example, 'x-3 indicates a line three in front of the line marked *x*.

Patterns are used to refer to a line containing a given text pattern. You can surround a pattern with slashes */pat/* to indicate a forward search to the next line that contains the pattern, or you can surround the pattern with question marks *?pat?* to indicate a reverse search. You can add an offset to a pattern; for example, the pattern ?Sam?-2 indicates a line two in front of the preceding line containing the text *Sam*.

. is a shorthand notation for the current line in the buffer.

$ is a shorthand notation for the last line in the buffer.

% is a shorthand notation for the entire (1,$) buffer.

The following example illustrates each of these address forms. It also demonstrates the **print, mark,** and **quit** commands. When the **print** command is supplied with one address, it prints that line and makes that line the current line; when it is supplied with two addresses, it prints those lines and then makes the last line printed the current line. The **mark** command takes a single-character argument, which can subsequently be used to reference the current line.

You can abbreviate most **ex** commands, often down to the command's first letter. For example, the abbreviation for the **print** command is p, and the abbreviation for **quit** is q. Both full names and abbreviations are shown in the following dialogue. When two commands have the same first letter, such as **append** and **abbreviate,** the command with the stronger **ed** heritage is usually the one with the single-character abbreviation.

```
$ cat fivelines
This is one
and two,
three,
four,
and five.
$ ex fivelines
"fivelines" 5 lines, 44 characters
:.=
5
:. print
and five.
:3 print
three,
:-2 p
This is one
:/ou/
four,
:2 p
and two,
```

```
:mark c
:'c+,$ p
three,
four,
and five.
:quit
$ _
```

The beginning of this example shows that you are initially positioned at the end of the file when you edit it with **ex**. In **vi** you are initially positioned at the beginning of the file.

COMMAND SYNTAX

ex commands can be broadly divided into two classes—those that take addresses, such as **delete**, and those that don't, such as **quit**. The general form of commands that take addresses is

```
n1 cmd
n2,n3 cmd
```

n1, *n2* and *n3* are line specifiers as discussed above.

Commands that operate on a range of lines, such as **delete**, take either one or two line specifiers, while commands that do something before or after a given line, such as **append**, take only one line specifier. Some commands take optional parameters following the command name. These will be discussed individually.

Commands generally appear one per line, although several separate commands can be entered on a single line by separating them with a | (vertical bar). You can correct typing mistakes by using your usual erase character (often backspace or delete). All command lines must be followed by a carriage return, which isn't shown in the examples in this manual page.

From within the **vi** realms of the editor you can access **ex** line commands by prefacing them with a colon. Native **ex** (but not **ed**) also allows a colon preface to accommodate fingers accustomed to **vi**.

Some commands have a variant form that is activated by placing a **!** after the command. For many commands, the variant form tells **ex** that you know what you're doing. For example, **quit!** tells **ex** to quit, even if there are unsaved changes in the buffer. Most other variants are relatively obscure. For example, in the **global** command the **!** means "do the following on lines that don't match". In the **insert** command the **!** means "toggle autoindent mode." You should try to avoid confusing **!**'s role in forcing variant forms of commands, and its use as a command name. (Fortunately, the **!** command doesn't have a variant.)

ED COMPATIBILITY

Today most UNIX systems contain both ed and ex. For historical reasons, ed is often used in shell scripts for simple automated editing tasks. ed is also required knowledge for systems programmers because on many systems ex/vi is not available in single-user mode without mounting additional filesystems. Today it is probably preferable to learn ex, and then learn which ex features are missing in ed, rather than to learn ed directly.

ex is a straightforward extension of ed. If you know ed, you can use almost all of that knowledge in ex because ex is mostly upwardly compatible with ed. However, if you learn ex, you may be surprised when you use ed, because ed doesn't contain many of the ex commands. In the more detailed command reference section of this manual page, the ed-like subset of ex is identified by a $\boxed{ED}$ symbol at the end of the citation. (Most commands with a single-character abbreviation are native ed commands. Those without a single-character abbreviation definitely don't appear in ed because ed command names are all a single character.)

Although ed is present on any computer that claims to run a UNIX system, even ed varies from version to version. For example, the early ed lacked an undo command and the ability to encrypt/decrypt its files. The $\boxed{ED}$ mark in the following command reference table reflects the features of the latest System V version of ed.

Some ed commands have variants, which are accessed by capitalizing the command letter. For example, the Q command means you really want to quit, even if the buffer has been modified but not yet saved. This system is different from ex and its ! suffix for accessing variants.

In the following command descriptions, the left column shows the major forms that each command takes, and the right column describes the commands. When a command has both an abbreviation and a full name, the abbreviation appears in the left column and the full name appears at the start of the description in the right column. Commands that take addresses have the default addresses shown in parentheses. If you don't explicitly specify an address (or address range), the command uses the defaults.

TEXT DISPLAY COMMANDS

^D
Striking the end of file character makes the editor scroll through the file. The number of lines that are printed depends on the scroll option, which is set by default to a half screenful.

(+,+)
Specifying lines without mentioning a command prints those lines. Simply hitting carriage return will print the next line in the file.

($)=
The line number of the specified line will be printed. By default, the number of the last line in the buffer will be printed, but the most common form of this command is probably .= to print the line number of the current line.

(.,.)l
list   Display tabs as ^I and newlines as $. This lets you distinguish between tabs and spaces, and it lets you identify white space at the end of a line. (ED)

(.,.)nu
(.,.)#
number   The number command prints the specified lines preceded by each line number. The ed version of this command is the n command (but the n command in ex has a totally different meaning). The # command is another ex abbreviation for the number command. (ED)

(.,.)p
print   The specified lines are displayed on the terminal.   (ED)

(.+1)z
(.+1)z *n*
(.)z-
(.)z=
(.)z^
Display a block of text. The default block length is specified by the window option, although the block can be specified to be *n* lines using the second form shown on the left. By default, the block of text starts with the line after the current line, so you can page through a file by repeatedly entering the z command. You can also specify where the specified line will appear in the block. The command z- will display the specified line at the bottom of the block. The command z= will display the specified line in the middle of the block, set off above and below with lines of dashes. The command z^ will display the block of text that ends window lines in front of the specified line.

Here is a short example of some text display commands:

```
$ ex fivelines
"fivelines" 5 lines, 44 characters
:1,3 list
This is^Ione$
and two, $
three,$
:1,$nu
    1   This is one
    2   and two,
    3   three,
    4   four,
    5   and five.
:--,.p
three,
four,
and five.
:quit
$ _
```

Notice on line one of this example that what appears to be simply a space is actually a tab. Notice also that the second line contains a blank at the end of the line.

TEXT ENTRY COMMANDS

The three text entry commands shown below change the mode of the editor from command line mode to text entry mode. In text entry mode, each line of input is added to the file, until a line containing a single period is entered. Unlike the format of the rest of the command citations, the format of the left column here sketches the **ex** text entry dialog — command line, (multi) line text entry, termination of text entry by a line consisting of a period.

(.)a
text
.

append   The given *text* is added to the buffer following the specified line. Text entry mode ceases when a line consisting of a single period is entered. The variant version of this command, a!, toggles the autoindent mode during the text entry.   (ED)

(.,.)c
text
.

change   The specified lines are changed to the given *text*. Text entry mode ceases when a line consisting of a single period is entered. The variant version of this command, c!, toggles the autoindent mode during the text entry.   (ED)

(.)i
text
.

insert   The given *text* is added to the buffer in front of the given line. Text entry mode ceases when a line consisting of a single period is entered. The variant version of this command, i!, toggles the autoindent mode during the text entry.   (ED)

u

undo   The last alteration to the buffer is undone. The global, visual, and open commands are considered a single change. undo works with the **ex** buffer; commands such as **w** that interact with the UNIX filesystem cannot be undone.   (ED)

The following example demonstrates the text entry commands.

```
$ ex fivelines
"fivelines" 5 lines, 44 characters
:0 append
The new line one.
.
:2,4c
This line replaces the old lines 1-3.
.
:3p
four,
:i
Make this three, please.
.
:1,$p
The new line one.
This line replaces the old lines 1-3.
Make this three, please.
four,
and five.
:write
"fivelines" 5 lines, 97 characters
:quit
$ _
```

CUT AND PASTE COMMANDS

(.,.)t *line*
(.,.)co *line*

copy   Take a copy of the addressed lines and place it after the specified *line*, which may be zero if you want the copy placed at the beginning of the buffer. In ex you can use t or co as an abbreviation for the copy command; in ed, the command is called t. (ED)

(.,.)d
(.,.)d *buf*
(.,.)d *n*
(.,.)d *buf n*

delete   Delete the specified lines and save them in an unnamed buffer. In ex (but not ed) you can specify a buffer name to store the deleted text. If the buffer name is a single upper-case character, the text will be appended to the buffer, but if it is a single lower-case character, the deleted text will overwrite the buffer's current contents. You can also specify a count to specify the number of lines to be deleted. (ED)

(.,+)j
(.,+)j!

join   The specified lines will be joined to form a single line. At each joint the original white space will be replaced by two spaces if there was a period at the end of the line, no white space if there was a) at the start of the next line, or one space otherwise. The variant form of this command doesn't perform any special processing on the white space at the beginning and end of the original lines. (ED)

(.,.)m *line*

move   The specified lines will be moved from their original place in the buffer to just after the specified *line*, which may be 0 if you want the text moved to the beginning of the buffer. (ED)

(.)put
(.)put *buf*

put   The previously deleted or yanked lines will be put into the file after the specified line. The unnamed buffer will be used unless you explicitly mention a buffer name.

(.,.)ya
(.,.)ya *buf*

yank   The specified lines will be yanked from the file and saved in an unnamed buffer. The file isn't altered by a yank. You can also specify a buffer name for saving the text.

Here is an example of several cut and paste commands:

```
$ ex girls
"girls" 5 lines, 32 characters
```

```
:1,$nu
    1   everything
    2   spice
    3   sugar
    4   nice
    5   and
:3m0
sugar
:$m1
and
:y
:put
and
:1,$nu
    1   sugar
    2   and
    3   and
    4   everything
    5   spice
    6   nice
:3,4d
spice
:put
everything
:1,$p
sugar
and
spice
and
everything
nice
:1,4join
sugar and spice and
:2,3j
everything nice
:w
"girls" 2 lines, 36 characters
:q
$ cat girls
sugar and spice and
everything nice
$ _
```

MODIFYING LINES

(.,.)s/*pat*/*repl*/   substitute   Substitute *repl* for *pat* on the specified
(.,.)s   lines. *pat* may be a regular expression, as explained
(.,.)&   in the *Regular Expressions* section of this manual
page. *repl* is ordinary text, except for a few characters that are described in the *Replacement Text* section of this manual page. The *repl* text may consist
of multiple lines, although each newline in *repl*
must be escaped with a backslash. Omitting *pat*
and *repl* will repeat the most recent substitution, as
will the & (which is not part of ed) command.
Although the / is shown separating the *pat* from
the *repl* text, any character may be used. (The separator should be escaped with a backslash if it
appears in *pat* or *repl*.) You may place a g after the
command if you want all instances of *pat* replaced
with *repl*; ordinarily only the first *pat* on each line
will be replaced. You may place a c after the command if you want to confirm (by typing in y or n
when requested) each substitution.   (ED)

(.,.)>   The specified lines will be shifted to
(.,.)<   the right (>) or left (<). You can shift more than
one shiftwidth unit (usually a tab) at a time by
repeating the > or <. Thus, the command >>> will
shift the current line three places to the right. Left
shifts never discard text other than white space.

GLOBAL COMMANDS

(1,$)g/*pat*/ *cmds*
(1,$)g!/*pat*/ *cmds*
(1,$)v/*pat*/ *cmds*

global   The global command initiates a two-step operation. During phase one, the specified lines (by default the entire file) are examined to see if they match the given *pat*, which may contain the regular expression features discussed in the *Regular Expressions* section of this manual. Those lines that match *pat* are marked. During phase two, the given editor *cmds* are performed at each marked line. The *cmds* may be any ex command other than undo or global. You can escape newlines with a backslash if your list of *cmds* must appear on multiple lines. If *cmds* contains append, insert, or change commands, then each line of added text must have a trailing backslash to escape the newline. If *cmds* is omitted, then each of the matched lines will be printed. The v command (or its equivalent, g!) is the same, except that *cmds* are executed on each line that does not match the specified *pat*. (Remember the -v flag of grep prints lines that don't match.) undo can undo all of the effects of a single global command. ED

(.)mark *x*

mark   The specified line will be marked for later identification with the letter *x*. Marks aren't visible in the file; rather they are ways for ex to remember locations so that you can refer to them by name. You can refer to a marked line using the ' feature; for example 't refers to the line marked as *t*. (The ed name for the mark command is k.) ED

MACROS AND ABBREVIATIONS

ab *word repl*
ab
unab *word*

abbreviate The *repl* text, which may consist of several words, is stored as an abbreviation for *word*. During a text insertion in visual mode, each time you enter the given *word* surrounded by white space (or newlines) it will be replaced by its abbreviation. Abbreviations don't have any effect on the operation of text insertions during ex line editing mode. Without the *word* and *repl* a list of current abbreviations will be printed. The unab command will remove an abbreviation for *word*.

map *key repl*
map! *key repl*
map
map!
unmap *key*
unmap! *key*

map The *repl* text, which may consist of several words, will be stored and used as a replacement whenever *key* is pressed in visual command mode. *key* should be a single character, or the multicharacter sequence produced by a single keystroke, or #*n*, meaning the code produced by function key *n*. The map! variant command creates a map that is active during visual insert mode instead of during visual command mode. You can list the active maps using the map or map! commands without supplying *key* and *repl*, and you can remove a map using the unmap or unmap! commands.

OPERATION

(.)o   open   Leave **ex** line editing mode and enter open line editing mode. In open line mode, the bottom line of the screen acts as a one-line window into the file, and you can use the native **vi** commands. You can return to line editing mode by typing an upper-case Q while in command mode, or by striking <ESC>Q during open line text entry.

q
q!   quit   Leave the editor and return to the shell. **quit** will print an error and refuse to quit if the buffer has been modified since it was last saved. You can use the **ex** variant **q!** (or the **ed** variant **Q**) to leave while unconditionally discarding any buffer modifications.   (**ED**)

set *option*
set no*option*
set *option* = *value*
set *option* ?
set all
set   set   The set command allows you to set or unset the editor's options. The meanings of each option are detailed on the **vi** *Options* manual page. For options that are on/off, such as **number**, you can set the option on with the command **set number** or set the option off with the command **set nonumber**. For options that have values, such as **window**, you can set them with the command **set window=24**. The special command **set all** will display all available options and their current settings, while the **set** command without arguments will print all arguments that differ from the default. You can also enter a **?** after an option name if you want to see the value of that one option.

source *file*   source   **ex** commands will be read from the given file. The file may not contain another **source** command.

sh   shell   A secondary shell will be spawned to execute your UNIX commands. Note that this shell will be different from your original login shell. When you have completed executing shell commands, you can resume editing by exiting from the shell, either by entering the **exit** command or by striking ˆD to force end of file.

stop stop!	**stop** On systems that support job control this command will suspend the editor and return to the shell command interpreter. When you have finished executing shell commands, you can resume your editing session by entering the fg (csh or Bourne) shell command. If the autowrite option is set, the editor will save a changed buffer before suspending itself, unless the variant form of the command is specified.
ta *tag*	**tag** A tags file is a small database that records the locations of various items in a text file. In practice, most tags files are created by the ctags program, which records the locations of all of the subroutines in a group of files. When you enter the ex editor's tag command, the current line moves to the specified tag, even if it is in another file. For example, the command ta xputs will move to the *xputs* routine. By default, the tags file is named 'tags', although the tags option can be set to the names of additional tags files.
ve	**version** The version command prints the editor's version number and last modification date.
vi vi *file*	**visual** The visual command enters the vi realms of the editor. You can return to line editing mode by typing an upper-case Q while in visual command mode, or by striking <ESC>Q during visual mode text entry. You can also specify a filename if you want to enter visual command mode to edit that file.
x	**xit** If the buffer has been modified since it was last saved, save it, and then leave the editor. (ed also has an x command, but it relates to encryption, not to exiting from the editor.)

!*cmd*

Execute the given UNIX command. When the command execution completes, the editor will print a ! alone on a line to delimit the end of *cmd's* output and then the editing session will resume. Within the text of *cmd* a % will be replaced by the current filename, # will be replaced by the alternate (usually the previous) filename, and ! will be replaced by the entire previous command. Note that this command doesn't alter the buffer; it is simply a convenient way to enter a UNIX command from within the editor. (Older versions of ed don't allow typical shell syntax for *cmd*.) (ED)

adr,adr!*cmd*

Send the specified lines of the buffer to the given UNIX command, and then take the output of that UNIX command as a replacement for the given lines. This is the only command that operates on a region of the buffer but does not have a default region—you must specify the address (or addresses) explicitly.

FILES

<table>
<tr><td>

args

</td><td>

`args`   Print the list of files to be edited. Multiple files can be mentioned on the `ex/vi` command line, and this list is reproduced from inside `ex/vi` using the `args` command. The file being edited is surrounded by square brackets.

</td></tr>
<tr><td>

e *file*
ex *file*
e! *file*
e
e +*n file*
e +/*pat file*

</td><td>

`edit`   Edit the named file. The editor will refuse to perform this command if the buffer has been modified but not yet saved. The variant command `e!` (or `E` in the `ed` editor) will start editing a new file even if the current buffer has been modified. If no file is mentioned, then filename defaults to the current filename. You can also specify a line number or a context pattern if you want to start editing at that place in the file. (The editor's `vi` command can also mention a file if you want to change to the `vi` side of the editor and start working on a new file.) Within the text of the filename the character % will be replaced by the current filename and the character # will be replaced by the alternate (usually the previous) filename. (ED)

</td></tr>
<tr><td>

f
f *file*

</td><td>

`file`   Print the name and status of the current file. If you also mention a filename, you change the filename associated with the buffer, and change the status of the buffer to *modified*.   (ED)

</td></tr>
<tr><td>

n
n!
n *filelist*
n +*n*
n +/*pat*

</td><td>

`next`   Start editing the next file specified on the command line. You will get an error message if the current buffer has been modified but not yet saved. The `n!` variant will start editing the next file even if the buffer has been modified. You can specify a list of files, which will then be used as the editor's file list, and you will start editing the first file in the list. You can also specify a line number or a context pattern if you want to start editing at that place in the file.

</td></tr>
</table>

preserve	**preserve** The edit buffer will be saved in a special preservation area. This command is useful if you are having trouble saving your work. Typical problems that **preserve** can circumvent are write-protected files, write-protected directories, and full filesystems. Use **recover** to retrieve your preserved file. (Or start a fresh editing session using the **-r** option of **ex** or **vi**.)
(.)r *file* (.)r !*cmd*	**read** The contents of the file will be added to the current buffer following the specified line. Unlike the **edit** command, which effectively starts a new editing session, **read** simply adds text to the current buffer. If the buffer has not yet been named, the filename used in the **read** command will become the filename associated with the buffer. If the buffer is empty, the **read** command is equivalent to the **edit** command. Specify 0 as the line number if you want the material to be added to the buffer in front of existing text. The second form shown on the left will add the output of the given UNIX command to the buffer. (Notice the space before the !). **ED**
recover *file*	**recover** The named file will be recovered from the special file preservation area. This command is useful after a crash, to recover a file that was saved automatically, or after using the **preserve** command.
rew rew!	**rewind** Start editing the first file in the list of files to edit. This command will issue an error message if the buffer has been modified but not yet saved. The variant form of the command will start editing the first file in the list even if the buffer has been modified.

```
(1,$)w
(1,$)w file
(1,$)w>>
(1,$)w>> file
(1,$)w!
(1,$)w !cmd
(1,$)wq
(1,$)wq!
```

`write`   The specified lines (by default the entire buffer) will be written to the file associated with the buffer. You can also specify a filename if you want to write to an alternate file. You can place the symbol `>>` after the `write` command if you want to append the buffer to the end of an existing file. Error checking is performed to warn you if you try to write a buffer to an existing file other than the original file. Use the `w!` variant to force the write. You can also write the buffer into a UNIX pipeline by replacing the filename with `!cmd` where *cmd* is any UNIX command, preferably one that reads its standard input. (Note the difference between appending the `!` to the `write` command, which forces a write, and prepending the `!` to a UNIX shell command, which sends the buffer to that command.) You can append a `q` to the command to also quit when the write is complete, or `q!` to write unconditionally and then quit. **(ED)**

REGULAR EXPRESSIONS

A regular expression is a text pattern that can match other text patterns. Ordinary characters stand for themselves, so a text pattern consisting solely of ordinary characters will simply match itself. However, matching gets more interesting when metacharacters are involved. A metacharacter is a character that is treated specially. For example, ˆ (discussed first below) is a metacharacter that forces a match to succeed only if the target is the first text on a line.

Regular expressions have two roles in the editor: as contextual line specifiers and in the substitute command. When used as a line specifier, the regular expression is enclosed in // (for a forward search) or ?? (for a reverse search). For example, the line specifier /fort/ specifies the next line containing the text *fort*. The substitute command replaces one chunk of text with another. The original text is specified as a regular expression; the replacement text is not. (However, a few characters in the replacement are treated specially—see the *Replacement Text* section of this manual page.)

Besides the metacharacters tabulated below, `ex` has several option settings that affect pattern matching. The `ignorecase` option can be set to make matches insensitive to case. When `noignorecase` is set, matches must be exact: *abc* won't match *Abc*. When `magic` is set, all of the metacharacters discussed below are active, but when `nomagic` is set, then only the ˆ and $ metacharacters are active. See the `vi` *Options* manual page for more information on these options.

THE EX/VI
EDITOR

^   A *caret* anchors a search target to the beginning of a line. Thus, the pattern ^the will match only the letters the when they occur at the beginning of a line. The caret is magic only when used as the first character of a target (or when used in a *character set*, where it has a different meaning).   (ED)

$ A *currency symbol* anchors a search target to the end of a line. Thus, the pattern PP$ will match the letters PP only when they occur at the end of a line.   (ED)

.   A *period* matches any single character. Thus, the pattern b.d will match bed, bid, bad, and any other three letters that begin with b and end with d.   (ED)

[set]   A *left square bracket* introduces a *character set*. The end of the set is indicated by a right bracket. A character set matches any *one* of the characters in the set; for example, [aeiou] matches any single vowel. A hyphen may separate two characters to indicate that range of characters; for example, [0-9] indicates any one of the numerals. A caret as the first character of a character set means "the character set consists of all characters not explicitly mentioned." Thus, the character set [^A-Z] matches anything other than a capital letter.   (ED)

*   An *asterisk* matches zero or more repetitions of the previous single-character matching expression. The asterisk is often used after a period, to match anything, or after a character set, to match any number of occurrences of that set. Thus, the pattern [aeiou][aeiou]* will match any sequence of one or more vowels.   (ED)

\<   The pair of characters *backslash, less than* anchors a pattern to the beginning of a word.

\>   The pair of characters *backslash, greater than* anchors a pattern to the end of a word.

\   A *backslash* is used to escape the following character.   (ED)

\(A *backslash* followed by a *left parenthesis* introduces a subexpression, which is terminated by \) . Subexpressions have no effect on the regular expression matching, but they are useful when you want parts of the regular expression to appear in the replacement text.   (ED)

REPLACEMENT TEXT

Although the replacement text of a subsitute command is not a regular expression, it can contain several special characters.

    &   An ampersand in the replacement text will be replaced by the text matched by the regular expression. (ED)

    ~   A *tilde* in the replacement text will be replaced by the previous replacement text.

    \n   A *backslash* followed by a numeral will match the *n*-th subexpression of the regular expression. (ED)

    \u   The following character will be converted to upper case.

    \l   The following character will be converted to lower case.

    \U   The following text will be converted to upper case, until a \e or \E is encountered.

    \L   The following text will be converted to lower case, until a \e or \E is encountered.

The following example demonstrates several aspects of regular expressions and some of the special characters in the replacement text.

```
$ ex Abe
"Abe" 4 lines, 138 characters
:1,$p
four scor and SEVEN yeaars ago
hour four fathers brought for the anew
nation, dedicated to the proposition that
allmen are kreated equal.
:1s/f/F
Four scor and SEVEN yeaars ago
:s/ a/e a/
Four score and SEVEN yeaars ago
:s/S.*N/\L&/
Four score and seven yeaars ago
:s/aa/a/
Four score and seven years ago
:s/ //
Fourscore and seven years ago
:+s/h//
our four fathers brought for the anew
:s/four //
our fathers brought for the anew
:s/for .*/forth a new/
our fathers brought forth a new
```

```
:+
nation, dedicated to the proposition that
:s/, / conceived in liberty and\
/
dedicated to the proposition that
:-,+
nation conceived in liberty and
dedicated to the proposition that
allmen are kreated equal.
:s/ll/& /
all men are kreated equal.
:s/k/c/
all men are created equal.
:w
"Abe" 5 lines, 155 characters
:q
$ cat Abe
Fourscore and seven years ago
our fathers brought forth a new
nation conceived in liberty and
dedicated to the proposition that
all men are created equal.
$ _
```

VI

NAME

vi — full screen interface to the ex/vi text editor

SYNOPSIS

vi [options] [files]

DESCRIPTION

The ex/vi family of editors has two major user interfaces: ex, which is a line-oriented interface, and vi, which is a full screen interface. This manual page primarily discusses the vi aspects of the editor; ex is discussed on its own manual page. The vi *Options* manual page has a list of the options that can be set to alter vi's behavior.

COMMAND LINE OPTIONS

-t *tag*

The editor commences at the tagged location in the appropriate file. This option usually replaces a command line filename. *tag* must be a tagname that is found in a tags file. The default tags files are the file named 'tags' in the current directory and the file '/usr/lib/tags'. Alternate tags files can be specified in the '.exrc' editor startup script. (The '.exrc' file is discussed in the *Environment Variables* section of this manual page.)

-r

When vi is terminated by a hangup or by a system crash, it saves the current edit buffer and then sends mail to the users notifying them that an edit buffer has been saved. A list of saved edit buffers is printed by vi when you specify the -r option without mentioning a filename. The -r option combined with a filename tells vi to recover that file from the recovery area.

-x

vi will prompt for a key, which will then be used to decrypt all files that are read in, and encrypt all files that are written out.

-R

The input file will be considered read-only. All write commands will fail unless you use the w! form of the write command to override the write protection. You can unset the read-only mode by setting the noreadonly option. If you invoke vi using the name view then the read-only option will be set automatically.

THE EX/VI
EDITOR

+excmd
>   The editing session will commence by executing the given ex editor command. The most common uses of this option are specifying a search target (e.g., +/Jones to find the first occurrence of *Jones* in the file) or line number (e.g., +50 to start editing on line 50). The editor will be positioned on the last line of the buffer prior to executing the command.

-1   Sets the showmatch and lisp options so that it is easier to edit lisp programs.

-w*n*   Sets the window size to *n*.

-    Sets the noautoprint mode. This makes ex quieter, which is useful when processing edit scripts.

OVERVIEW

vi attempts to portray on the screen of your terminal a window showing the current appearance of the file being edited. There are two major vi modes: visual command mode and text entry mode. (There are also several ex specific modes, but they are not discussed here.) During visual command mode, everything that you type is interpreted as a command. Visual commands are not echoed on the screen; just their effect is visible. In text entry mode, everything that you type (with a few exceptions) is added to the text. Entering a Text Entry Command (Section 5) changes from visual command mode to text entry mode; pressing <ESC> terminates text entry mode and resumes visual command mode.

While you are editing a file with vi, you are actually working with a copy of that file, which is stored in the edit buffer. Changes made to the edit buffer don't alter the original file until you issue a write command. You should periodically write out the edit buffer to the disk file so that your work will be safe—from computer crashes or your own mistakes. If you make a disastrous alteration to the edit buffer, do *not* write out the buffer to the original file (you might want to write it out to another file, just in case). At the end of your editing session you should write out the buffer to the original file. vi will warn you if you try to exit without saving a modified edit buffer.

Before using vi, you must properly set the environment variable $TERM to indicate the type of terminal that you are using. If $TERM is unset, or, even worse, if it is set incorrectly, vi will not be able to function properly. The $TERM variable is often set in your '.profile' (or '.login' for csh users) login script. The second chore that must be done before using vi is to initialize the terminal. The importance of terminal initialization depends on which terminal you are using; some will not operate properly until initialized, while on others the initialization is superfluous. On System V there is the tput program. The most recent versions of tput have the command line option init, which will perform the initialization. On older versions of System V the sequence of commands tput is1;tput is2;tput is3 will usually be sufficient. Berkeley systems have the tset program.

It will perform the initialization, but the syntax is awkward.

Commands in visual command mode are typically one or a few keystrokes long. You do not have to enter a final <CR> for most commands. They are executed as you type the keys. Because visual mode commands are not echoed on the screen and they are executed immediately, it is easy to enter commands incorrectly. It is especially important to strike the correct keys because there is no way to take back a keystroke (or to even see what you have typed). You can always cancel a partially entered command by striking <ESC>.

Since vi has several modes, it is possible for the novice to move unintentionally from one to the other. All of the commands in this reference assume that you are in vi visual command mode. That's where you want to be unless you care to learn the powerful ex line editing commands. If you get into ex command line mode (you know you are in ex command line mode if a : is printed each time you hit <CR>, or if <ESC> is echoed as ^[), enter the command vi<CR> to re-enter visual mode. (If that doesn't work, try <CR>.<CR>vi<CR>.) If you get into open line editing mode (you know you are in open line editing mode when cursor movement commands constantly redraw the bottom line of the screen), enter the command Q (or <ESC>Q) to move to ex command line mode and then enter the command vi<CR> to return to visual mode.

Commands that start with a : or a ! are displayed on the bottom line of the screen as they are entered. For these commands, you can use the backspace to make corrections as you enter the command, you can abort the command by striking the interrupt character (usually ^C or <DEL>), and you must hit <CR> (carriage return) when the command has been completely entered.

Many vi commands accept an optional *numeric prefix*. Usually a numeric prefix means execute the command that many times; otherwise the command will be executed once. Occasionally a numeric prefix has a different meaning. The exact meaning of the numeric prefix is detailed below only when it does something other than repeat the command. Commands that accept a numeric prefix are indicated in the following table with a • in front of the citation. As you enter a numeric prefix, vi does not echo the value of the numeric prefix on the screen, so type carefully.

The commands c, y, d, <, >, and ! (change, yank, delete, shift left, shift right, and filter the buffer) are called *operators* because they operate on regions of text. An operator must be followed by a suffix, symbolized by § in the following table, that indicates the text region. The suffix may be any of the Cursor Movement Commands, any of the Text Search Commands, or either of the *goto* Marked Text Commands. (The suffix need not be a single keystroke.) The <, >, and ! operators always affect whole lines; thus, they allow only suffixes that specify line positions. When an operator is doubled, it affects entire lines. Thus, cc will change the current line, and 5yy will yank five lines starting with the current line.

Many people who use vi extensively over long periods of time don't take advantage of vi's operators. That's unfortunate because the operators are relatively easy to use, powerful, and flexible. The most important part of using an operator is knowing the cursor movement commands well enough to know exactly how to specify a given region of text. Once you've mastered cursor movement, you've nearly mastered operators. For example, d$ will delete from the current cursor position to the end of the line, d^ will delete from the current cursor position to the end of the line, dfq will delete from the current cursor position to the next letter *q* on the line, dG will delete from the current line to the end of the file, and d100G will delete from the current line to line 100. Take some time to learn to use vi operators; they are often useful.

Several conventions are used in this manual page. The notation ^X means Ctrl-*X*, where *X* may be any character. The notation <CR> signifies a carriage return, <DEL> is the delete key, <ESC> is the escape key, and <SPACE> is the space key. The notation *text* in the Text Entry Commands means any printable characters; any escaped (using ^Q or ^V) control characters; or tabs, spaces, or carriage returns. While you are entering *text*, only those controls described under Commands Used During An Insertion are available. You must terminate the insertion before using the full visual command set.

1. CURSOR MOVEMENT COMMANDS

h j k l	• Cursor left, down, up, right.
← ↓ ↑ →	• Cursor left, down, up, right.
^H ^N ^P \<SPACE\>	• Cursor left, down, up, right.
^J	• Cursor down.
+ \<CR\>	• Cursor to first non-blank on following line.
-	• Cursor to first non-blank on previous line.
G	• Goto line. (Goto end without preceding count.)
w b e	• Move forward word, backward word, or to end of word. (A *word* is a sequence of letters and digits, or group of punctuation symbols.)
W B E	• Move forward word, backward word, or to end of word. (A *word* is any text delimited by white space.)
0	Cursor to beginning of line.
^	Cursor to first non-blank on line.
|	• Cursor to column 1, or column specified by count.
$	• Cursor to end of line, or if count is supplied, then cursor to end of count-th following line.
( )	• Cursor moves backward or forward to beginning of sentence.
{ }	• Cursor moves backward or forward to beginning of paragraph.
[[ ]]	• Cursor moves backward or forward to beginning of section.
H M L	• Move cursor to home (top line of screen), middle line, or lowest line. For H a count means move to that many lines from top of screen; for L a count means move to that many lines from bottom.

2. MARKED TEXT

m*a*	Mark location with mark named *a*, where *a* may be any lower-case letter.
″	Goto line from previous context.
′*a*	Goto line marked *a*.
``	Goto character position from previous context.
`*a*	Goto character position marked *a*.

3. TEXT SEARCHES

f*c* F*c*	• Move cursor forward or backward to find character *c* on current line.
t*c* T*c*	• Move cursor forward or backward to position left of character *c* on current line.
;	• Repeat last intra-line search.
,	• Repeat last intra-line search backwards.
/*pat*\<CR\>	Forward search for pattern *pat*.
?*pat*\<CR\>	Reverse search for pattern *pat*.
n N	Repeat last search in same or opposite direction.
%	Search for balancing parenthesis () or brace {} when cursor is positioned on parenthesis or brace.

4. SCREEN MANAGEMENT COMMANDS

^F ^B	• Forward or backward screenful.
^U ^D	• Up or down ½ screenful. (Preceding count, which is remembered, specifies how many lines to scroll.)
^Y ^E	• Up or down one line.
z<CR> z. z-	• Move current line to top, middle, or bottom of screen. A numeric prefix to z specifies which line; a numeric suffix to z specifies a new window size.
^R	Redraw screen. Closes up empty screen lines created during editing on dumb terminals.
^L	Completely rewrite screen. (Needed after a transmission error, or after some other program writes to the screen.)

5. TEXT ENTRY COMMANDS

rc	• Replace character under cursor with c.
a*text*<ESC>	• Append *text* following current cursor position.
A*text*<ESC>	• Append *text* at the end of the line.
i*text*<ESC>	• Insert *text* before the current cursor position.
I*text*<ESC>	• Insert *text* at the beginning of the current line.
o*text*<ESC>	Open up a new line following the current line and add *text* there.
O*text*<ESC>	Open up a new line in front of the current line and add *text* there.
s*text*<ESC>	• Substitute *text* for character under cursor.
c§*text*<ESC>	• Change the given object to *text*. § is any character position specifier. For example, the command cwBob<ESC> will change the next word to *Bob*.
C*text*<ESC>	• A synonym for c$. Replaces from cursor position to end of line with *text*.
S*text*<ESC>	• A synonym for cc. Replaces lines with *text*.
R*text*<ESC>	• Replace the original material with *text*.
>§	• Shift lines right. § is a line specifier.
<§	• Shift lines left. § is a line specifier.
=	• Reindent line according to lisp conventions.
J	• Join lines together.
!§*unixcmd*<CR>	• Filter lines of text through a UNIX pipeline. The pipeline's output replaces the original text. § is a line specifier.
~	Change the case of the character under the cursor and move right one position.
.	• Repeat the last change.
&	Repeat last ex substitute command. A synonym for :&<CR>.

6. COMMANDS USED DURING AN INSERTION

^Q ^V	Quote the next character. For example, in text insert mode ^V^L will put a linefeed (^L) in the text.
\	Quote a following ^H, erase, or kill.
^W	Erase last entered word.
^H	Erase last entered character.
<CR>	Start a new line.
^T	In autoindent mode, indent shiftwidth at beginning of line.
^I	Tab

^D	In autoindent mode, move back one tab from beginning of line.
0^D	In autoindent mode, move to left margin and reset autoindent amount to zero.
^^D	In autoindent mode, move to left margin, but don't change autoindent amount. (Caret Ctrl-D)
\<ESC\>	Terminate insertion.
\<DEL\>	Abnormally terminate insertion.

7. TEXT DELETION COMMANDS

d§	•Delete the given object. § is any position specifier.
x	•A synonym for d\<SP\>. Delete character under cursor. (Preceding count repeats, but only on current line.)
X	•A synonym for d\<BS\>. Delete character to left of the cursor. (Count repeats, but only on current line.)
D	A synonym for d$. Deletes from the cursor to the end of the line.
u	Undo last change.
U	Restore Line.

8. BUFFERS

y§	•Yank text into buffer. § is any position specifier.
Y	•A synonym for yy. Yanks lines of text into a buffer.
p P	Put back text from buffer and place it after (lower-case p) or before (upper-case P) current line or character position.
"a	A prefix to yank (y), delete (d), put (p), or change (c) to indicate that the buffer named *a* should be used. (*a* is any lower-case letter.)
"A	A prefix to yank (y), delete (d), or change (c) to indicate that the selected text should be appended to the buffer named *A*. (*A* is any upper-case letter.)

9. SHELL ESCAPES

:!cmd\<CR\>	Escape to perform one UNIX command.
:sh\<CR\>	Start a subshell. You may enter commands, then exit from the subshell to return to vi.

10. STATUS

^G	Display filename, modified message, line number, and percentage location in file.
^Z	On UNIX systems that support job suspension, this will suspend vi.
Q	Change from vi mode to ex mode.
\<DEL\>	Striking the interrupt character returns to vi command mode from a search or from inserting text. Many people prefer to use \<Ctrl-C\> as their interrupt character.
\<ESC\>	Sound bell or terminate insertion.
:set\<CR\>	List options set differently from default.
:set all\<CR\>	List settings of all options.
:set *opt = val*	Set option named *opt* to *val*. (*Options* are discussed on their own manual page.)

11. MACROS

@b	Execute the commands stored in the buffer named *b*.
:map key repl<CR>	Create a command macro that will be invoked when you hit *key*. *key* is a single keystroke, the escape code generated by a function key, or *#n*, which means function key *n*. When you hit the key, the commands stored in *repl* will be executed. Use ˆv to escape special characters (e.g., <ESC>, <CR>) in *repl*.
:map<CR>	List the current command macros.
:unmap key<CR>	Delete a command macro.
:map! key repl<CR>	Create an insertion macro that will be invoked when you hit *key* in insert mode. *key* is coded as detailed above for map. *key* becomes a single keystroke abbreviation for *repl*.
:map!<CR>	List the current insertion macros.
:unmap! key<CR>	Delete an insertion macro.
:ab word repl<CR>	Create an abbreviation for *word*. During a text insertion, whenever you type *word* surrounded by white space or newlines, it will be replaced with *repl*. *word* can be more than one character. Use ˆv in *repl* to escape special characters.
:ab<CR>	List the current abbreviations.
:unab word<CR>	Delete an abbreviation.
#n	Manually simulate a function key on a terminal that lacks function keys.

12. FILE MANIPULATION

:w<CR>	Write edit buffer to original file.
:w filename<CR>	Write edit buffer to named file.
:w! filename<CR>	Write edit buffer to named file. Overwrite existing file.
:wq<CR>	Write edit buffer to original file and then quit.
:e filename<CR>	Start editing a new file. A warning will be printed if edit buffer has been modified but not yet saved.
:e! filename<CR>	Start editing a new file regardless of whether buffer has been saved since it was last modified.
:e #<CR>	Edit alternate file. The alternate file is the previous file that you were editing, or the last file mentioned in an unsuccessful :e command.
:n<CR>	Edit the next file mentioned on the command line.
:n filelist<CR>	Specify a list of files to edit, as if they had been mentioned on the command line.
:r filename<CR>	Add a file to the edit buffer.
:r !cmd<CR>	Read the output of a command into the edit buffer.
:q<CR>	Quit. (A warning is printed, and you will remain in the editor if the edit buffer has been modified but not yet saved.)
:q!<CR>	Quit. (No warning.)
ZZ	Save edit buffer and quit. Equivalent to :x<CR> or :wq<CR>.

`:cd dir<CR>`   Change directory to *dir*. A warning will be printed, and the move will not occur if the file has been modified but not yet saved.

ENVIRONMENT VARIABLES

Before using vi, the environment variable $TERM must be correctly set for your terminal. If $TERM isn't set, then vi will complain when it starts to run, and you will be put in ex command line mode. If $TERM is set incorrectly, then when vi starts it is likely that your screen display will be garbled. If either of these two problems arises, you should probably enter the command :q<CR> and get help. Since there are several families of similar terminals, it is possible for $TERM to be wrong even if everything appears correct for a while. Get help from an expert if your screen doesn't seem to behave as expected.

On Berkeley systems the screen management routines are based on the *termcap* terminal capabilities database. The most commonly used terminals at your site should be listed near the beginning of the '/etc/termcap' database to help vi start faster. If the environment variable $TERMCAP exists and its first character isn't a slash, it is checked to see if it contains the termcap entry for the $TERM terminal Placing a termcap entry into the $TERMCAP variable lets vi start faster because it doesn't need to search sequentially through the '/etc/termcap' terminal capabilities database. If the $TERMCAP variable does start with a slash character, then vi assumes it names a terminal capabilities database file, and uses that database instead of the default database.

On System V the *terminfo* terminal capabilities database is used. Unlike a termcap database, which stores all of the information in a single large file, the terminfo database stores each description in a single file. The directory '/usr/lib/terminfo' is the root terminfo directory, and the '/usr/lib/terminfo/a' directory stores termcaps whose names start with *a*. If $TERMINFO is set, vi will look in that directory for the root directory of the terminfo description files. If a description isn't found in the $TERMINFO subtree the '/usr/lib/terminfo' subtree will be searched as usual.

The environment variable $EXINIT may contain the name of a file containing ex commands. If $EXINIT doesn't exist, vi will read commands from the file '.exrc' in your home directory. Then in either case the editor will read any commands in the file '.exrc' in the current directory. '.exrc' startup files typically contain set commands to set desired vi options.

VISUAL COMMANDS INDEX

VI OPTIONS

NAME

vi options — option settings for the ex/vi editor

SYNOPSIS

```
:set all
:set opt
:set noopt
:set opt=val
```

DESCRIPTION

The ex/vi text editor has various options that can be set to customize its operation. The set command in ex/vi is used to display or change option settings. set can be used interactively, or set commands can be placed in the '.exrc' script so that they will be set automatically each time vi or ex starts to execute.

Several options can be set from the ex/vi command line:

-R Sets the readonly option.

-l Sets the showmatch and lisp options for lisp editing.

-w Sets the default window size.

THE EX/VI
EDITOR

OPTION	ABB.	MEANING
autoindent	ai	autoindent makes vi automatically indent each new line to the same level as the previous, or to the same level as the one the cursor was on when a new line was opened. ^T will increase the indentation one shiftwidth. ^D at the beginning of a line will cause the indent to retreat left one stop. ^D will retreat to the left margin. The default is noai.
autoprint	ap	When autoprint is set, lines are printed after being modified by one of the following ex commands: d, c, J, m, t, u, <, or >. This option applies only in line editing mode, and the effect is as if a trailing p were added to each of the above ex commands. The default is ap.
autowrite	aw	When autowrite is set, vi will automatically write out the current file before executing commands that might switch to another file, or before executing a shell escape command. The default is noaw.
beautify	bf	beautify tells vi to discard all control characters (other than tab, newline, and form-feed) from the input. The default is nobf.
directory	dir	directory tells vi where to place its temporary files. The default is /tmp.
edcompatible		This makes the ex substitute command more closely resemble ed's. The default is noedcompatible.
errorbells	eb	errorbells tells vi to ring the terminal's bell for a larger set of errors. The default is noeb.
flash		Flash the screen instead of ringing the bell, on those terminals that are capable of flashing the screen. (Only available on newer versions of vi.) The default is flash.
hardtabs	ht	hardtabs defines the hardware tab stops for your terminal. The default is 8 spaces.

OPTION	ABB.	MEANING
ignorecase	ic	ignorecase tells vi to ignore case distinctions in searches and substitutions. The default is noic.
lisp		lisp alters the indent strategy in indent mode for lisp programs. The default is nolisp.
list	li	list mode displays tabs and linefeeds explicitly. Tabs are displayed as ^I, and linefeeds are displayed as $. The default is noli.
magic		In magic mode all regular expression characters are active. In nomagic mode only ^, $, and \ are metacharacters. In nomagic mode a metacharacter (e.g., ?) can be restored its power by preceding it with a backslash (e.g., \?). The default is magic.
mesg		mesg allows messages to be written on your screen during vi sessions. The default is nomesg.
number	nu	number numbers lines on the display. The default is nonu.
open		open mode allows you to issue the open or visual commands from ex line editing mode. noopen prevents these commands so that novices will be less confused by modes. (Called novice on System V.) The default is open.
optimize	opt	optimize uses cursor positioning escape sequences at the end of each line to move to the beginning of the next line. This is more efficient on many terminals. The default is opt.
paragraphs	para	paragraphs tells vi the names of the nroff/troff paragraph macros. When you move to the beginning or end of a paragraph (using the { or } commands), vi searches for the closest paragraph marker in the paragraphs list, or for a blank line. In the list, pairs of characters are macro names (e.g., IP). The default is IPLPPPQPP LIbp, which covers standard -ms or -mm paragraphs, -mm list items, and manual page breaks.

OPTION	ABB.	MEANING
prompt		prompt tells vi to print the : prompt when it is waiting for line editing commands. The default is prompt.
readonly	ro	When readonly is set, the editor will refuse to write to a file (unless you use the w! command). readonly can be set like any other option, or it can be set by invoking vi with the -R command line option. The default is noreadonly.
redraw		redraw tells vi to constantly keep the screen display up to date, even on dumb terminals. This option generates much output on a dumb terminal. The default is noredraw.
remap		remap makes vi repeatedly scan the text of macros to see if any further macros are invoked. noremap scans each only once, thus making it impossible for one macro to invoke another. The default is remap.
report		When a command modifies more than report lines, vi prints a message. The default is 5.
scroll		scroll is the number of lines the display scrolls in ex mode when you type the EOF character. The default is ½ window.
sections		sections is a list of nroff/troff macro names that vi searches for when you enter the [[and]] commands to move to the beginning and end of the section. In the sections list, pairs of characters denote macro names (e.g., SH). The default is SHNHH HU, which covers the heading start commands of -ms and -mm.
shell	sh	shell contains the name of the default shell. When vi starts to execute, shell is copied from the $SHELL environment variable.
shiftwidth	sw	shiftwidth is the size of the software tab stop. The default is 8.

OPTION	ABB.	MEANING
showmode		showmode displays the current edit mode on the status line. When terse is set, the mode is represented by a single character. (Only available on newer versions of vi.) The default is noshowmode.
showmatch	sm	When showmatch is set, vi will automatically move the cursor to the matching (or { for one second each time you type a) or }. This is useful for programmers, especially for lisp programmers. The default is nosm.
slowopen	slow	The slowopen mode is an alternate output strategy for open or visual mode. It improves vi on dumb terminals by reducing the amount of screen updating during text inputs. Its value and default depend on terminal type.
tabstop	ts	Tab characters in the input file produce movement to the next tabstop boundary. Reducing tabstop to two or four often makes it easier to view heavily indented material, such as C programs. The default is 8.
taglength	tl	taglength is the number of significant characters in a tag. Zero means the entire tag is significant. The default is 0.
tags		tags is a list of files containing tags. The default list is '/usr/lib/tags'.
term		term is the name of the output terminal. Its initial value comes from the $TERM environmental variable.
terse		terse makes vi produce shorter error messages. The default is noterse.
timeout		When timeout is set, the complete character sequence invoking a macro must be entered within one second. The default is timeout.
warn		When warn is set, vi will warn you if you enter a ! (shell) command without first saving your text. The default is warn.

OPTION	ABB.	MEANING
window		window is the size of the text display in visual mode. The default varies according to the baud rate. It is eight lines at speeds less than 1200 baud, sixteen lines at 1200 baud, and the full screen at more than 1200 baud.
w300		w300 is a synonym for window, but it is effective only if the baud rate is less than 1200. The default is 8.
w1200		w1200 is a synonym for window, but it is effective only if the baud rate is 1200. The default is 16.
w9600		w9600 is a synonym for window, but it is effective only if the baud rate is higher than 1200. The default is full screen.
wrapscan	ws	wrapscan makes vi search the entire file every time. Searches always start from the current line and proceed to the end (or beginning) of the file. When wrapscan is set and a vi search reaches the end (or beginning) of the file, the search continues from the beginning (or end) to the current line. The default is ws.
wrapmargin	wm	When you are entering text and the cursor position gets to within wrapmargin characters of the right margin, vi will automatically insert a line break (between two words). This allows you to type continuously without striking return to form each line. wrapmargin applies only to text entry in visual mode, not in line editing mode. The value 0 disables automatic line break insertion. The default is 0.
writeany	wa	When writeany is set, vi will allow you to overwrite existing files without warning you. The default is nowa.

NOTE

When you assign a value to an option, there can't be any white space on either side of the equal sign. The command

```
:set wm=10
```

will work, but the command

```
:set wm = 10
```

will complain "=: No such option".

SECTION VII

TEXT PROCESSING COMMANDS

295

Text processing was one of the first practical applications of the UNIX tools philosophy. The UNIX text processing facility is built from a handful of separate programs that together form a full-featured typesetting system.

The UNIX system features a two-stage approach to text processing. The first stage is document preparation—creating a text file that contains ordinary text interspersed with formatting commands. The second stage is text formatting—processing the document file with formatting software that carries out the formatting instructions embedded in the document.

Some of the most important components of this system have already been described. The text file commands, described in Section III, are often used to help manage and analyze document files, and the ex/vi text editor, described in Section VI, is often used to prepare the document files.

The facilities described in this section are used during the document formatting stage of the process. The key to this system is troff, a program that formats a text file according to its embedded instructions. troff is designed to work with typesetters and laser printers, while its alter ego, nroff, works with conventional printers.

troff's own formatting codes are very low-level. They closely match the feature set of most typesetters, but they aren't very result oriented. For example, troff doesn't have a command that performs the half-dozen basic chores that are necessary when starting a new paragraph. It doesn't contain facilities for page headings, footers, or footnotes. Of course, these features can be hand crafted from troff's basic command set, but few users want to master that much detail. Instead, a few troff masters have created macro packages, which provide a result-oriented interface on top of the low-level troff feature set.

There are three commonly used, general-purpose macro packages, -ms, -mm, and -me. The -ms macro package is the oldest. It was developed shortly after troff was developed, and it has been widely used ever since. -ms is available on all Version 7 and Berkeley systems, and it is sometimes available on System V. -mm was developed by Bell Laboratories to overcome some of the shortcomings in -ms. It has an extremely wide variety of features, including a very flexible set of macros for managing lists. -mm is principally available on System V, although it sometimes appears on Berkeley systems. The newest macro package is -me. It was developed by Eric Allman of Berkeley to provide more features than -ms without the baroque tendency of -mm. -me is widely available on Berkeley-derived systems, but is rarely present elsewhere.

For almost all UNIX text processing users, one of the three macro packages mentioned above should be their primary interface to the text processing system. Few users need to know many native troff formatting commands; the command repertoire of their macro package is much more important. In this manual, the descriptions of nroff and troff center on their command line options. Their basic formatting codes are not described. Instead, you should consult the appropriate macro package manual page.

Only the -ms and -mm macro packages are described here. (The -me macro package is not as widely available as the -ms and -mm macros, and it is already supported by excellent documentation.) The formatting commands of each package are described, with topically related commands grouped together. Please note that -ms and -mm are not UNIX commands; they are macro packages that can be invoked during document formatting by using the `-ms` or `-mm` command line option of `nroff` or `troff`. (To further confuse this issue there is the `mm` command, which provides an alternate interface to `nroff` or `troff` for -mm users.)

The general-purpose macro packages, and `troff` itself, are designed to meet typical text processing needs. More specialized needs, such as typesetting mathematics, are addressed by *preprocessors*. The two most widely used preprocessors, `tbl` and `eqn`, are discussed in this manual. `tbl` is a preprocessor for typesetting tables. It scans through tabular material to compute the optimal width for each column, thereby eliminating tedious trial and error guesswork. `tbl` also knows how to box tables, center tables, and set certain columns in a given font. `eqn` is used for typesetting mathematics. It translates a description of an equation layout into basic `troff` commands. `eqn` doesn't know much about mathematics, but it understands how to place one symbol in relation to another.

The material in this section is designed more as a reference than as a tutorial for novices. Learning this material from scratch is a difficult, but rewarding, job. There are several tutorial papers on most of these facilities, plus a handful of introductory books including my book, *The UNIX Text Processing Tools*.

EQN

NAME

eqn — translate equation descriptions into `troff` commands

SYNOPSIS

eqn [options] [files]
neqn [options] [files]

DESCRIPTION

eqn is a `troff` preprocessor. It translates a description of an equation layout into a series of primitive `troff` commands that specify exactly how the equation should be printed. eqn output is usually piped to `troff` (for printing) or redirected to '/dev/null' (for viewing error messages while debugging). The neqn program performs the same function for `nroff`.

If *files* are mentioned on the command line, eqn will read its input from them, otherwise eqn will read from the standard input. When eqn and `tbl` are both used, `tbl` should appear first in the pipeline.

eqn recognizes the following command line options:

-dxy

The inline starting delimiter is set to x, and the inline concluding delimiter is set to y. Thus, the command line option -d$$ will set both delimiters to the currency symbol.

-pn

This option controls how much subscripts and superscripts are reduced from the previous size. The default is three, but two or one would be more appropriate if you have subsubscripts.

-sn

This option sets the global size for equations to n. This command line option is equivalent to the `gsize` statement.

-fn

This option sets the global font for equations to n. This command line option is equivalent to the `gfont` statement.

INPUT FORMAT

eqn alters only the part of its input that lies between delimiters. All other input is passed through untouched. eqn recognizes two separate delimiter pairs—the macro commands, `.EQ` and `.EN`, which delimit equations entered alone on one or more lines, and two single-character inline delimiters that are specified on the command line or in a `delim` statement. The following `eqn` input will set the inline delimiters to currency symbols:

```
.EQ
delim $$
.EN
```

Currency symbols would be a bad choice for an economics paper (because the $ in the phrase "a $500 capital loss" will look like the start of an equation), but the $ is often used as the inline equation delimiter in other (nonmonetary) disciplines. You can disable the delimiter at any point with the command

```
.EQ
delim off
.EN
```

Delimiters must be paired; havoc will ensue if the starting or ending delimiter is missing. The `checkeq` program can examine `eqn` input files and report unpaired delimiters.

Equations that are surrounded by the `.EQ` and `.EN` macro commands will be positioned according to which macro package you are using. In `-ms` the default is centered horizontally with some extra space above and below, but the macro arguments `I` or `L` can be used to specify indented or left flush. In `-ms` you can also supply a label for the equation, which should follow the adjustment keyletter. In `-mm` the `.EQ` and `.EN` macros must be surrounded by `-mm` display macros, `.DS` and `.DE`, which will control the placement of the equation. In both `-ms` and `-mm`, equations that are identified by the inline delimiters—such as the equation `$x sup i$`—will be output inline: x^i.

`eqn` divides its input (the part of the document that falls between delimiters) into words. Each word that is part of `eqn`'s vocabulary is treated specially and all other words are simply output in italic. Apply spaces liberally to the input so that `eqn`'s notion of a word and yours are the same. Unlike many languages, `eqn` will read (x sup 2) as three symbols (not five). The superscript will be 2), which is not often what is intended. You can use ~ or ^ in place of input spaces, with the side effect that extra horizontal space will appear in the output. (~ produces twice the extra output space as ^.)

A sequence of items can be logically collected into a single entity by surrounding the items with {}. This allows each *thing* in an `eqn` construct to be arbitrarily complicated. You can remove any special `eqn` meaning from something by surrounding it with "". For example the word `sin` is usually set in Roman (instead of italics) because it is a common function name. You can defeat its special treatment by using "sin" instead of sin.

If you want a group of equations to line up at a given point, you can use the keyword mark at the lineup point in the first equation, and then use the keyword lineup at the lineup point of the following equations. (Note that lineup can only move an equation to the right.)

LAYOUT COMMANDS

x sub *y*

x sup *y*

    sub and sup make *y* a subscript or superscript of *x*.

x over *y*

    over places *x* over *y*, with a horizontal line between. (Use a pile to stack things without a separating horizontal line.)

symbol from *x* to *y*

    The from and to keywords produce labels for symbols such as integrals, or summations.

sqrt *x*

    The sqrt keyword places *x* inside a traditional square root symbol. (eqn can't produce a tall and attractive square root symbol.)

left *symbol*

right *symbol*

    left and right produce tall bars, curly braces, square brackets, parentheses, or other symbols as specified, to appear to the left or right of a tall construct. Although you can use left without right, you must at least have a left "" before a right something.

pile { *thing* above *thing* ... }

    A pile is a vertical stack of *things*. You can replace the keyword pile with rpile for a right flush pile, or with lpile for a left flush pile. A cpile is a centered pile.

matrix {

    col { *thing* above *thing* ... }

    col { *thing* above *thing* ... }

    ...

}

    A matrix is a two-dimensional array of elements. Each column started with the col or ccol keyword will be centered, each started with lcol will be left flush, and each started with rcol will be right flush. Each column must have the same number of elements.

$$x_{ij} * y_{jk} = z_{ik}$$

```
.EQ
x sub ij * y sub jk ~=~ z sub ik
.EN
```

$$ax^2 + bx^1 + cx^0 = 0$$

```
.EQ
ax sup 2 + bx sup 1 + cx sup 0 ~=~ 0
.EN
```

$$\frac{1}{3} = 0.33333333333333333$$

```
.EQ
1 over 3 ~=~ 0.33333333333333333
.EN
```

$$\sum_{i=0}^{\infty} x_i = 0.5$$

```
.EQ
sum from i=0 to inf x sub i ~=~ 0.5
.EN
```

$$\left[\frac{1}{2} \right.$$

```
.EQ
left [ { 1 over 2 }
.EN
```

$$\begin{bmatrix} 0, & i<0 \\ 1, & i=0 \\ -1, & i>0 \end{bmatrix}$$

```
.EQ
left "" pile {
    { 0, ~~i < 0} above
    { 1, ~~i = 0} above
    { -1, ~~i > 0}
    } right ]
.EN
```

$$\begin{matrix} 0 & -\frac{1}{2} & -\frac{\sqrt{2}}{2} \\ \frac{1}{2} & 0 & -\frac{1}{2} \\ \frac{\sqrt{2}}{2} & \frac{1}{2} & 0 \end{matrix}$$

```
.EQ
matrix {
    col { 0 above { 1 over 2 } above { sqrt 2 over 2 } }
    col { {- {1 over 2}} above 0 above {1 over 2} }
    col { {- {sqrt 2 over 2}} above {- {1 over 2}} above 0}
}
.EN
```

FONTS AND SIZES

roman *thing*

italic *thing*

bold *thing*

The following *thing*, which should be surrounded by {} if it is more than one word, will be set in the named font. Words are usually set in italics, except for special symbols and recognized function names, such as *sin*.

font X *thing*

> The following *thing*, which should be surrounded by {} if it is more than one word, will be set in the font X. The name X must be a single-character troff font name.

size N *thing*

> The following *thing*, which should be surrounded by {} if it is more than one word, will be set in point size N. A signed digit will increase or decrease the current point size by that amount.

fat *thing*

> The following *thing*, which should be surrounded by {} if it is more than one word, will be fattened by overstriking. fat is usually used when you want an emphasized italic or an emphasized special symbol. bold is better for emphasizing ordinary Roman (upright) letters.

gsize N

gfont X

> gsize and gfont set the default point size and font for equations. Unlike other settings, gfont and gsize persist until changed.

$\nabla \cdot dt \neq \nabla \cdot \mathbf{ds}$

```
.EQ I
del ~cdot~ dt ~!=~
fat del ~cdot~ bold ds
.EN
```

POSITIONING

fwd N

back N

up N

down N

> Move in the given direction N hundredths of an em. Thus, fwd 100 will move one em to the right. These tweaks allow you to tune the appearance of equations. eqn output is usually too dense, which is best corrected with ~ space indicators in the input, rather than with these commands.

DEFINITIONS

define *name* 'words'

ndefine *name* 'words'

tdefine *name* 'words'

> eqn has a simple macro facility that allows one piece of text to stand for another. This is primarily used as a shortcut when entering equations, or to

reduce the chance of error in repetitive equations. Following a definition, you can use *name* in place of the quoted words. The most likely error when making a definition is to define something as itself. Whereas `define` is for both eqn and neqn, `ndefine` is only for neqn, and `tdefine` is only for eqn. `ndefine` and `tdefine` let you specify equations differently for the two formatters.

SPECIAL SYMBOLS

alpha	α	omega	ω
beta	β	omicron	o
chi	χ	phi	ϕ
delta	δ	pi	π
epsilon	ϵ	psi	ψ
eta	η	rho	ρ
gamma	γ	sigma	σ
iota	ι	tau	τ
kappa	$\varkappa$	theta	θ
lambda	λ	upsilon	υ
mu	μ	xi	ξ
nu	ν	zeta	ζ
DELTA	Δ	PSI	Ψ
GAMMA	Γ	SIGMA	Σ
LAMBDA	Λ	THETA	Θ
OMEGA	Ω	UPSILON	Υ
PHI	Φ	XI	Ξ
PI	Π		
>=	$\geq$	<=	$\leq$
==	$\equiv$	!=	$\neq$
->	$\rightarrow$	<-	$\leftarrow$
<<	$\ll$	>>	$\gg$
+-	$\pm$	approx	$\approx$
inf	∞	partial	∂
half	$\frac{1}{2}$	times	$\times$
prime	$'$	cdot	$\cdot$
del	∇	grad	∇
...	$\cdots$	,...,	$,\cdots,$
sum	$\sum$	int	$\int$
union	$\bigcup$	inter	$\bigcap$
prod	$\prod$	nothing	

DIACRITICAL MARKS

a dot	$\dot{a}$	b dotdot	$\ddot{b}$
c hat	$\hat{c}$	d tilde	$\tilde{d}$
e vec	$\vec{e}$	f dyad	$\overrightarrow{f}$
g bar	$\bar{g}$	h under	$\underline{h}$

KNOWN FUNCTIONS

The following function names are recognized by eqn and they will be set in Roman unless you quote them or specify another font using one of the font selection keywords.

and	arc	cos	cosh	coth	det	exp	for
if	Im	lim	ln	log	max	min	Re
		sin	sinh	tan	tanh		

MM, MMT

NAME

mm — a simplified interface to the nroff formatter

mmt — a simplified interface to the troff formatter

SYNOPSIS

mm [options] [file . . .]

mmt [options] [file . . .]

DESCRIPTION

On UNIX System V you can use the mm or mmt programs to format and print your -mm documents. mm formats a document with nroff for ordinary printers, and mmt formats a document with troff for more sophisticated printers such as laser printers or typesetters. mm and mmt were designed to simplify text processing, but some people find them confusing because they present yet another command line interface to an already complicated system.

The options must precede the filenames, and the special filename - can be used to force mm or mmt to read from the standard input. By default, the input is processed using the compacted version of the -mm macros.

The following options are common to mm and mmt.

-e   Preprocess the input with eqn.

-t   Preprocess the input with tbl.

-y   Use the noncompacted version of the -mm macros instead of the compacted version.

Any unrecognized options will be passed along to nroff or troff. Here are a few of the common nroff/troff options that are used on the mm or mmt command line.

-olist

Output is produced for the pages mentioned in the *list*. The *list* is a comma-separated list of pages, or page ranges. (A page range is n-m, which means from page *n* through page *m*.) For example, the option -o1,3,5-11,19 means print pages one, three, five through eleven, and nineteen.

-nN The first page of the document is numbered N.

-s*N* The output process is stopped every *N* pages so that you can change the paper. (Not functional on all versions of troff.)

-r*aN*

> The nroff/troff internal register named *a* is set to the value *N*. *a* is any single-character register name, and *N* is any value.

The following command line options apply only to mm:

-T*term*

> Prepare output for the terminal named *term*. A list of supported terminals can be generated by listing the files in the '/usr/lib/term' directory. If this option is not specified, then output will be generated for the terminal listed in the $TERM environment variable. When all else fails, output will be for a model 450.

-c The col program will be invoked as an output filter. col is automatically invoked for some terminals.

-12 Produce output in twelve pitch, if possible.

-E Produce equally spaced lines on capable printers. (Equivalent to the nroff's -e option.)

—MM

NAME

-mm — the memorandum macros (System V)

SYNOPSIS

```
nroff -mm [ options ] [ file ... ]
troff -mm [ options ] [ file ... ]
mm [ options ] [ file . . . ]
mmt [ options ] [ file . . . ]
```

DESCRIPTION

The -mm macros are used with `nroff` and `troff` to conveniently prepare documents. They currently are the standard macros on System V, and they are available on some Version 7 and Berkeley UNIX systems.

It is important to understand clearly the difference between the -mm *macros*, which are `troff` language directives that specify the formats for pages, paragraphs, and lists, and the `mm` (or `mmt`) *program*, which is actually a simplified command line interface to the `nroff` or `troff` formatter. `mm` (the program) makes it easier to type the UNIX command line that invokes the formatter. It is discussed on its own manual page. -mm (the macros) are discussed here.

-mm has commands that produce section headings, paragraphs, page headings, displays, and lists. The appearance of these features can be altered to suit your requirements. -mm supports the `eqn` and `tbl` preprocessors.

-mm documents contain plain text interspersed with -mm commands. Most -mm commands stand alone on a line that starts with a period, and the names of -mm commands are one or two upper-case letters. For example, the

```
.P
```

command tells -mm that the following text is a paragraph. -mm will automatically perform the required operations: checking for space on the page, leaving extra space above the paragraph, and possibly indenting the first line of the paragraph.

There are several ways to access the -mm macros. One method is to use the **-mm** flag on the `nroff` or `troff` command line. On some versions of System V a compacted version of -mm is available. The compacted version, which is accessed with the **-cm** command line flag, is preferable because it loads faster. Another

TEXT
PROCESSING

way is to use the mm (or mmt) front end program. mm (or mmt) will automatically invoke nroff (or troff) with the appropriate arguments.

Yet another way to access the -mm macros is to include literally the text of the -mm macros using the following troff include command near the beginning of your document:

```
.so /usr/lib/tmac/tmac.m
```

Many -mm page layout features require that particular troff number registers be initialized before the -mm macros are loaded, if the defaults are not acceptable. Thus, these registers must be set on the command line, or the assignments can be placed in the document file just before the troff include command shown above. If you choose to include -mm directly in your document, you must avoid the mm (or mmt) program, and you shouldn't use the -mm (or -cm) option on the nroff or troff command line.

HEADINGS AND PARAGRAPHS MACROS

.H *N text*	Numbered heading. *N* is the heading level, *text* is the heading text.
.HU *text*	Unnumbered heading. *text* is the heading text.
.P	Start a paragraph in the prevailing style.
.P 0	Start a flush left paragraph.
.P 1	Start an indented paragraph.
.nP	Start an automatically numbered paragraph.

TYPE STYLES MACROS

.R .I *A B C D E F* .B *A B C D E F* .IB *A B C D E F* .BI *A B C D E F* .RB *A B C D E F* .BR *A B C D E F* .RI *A B C D E F* .IR *A B C D E F*	The commands .R, .I, and .B switch font to Roman, Italic, or Bold. For I or B optional arguments can be supplied to make a temporary switch. If *A* is supplied, it alone will be in italic or bold. If *B* is also supplied it will follow *A*, without a separating space, and be in the surrounding font. If *C* is supplied, it will immediately follow *B* in italic or bold, and so forth. .IB, .BI, and so on are similar except that the fonts alternate between the two fonts specified in the macro name, rather than between a named font and the surrounding font.
.SM *A*	Print *A* in (1 pt.) smaller text.
.SM *A B*	Print *A* smaller followed by *B* normal.
.SM *A B C*	Print *B* smaller sandwiched between *A* and *C* normal.

.S *p v*	Set the default point size and vertical spacing. The optional argument *p* controls the point size, and *v* controls vertical spacing. By default the point size is ten, and the vertical spacing is the point size plus two. The arguments may be:
	    number — set the point size to that number
	    ±*number* — change the size by that amount
	    P — restore the previous size
	    D — restore the default size
	    C — maintain current size
	Without arguments, the previous point size and vertical spacing will be restored. If only the *v* argument is omitted, the vertical spacing will be set to the default.

DISPLAY AND FOOTNOTE MACROS

.DS *t f i*
text
.DE

.DF *t f i*
text
.DE

.DS and .DF start regular and floating displays. All displays are ended by the .DE command. Both display types accept three optional arguments. The first argument, *t*, specifies the type of the display. It must have the value I for an indented display, C for individually centered lines, CB for centered as a block, or L for left flush (the default). If the fill argument *f* is F, the display will be filled instead of the default nofill. The third argument, if present, will right-indent the display that many ens.

.EQ *label*
text
.EN

text will be processed by the eqn preprocessor. Unless *text* is a define or a delimiter, it must be surrounded by a display. An optional *label* argument to .EQ will be printed as an equation label (usually) on the left.

.PS
text
.PE

text will be processed by the pic line drawings preprocessor.

.G1
text
.G2

text will be processed by the grap graph drawing preprocessor.

.TS
text
.TE

text will be processed by the tbl preprocessor. Displays must surround the table if you want it kept together.

.FS *label*
text
.FE

text is a footnote that will be placed at the bottom of the page. In the main text, the string *F can be used to automatically number the citation. Optional *label* should be used when footnotes aren't numbered automatically.

TEXT PROCESSING

OVERALL DOCUMENT FORMAT MACROS

.1C	Switch to one-column (the default) or two-column format.
.2C	
.WC x	Control width of displays and footnotes in two-column mode. The x argument can be:

N	Restore the default settings: -WF, -FF, -WD, and FB.
WF	Make footnotes two columns wide in .2C mode.
-WF	Make footnotes one column wide in .2C mode.
FF	Make all footnotes on a page be the same width as the first footnote. This will override -WF or WF.
-FF	Allow a mix of footnote styles on a page.
WD	Make displays two columns wide in .2C mode.
-WD	Make displays one column wide.
FB	Make floating displays cause a break when they are output on the current page.
-FB	Prevent floating displays output on the current page from causing a break.

.PH "'*L*'*C*'*R*'"	These macros produce *H*eaders and *F*ooters on all, *O*dd or *E*ven pages. Each three-part header consists of text *L* for the left, *C* for the center, and *R* for the right. In a header or footer \\\\nP will print the page number.
.OH "'*L*'*C*'*R*'"	
.EH "'*L*'*C*'*R*'"	
.PF "'*L*'*C*'*R*'"	
.OF "'*L*'*C*'*R*'"	
.EF "'*L*'*C*'*R*'"	

LIST MACROS

.BL *i ns*
list
.LE

Each item in a bullet list is marked with a bullet (●). Optional arguments *i* and *ns* specify an indent and no-space (no extra space between list elements) mode.

.DL *i ns*
list
.LE

Each item in a dash list is marked with a dash (−). Optional arguments *i* and *ns* specify an indent and no-space mode.

.ML *M i ns*
list
.LE

Each item in a marked list is identified by the mark *M*. Optional arguments *i* and *ns* specify an indent and no-space mode.

.AL *t i ns*
list
.LE

Item marks in an automatic list are sequenced automatically. The optional argument *t* must be 1 (numeral one) for arabic numerals, a or A for lower- or upper-case alphabetic, or i or I for lower- or upper-case Roman numerals. The default type is numeric. Optional arguments *i* and *ns* specify an indent and no-space mode.

.VL *I mi ns*
list
.LE

A variable item list uses marks supplied with each .LI macro. The argument *I* that specifies the indent must be supplied. Optional arguments *mi* and *ns* specify the indent for the mark and no-space mode. Exdented paragraphs are produced if the .LI macros don't have marks.

.LI *m if*

The .LI macros appear within the list macro pairs described above to introduce each item in the list. For example, a five-item bullet list will have five .LI macros, one in front of each item in the list. The following is a typical list specification:

```
.DL
.LI
All -mm lists start with one of the five
list begin macros.
.LI
Each item in a -mm list is introduced by
the .LI macro.
.LI
The end of each -mm list is marked by
the .LE macro.
.LE
```

The argument *m*, specifies the mark. In a .VL list a mark is usually supplied with each item. In other list types, the mark will replace the customary mark. The optional argument *if* specifies that the supplied mark should appear in front of the customary mark, rather than replace the customary mark. Lists may be nested.

TABLE OF CONTENTS MACROS

.TC *sl sp tl t*

Headings whose level is less than or equal to the level stored in the C1 number register are saved. The stored table of contents is output by the .TC command. Four optional arguments control the format of the table of contents. Headings whose level is *sl* or less will have *sp* blank lines (nroff) or half lines (troff) above. *sl* and *sp* each have a default value of one. Headings whose level is *tl* or less will have their page numbers flush right. If *t* is zero, those page numbers will be preceded by a string of periods, otherwise by white space. The default value for *tl* is two, and the default value for *t* is 0. Arguments five through nine are printed as a centered title above the table of contents.

ACCENT MARKS

NAME	INPUT	OUTPUT	NAME	INPUT	OUTPUT
acute	e*'	é	grave	e*`	è
circumflex	o*^	ô	tilde	n*~	ñ
umlaut	u*:	ü	Umlaut	U*;	Ü
cedilla	c*,	ç			

FORMATTER DEPENDENT STRINGS

NAME	INPUT	nroff OUTPUT	troff OUTPUT
bullet	*(BU	⊕	●
em dash	*(EM	--	—

ÆRALL FORMAT NUMBER REGISTERS

D † Debug flag.

   0 No debugging.

   1 Debugging. Continue on error.

Hy   Hyphenation control. Default is 0.

   0 Do not hyphenate main text.

   1 Hyphenate main text.

L † Length of page. Units are lines (nroff) or scaled numbers (troff). Default value is 66 (nroff) or 11i (troff).

N † Page numbering style.

   0 All pages get prevailing header.

   1 Prevailing header used as footer on page 1, and all other pages get prevailing header.

   2 Page 1 doesn't get a header, but all other pages get prevailing header.

   3 All pages get section-page number in footer.

   4 If a user header is specified with .PH, it will appear on pages 2 onward. Otherwise, no page header will appear.

   5 All pages get section-page number in footer.

O † Page offset. The left margin will be offset from the edge of the page by the amount specified in the O number register. The units for O are ens (nroff) or scaled numbers (troff). The defaults are seven ens (nroff) and 0.5i (troff).

P † Page number. The P number register may be set on the command line, or reset in the document to alter the page numbering sequence.

S † Point size for troff. The default is 10.

U † nroff underline style for headings. The default is 0.

   0 Continuous underline.

   1 Underline only letters and digits.

W † Text width. The units are ens (nroff) or scaled numbers (troff). The default is six inches. Note that for nroff the width of an en is 0.1i in ten pitch and 0.08333i in twelve pitch.

   † All number registers marked with † must be set before -mm is loaded, either on the command line or in .nr commands preceding the inclusion of the -mm text.

HEADING FORMAT NUMBER REGISTERS

Ej   Heading eject. Headings at this level or lower will always appear at the top of the page. Default value 0.

Hb   Heading break level. Headings of this level or less will be followed by a break, making following text start on a new line. The default value is 0.

Hc   Heading centering level. Headings of this level or less will be centered. The default value is 0.

Hs   Heading space level. Headings of this level or less will be followed by a blank line (nroff) or a half vertical space (troff). The default is 2.

Ht   Heading type.
    0   Heading numbers will contain as many parts as the level of the heading. For example, a level three head would appear as 4.2.12.
    1   Heading numbers will contain only the rightmost part. For example, the heading mentioned above would be written as 12.

Hu   Heading level for unnumbered (.HU) headings. Unnumbered headings will be treated as if they were at this level for formatting, and for incrementing the heading counters.

PARAGRAPH FORMAT NUMBER REGISTERS

Np   Paragraph numbering style. The default is 0.
    0   Paragraphs will not be numbered.
    1   Paragraphs will be numbered.

Pi   Paragraph indent. Indented paragraphs, bullet lists (.BL), and dash lists (.DL) are indented by the amount specified in the Pi number register. The units are ens, and the defaults are 5 (nroff) or 3 (troff).

Pt   Paragraph type. Paragraphs started by the command .P (no argument) will be the type specified by the Pt number register. The default is 0.
    0   The first line of all default paragraphs will be left justified.
    1   The first line of all default paragraphs will be indented by Pi.
    2   The first line of all default paragraphs will be indented by Pi unless they immediately follow a heading, list, or display.

ꜱPLAY FORMAT NUMBER REGISTERS

De Floating display eject flag.

0 Text may appear on page following a floating display.

1 Floating displays will always be followed by a page eject.

Ds The amount of extra space that is placed above and below a static display. Units are lines for `nroff` and half vertical spaces for `troff`. Default value is 1.

Eq Equation label placement. Default is 0.

0 Label will be placed flush right.

1 Label will be placed flush left.

Si Standard display indent. Units are ens, and the defaults are 5 (`nroff`) or 3 (`troff`).

LIST FORMAT NUMBER REGISTERS

Li List indent. Automatic lists (`.AL`) and reference lists (`.RL`) will be indented by the amount specified in the `Li` number register. The indent is specified in ens, and the default amounts are 6 (`nroff`) or 5 (`troff`).

Ls List spacing. Lists that are nested `Ls` deep or less will have an extra line (`nroff`) or half vertical space (`troff`) placed before the list, and before each item in the list. If `Ls` is zero, lists won't be preceded by extra vertical space; if `Ls` is one, then only outer lists will be preceded by extra vertical space. The default is 6.

HEADING FORMAT STRING REGISTERS

HF The string stored in this register contains up to seven font codes, one for each heading level. The default string is 3 3 2 2 2 2 2, which means that level one and two heads will be bold, and other heads will be underlined (`nroff`) or italic (`troff`).

HP The string stored in this register contains up to seven point size codes, one for each heading level. The default is for bold standalone heads to be printed one point smaller than the text and for other heads to be the same size as the text.

—MS

NAME

-ms — the manuscript macros (Berkeley)

SYNOPSIS

```
nroff -ms [option] file . . .
troff -ms [option] file . . .
```

DESCRIPTION

The -ms macros are the original text formatting macros in the UNIX system. They are used with nroff or troff to conveniently format documents. -ms is available on all Version 7 systems and all Berkeley systems, but is not a standard part of System V. However, many System V users have access to -ms despite the fact that -mm is the supported System V macro package.

-ms makes it easier to prepare a document for the nroff or troff formatter. -ms has commands that produce section headings, paragraphs, page headings, and displays. The appearance of these features is easily controlled using number registers. -ms supports the most common preprocessors including eqn, tbl, and pic. Users of the refer reference preprocessor invariably use -ms or -me because -mm doesn't support refer.

-ms documents contain plain text interspersed with -ms commands. Most -ms commands are alone on a line that starts with a period, and the names are all one or two upper-case letters. For example, the

```
.PP
```

command tells -ms that the following text is a paragraph. -ms will automatically leave extra space, start a new page if you are too near the bottom margin, and then indent the first line of the paragraph. Similarly most other -ms commands direct it to perform many small actions that, taken together, create the desired effect.

Besides the dot commands, -ms also has special escape sequences that allow you to access accent marks. These commands may be mixed with ordinary text on a line, and they all start with a \ (backslash).

If you prepare a document that contains -ms commands, you must use the -ms option on the nroff or troff command line, as shown in the SYNOPSIS above. In a -ms document you may also use some of the native nroff/troff commands. You must avoid those commands that might interfere with aspects of the formatting that are managed by -ms, but the following commands are usually safe:

.bp	Start a new page.
.br	Cause a break. (Flush preceding text and start a new line.)
.sp *n*	Skip *n* lines.
.na	Don't adjust the right margin. (Ragged right)
.ad	Adjust the right margin. (Flush right)
.nr *xx n*	Set number register named *xx* to the value *n*.
.ds *xx s*	Set string register named *xx* to the value *s*.

Notice that -ms commands have upper-case names, but native `nroff/troff` commands have lower-case names.

The original Version 7 -ms was slightly enhanced at Berkeley. The accent marks were improved, footnote support was improved, page heading flexibility was increased, and table of contents support was added. In the following tables the Berkeley features are marked with a †. These features are not available in all versions of -ms.

HEADINGS AND PARAGRAPHS

.NH *n* *text* .LP	Numbered heading. *n* is the heading level, *text* is the heading text, followed by any paragraph command.
.SH *text* .LP	Section heading. *text* is the heading text, followed by any paragraph command.
.PP	Start a normal paragraph. First line is indented.
.LP	Start a normal paragraph. All lines are flush left.
.IP *label*	Start an indented paragraph. All lines are indented on the left. The optional *label* is printed to the left of the first line.
.XP	†Start an exdented paragraph. All lines but the first will be indented on the left.

TYPE STYLES

.R

.I *wd1 wd2*

.B *wd1 wd2*

Switch font to Roman, Italic, or Bold. For I or B, if *wd1* is supplied, it alone will be in italic or bold. If *wd2* is supplied, it will follow *wd1*, without a separating space, and be in the surrounding font.

.SM

.NL

.LG

Switch to a smaller, normal size, or larger typeface. .SM or .LG can be repeated to increase the size change.

.UL *word*

Underline a single *word*.

DISPLAYS AND FOOTNOTES

.DS *x* *text* .DE	Display *text* in no-fill mode. *text* will be moved to the following page, leaving a blank region, if it doesn't fit on the current page. Optional argument *x* may be L for a flush left display, I for a slightly indented display, C for a line-by-line centered display, or B for a block-centered display. The default is an indented display.
.LD .ID .CD	Display multipage *text*. .LD replaces .DS L .ID replaces .DS I .CD replaces .DS C
.KS *text* .KE	*text* will be moved to the following page if it doesn't fit on the current page, possibly leaving a blank space at the bottom of the current page.
.KF *text* .KE	*text* will float to the start of the following page if it doesn't fit on the current. Following text may be moved forward to fill the bottom of the page.
.EQ *x n* *text* .EN	*text* will be processed by the eqn preprocessor. Optional argument *x* may be I for an indented equation, L for a flush left equation, or C for a centered equation. Centered is the default. An argument *n* may follow the equation type. It will be placed flush left to identify the equation.
.TS *text* .TE	*text* will be processed by the tbl preprocessor.
.RS *text* .RE	*text* will be shifted to the right.
.FS *text* .FE	*text* is a footnote that will be placed at the bottom of the page. Berkeley -ms allows ** to automatically number footnotes.

TEXT
PROCESSING

OVERALL DOCUMENT FORMAT

.1C .2C	Switch to one-column (the default) or two-column format.
.DA *date*	The date will be printed at the bottom of the page. This is the default with nroff, but not with troff. The optional *date* argument overrides the current date.
.ND	The date will not be printed at the bottom of the page.
.OH 'L'C'R' .EH 'L'C'R' .OF 'L'C'R' .EF 'L'C'R'	†These macros produce *H*eaders and *F*ooters on *O*dd or *E*ven pages. Each three-part header consists of text *L* for the left, *C* for the center, and *R* for the right. In a header or footer, % will print the page number.
.AM	†This macro command must be placed at the beginning of any document that uses the new accent marks.

FIRST PAGE FORMATS

.RP	Use AT&T Released Paper style.
.TM	Use Berkeley Thesis style.
.TL *text*	Use *text* as the title.
.AU *loc ext* *text*	*text* specifies an author's name, and optional arguments *loc* and *ext* specify the author's address and phone number.
.AI *text*	*text* specifies the author's institution.
.AB *text* .AE	Use *text* as the abstract.
.SG	Insert the author's name (signature) in the text.

TABLE OF CONTENTS

.XS *n*   †*text* will be stored internally, to be used later as an
text   entry in the table of contents, with *n* the page number.
.XE   *n* defaults to the current page.

.XA *n*   †Within an .XS .XE pair of macros, .XA will store *text*
text   to be used later in the table of contents.

.PX   †Print the stored table of contents.

NUMBER REGISTERS

NAME	USE	TAKES EFFECT	DEFAULT VALUE (nroff)	DEFAULT VALUE (troff)
HM	Header Margin	Next Page	1i	1i
FM	Footer Margin	Next Page	1i	1i
PO	Page Offset	Next Page	0	26/27i
CW	Column Width (Two column style)	Next .2C	7/15 LL	7/15LL
GW	Gutter Width (Space between columns)	Next .2C	1/15 LL	1/15LL
PD	Paragraph Drop	Next Para.	1v	0.3v
DD	†Display Drop	Next Display	1v	0.5v
PI	Paragraph Indent	Next Para.	5n	5n
QI	Quote Para. Indent	Next Para.	5n	5n
PS	Point Size	Next Para.	10p	10p
VS	Vertical Spacing	Next Para.	12p	12p
LL	Line Length	Next Para.	6i	6i
LT	Title Length	Next Para.	6i	6i
FI	†Footnote Indent	Next .FS	2n	2n
FL	Footnote Length	Next .FS	11/12 LL	11/12 LL
FF	†Footnote Format	Next .FS	0	0

FORMATTER DEPENDENT STRINGS†

NAME	INPUT	nroff OUTPUT	troff OUTPUT
dash	*-	--	—
left quote	*Q	"	"
right quote	*U	"	"

HEADER STRINGS

NAME	USE	NAME	USE	NAME	USE
LH	Left Header	CH	Center Header	RH	Right Header
LF	Left Footer	CF	Center Footer	RF	Right Footer

TEXT PROCESSING

ORIGINAL ACCENT MARKS

The following accent marks are available in all versions of -ms. (Note that these original accents will be unavailable after using the .AM command.)

NAME	INPUT	OUTPUT	NAME	INPUT	OUTPUT
acute	*´e	é	grave	*`e	è
circumflex	*^o	ô	tilde	*~n	ñ
haček	*Cc	č	cedilla	*,c	ç
umlaut	*:u	ü			

NEW ACCENT MARKS†

These accent marks are available only on Berkeley versions of -ms, and they will work only if the macro command .AM is placed at the beginning of the document.

NAME	INPUT	OUTPUT	NAME	INPUT	OUTPUT
acute	e*'	é	grave	e*`	è
circumflex	o*^	ô	cedilla	c*,	ç
tilde	n*~	ñ	umlaut	u*:	ü
haček	c*v	č	angstrom	a*o	å
macron	a*_	ā	underdot	s*.	ṣ
o-slash	o*/	ø			

NEW SPECIAL SYMBOLS†

These special symbols are available only on Berkeley versions of -ms, and they will work only if the macro command .AM is placed at the beginning of the document.

NAME	INPUT	OUTPUT	NAME	INPUT	OUTPUT
question	*?	¿	exclamation	*!	¡
digraph s	*8	β	yogh	kni*3t	kni₃t
Thorn	*(Th	Þ	thorn	*(th	þ
Eth	*D-	Ð	eth	*d-	ð
AE ligature	*(Ae	Æ	ae ligature	*(ae	æ
OE ligature	*(Oe	Œ	oe ligature	*(oe	œ
hooked o	*q	ǫ			

NROFF

NAME

nroff — text formatter for ordinary printers

SYNOPSIS

nroff [options] [files]

DESCRIPTION

nroff is a text formatter that produces output on ordinary printers. It is typically used with printers that have fixed width characters in a single size. The troff formatter should be used with laser printers and typesetters that have proportional width fonts in various sizes.

nroff interprets a text file containing print directives and plain text. The text is printed according to the directives stored in the file. nroff must know which printer is being used because different printers have different command strings for print features such as half-line motions or overstriking.

The format codes in the text may be native nroff/troff codes, or they may also contain macro codes, which are defined by a macro package. The most common macro packages are -ms, the UNIX system's original macros; -mm, the current standard on System V UNIX systems; -me, an improved macro package developed at Berkeley; and -man, a macro package for formatting entries in the UNIX manual. If macro package commands are used in the document, the macro package must be mentioned on the nroff command line (or inside the document in a .so command) or the document will not format correctly.

The nroff command line options must precede the files, the standard input is assumed if no filenames are present, and the filename - means the standard input.

-o*list*
>   Output is produced for the pages mentioned in the *list*. The *list* is a comma-separated list of pages, or page ranges. (A page range is n-m, which means from page *n* through page *m*.) For example, the option -o1,3,5,11-19 means pages one, three, five, and eleven through nineteen.

-n*N* The first page of the document is numbered *N*.

-s*N* The output process is stopped every *N* pages so that you can change the paper.

-m*name*
> Use the standard macro package *name*. The most common uses of this option are **-ms** to access the manuscript macros, **-mm** to access the memorandum macros, **-me** to access Berkeley's -me macros, and **-man** to access the manual page macros.

-c*name*
> Use the compacted version of the standard macro package *name*. Compacted macros require less processing than the uncompacted macros invoked with the **-m** option. Use **-cm** (instead of **-mm**) to access the compacted memorandum macros. (System V UNIX only.)

-ra*N*
> The nroff/troff internal register named *a* is set to the value *N*. *a* is any single-character register name, and *N* is any value.

-i   Read the standard input after the files are processed.

-q   Echoing is suppressed during .rd insertions. This is necessary to prevent scrambled output when input and output are attached to the terminal. This option is used when you are generating form letters, and your "terminal" is actually a printer.

-T*name*
> nroff prepares output for the named terminal. On most systems, nroff is set up so its default terminal matches the locally available terminal. You can see what terminals are supported on your system by listing the contents of the '/usr/lib/term' directory. For printers that work at either ten or twelve pitch, you can usually select the pitch by adding the suffix *-10* or *-12* to the printer name.

-e   nroff prepares output that uses the full resolution of the output device. This may result in slower printing.

-h   nroff uses tab characters which may reduce the size of the output.

EXAMPLES

Format the 'unifld.t' document using the -mm macros for the twelve pitch mode of the DASI 450 printer. Send the output to the q450 print spooler. (q450 is a locally prepared script that calls the standard print spooler with the appropriate options to access the 450 printer.)

```
$ nroff -mm -T450-12 unifld.t | q450
$ _
```

Same as above, but print only pages two, six, and then eight through the end.

```
$ nroff -mm -T450-12 -o2,6,8- unifld.t | q450
$ _
```

Print 'sandy.let' on the terminal using the -ms macros. This will work only if you are logged onto the UNIX system using a TeleType model 37 terminal.

```
$ nroff -ms -T37 sandy.let
```
— The Document is printed on the terminal —
```
$ _
```

TBL

NAME

tbl — translate table descriptions into troff commands

SYNOPSIS

tbl [files]

DESCRIPTION

tbl is a troff preprocessor. It translates a description of a table into the troff or nroff commands that will produce the table. Although tables can be typeset manually, by setting tabs and using the troff spacing and line drawing primitives, better results are obtained much more easily with tbl. It automatically calculates the width of each column, it can span titles across several columns, and so on.

If *files* are mentioned on the command line, tbl will read its input from them. Otherwise, tbl will read from the standard input. When eqn and tbl are both needed to format a document, tbl should come first in the pipeline.

INPUT FORMAT

A tbl input file consists of ordinary text, which is passed through unchanged, and table specifications, which are enclosed in .TS and .TE delimiters. A table specification consists of an optional global options part, followed by the column format specification, followed by the data for the columns.

```
.TS
options ;
column formats .
data
.TE
```

The *options* part of the specification ends with a semicolon, and the *column formats* part ends with a period. Within the data section, the table elements for each row of the table appear on a line, with the parts for each column separated by a tab. In this manual page the tab character is represented visually as ⊤ . Although the column formats section specifies the overall format of the columns, there are also several format specifiers that may appear in the data section of the table.

GLOBAL OPTIONS

center
>   This option makes the table centered between left and right margins. Otherwise it will align near the left margin. The center option has no effect on the vertical position of the table.

expand
>   An expanded table has increased separation between the columns so that the table width matches the width of text on the page. The default column separation is three ens.

box
doublebox
>   The table is enclosed in a single or double box.

allbox
>   Every item in the table is enclosed in a box. There will be a horizontal line between all of the rows, and a vertical line between all of the columns.

tab(x)
>   The tab option specifies an alternate column separator character. This option is especially useful when you are constructing tables with many narrow columns because using tabs makes the lines in your input file wider than most terminals can display. Common alternate column separators are #, @, %, and _. The column separator should not appear in the table as data.

linesize(n)
>   The linesize option specifies an alternate point size for drawing the lines in a table.

delim(xy)
>   The delim option lets you tell tbl the eqn equation delimiters. x is the starting delimiter, and y is the end of equation delimiter. This is only necessary in a numeric column that contains equations. When tbl knows the eqn delimiters, it doesn't disturb the equation during its attempt to align a numeric column. Equations are usually placed in left aligned, centered, or right aligned columns.

COLUMN FORMATS

In most tables, the heading format varies from line to line, and then the format stabilizes in the data part of the table. This typical organization is mirrored in the column formats part of a table specification. The first line of the column format section specifies the format of the first line of the table, the next column format line is used for the next line of the table, and so on. When you run out of column format lines, the last is reused for the remainder of the table. For example, if there are three column format lines and twenty lines of data, the first two column format lines manage the first two lines of data (usually the table's title), and the third format specifier line is for lines three through twenty of the data.

However, for tables with a less regular appearance it is possible to change the format in the midst of the data section. A line that starts .T& introduces a new column formats section, which may be several lines long, and which is terminated, as usual, by a period. Such a table has the following form:

```
.TS
options ;
column format .
data
.T&
column format .
data
.TE
```

There may be as many additional column format sections as necessary.

The main column format specifiers are single characters, in upper or lower case, which specify the overall format (e.g., centered) of a column. After each main specifier there can be several modifiers, which specify attributes of a column (e.g., font or point size). The modifiers are discussed in the next section of this manual entry.

L   The data is left aligned.

C   The data is centered.

R   The data is right aligned.

S   The data from a previous column spans across this column.

N   The data is aligned at the rightmost period, or at the rightmost digit (if there is no period), or centered (if there is no period or digits). Useful for columns of numbers.

A   The data for this column is treated as if it were a block. The block is left aligned, but centered within the column. The data is aligned on its left edge, but the left edge may not be at the left margin of the column.

^   The data in this column from the previous row is vertically spanned across this row.

_   The data for this column will be a single horizontal line.

=   The data for this column will be a double horizontal line.

COLUMN FORMAT MODIFIERS

n The space between this column and the next is made to be *n* ens. The default is three ens.

| A vertical line is drawn between this column and the next.

| | A double vertical line is drawn between this column and the next.

T Put vertically spanned item at top, instead of centered between its uppermost and lowermost row.

F*x* Print this column using the named font. *x* may either be a font name or number.

I Print this column in italic.

B Print this column in bold.

P*n* Print this column in point size *n*.

V*n* Select vertical space *n* in text block.

W(*n*) Make this column *n* wide. *n* may use troff unit suffixes.

E Make all columns marked with E the same width.

FORMAT CONTROLS IN THE DATA

Alone on a line:

_ Draw horizontal line across the entire table.

= Draw double horizontal line across the entire table.

Column entries:

_ Draw a single horizontal line across the column. The line will join adjacent vertical or horizontal lines.

= Draw a double horizontal line across the column. The lines will join adjacent vertical or horizontal lines.

_ Draw a horizontal line across the column that will not touch adjacent horizontal or vertical lines.

\R*x* Draw a string of repeated *x*'s filling the column. *x* may be any character.

\ˆ This will produce a vertically spanned entry constructed from the above data.

Text Blocks:

T{   A T{ column entry indicates that the following lines contain a text block.

text Many nroff/troff commands, such as font change commands, may be

T}   safely used within a text block. The block is terminated by T} at the beginning of a line, possibly followed by a column separator and the data for the remaining columns.

EXAMPLES

```
.TS
box;
CBP+1 S S S
L CP-1 CP-1
L CP-1 CP-1
LBP-1
A N N N.
AUTO SALES DATA

_
T Dec. 20-31 T Dec. 20-31
T 1985 T 1984 T %Chg.
CHRYSLER CORP.
Chry-Plym Div. T 19,453 T 14,892 T 30.6
Dodge Div. T 11,695 T 9,638 T 21.3
\0\0Total Cars T 31,148 T 24,530 T 27
.TE
```

AUTO SALES DATA			
	Dec. 20-31	Dec. 20-31	
	1985	1984	%Chg.
CHRYSLER CORP.			
Chry-Plym Div.	19,453	14,892	30.6
Dodge Div.	11,695	9,638	21.3
Total Cars	31,148	24,530	27

```
.TS
center;
CW(4) S6 1 CW(4) S
CW(4) S6 1 CW(4) S
CfUU 1 1 CfUU 1.
Who T   T Operators
_  T   T _
u T user (owner) T  T \&- T remove permission
g T group T  T + T add permission
o T other T  T \&= T assign permission
a T all (ugo)
.TE
```

Who		Operators	
u	user (owner)	−	remove permission
g	group	+	add permission
o	other	=	assign permission
a	all (ugo)		

TROFF

NAME

troff — text formatter for laser printers or typesetters

SYNOPSIS

troff [options] [files]

DESCRIPTION

troff is a text formatter that prepares documents for printing on a typesetter or other printer with variable size characters and multiple fonts. nroff should be used to print documents on ordinary printers. troff interprets a text file that contains ordinary text interspersed with print directives. troff is often accessed through a locally prepared shell script that calls troff with the locally used options, routes the troff output through any intermediate processing stages, and then sends the output to the print spooler. Your locally prepared troff command script may have additional options.

The format codes in the text may be native nroff/troff codes, or they may also contain macro codes, which are defined by a macro package. The most common macro packages are -ms, the UNIX system's original macros; -mm, the current standard on System V UNIX systems; -me, an improved macro package developed at Berkeley; and -man, a macro package for formatting entries in the UNIX manual. If macro package commands are used in the document, the macro package must be mentioned on the troff command line (or inside the document in a .so command) or the document will not format correctly. These command line options must precede the files. The standard input is assumed if no filenames are present, and the filename - means the standard input.

-o*list*
  Output is produced for the pages mentioned in the *list*. The *list* is a comma-separated list of pages, or page ranges. (A page range is n-m, which means from page *n* through page *m*.) For example, the option -o1,3,5,11-19 means pages one, three, five, and eleven through nineteen.

-n*N* The first page of the document is numbered *N*.

-s*N* The output process is stopped every *N* pages so that you can change the paper. (Not functional on all versions of troff.)

-m*name*

Use the standard macro package *name*. The most common uses of this option are -ms to access the manuscript macros, -mm to access the memorandum macros, -me to access the -me macros, and -man to access the manual macros.

-c*name*

Use the compacted version of the standard macro package *name*. Compacted macros require less processing than the uncompacted macros invoked with the -m option. Use -cm to access the -mm macros. (System V UNIX only.)

-r*aN*

The troff internal register named *a* is set to the value *N*. *a* is any single-character register name, and *N* is any value.

-i   Read the standard input after the files are processed.

-q   Echoing is suppressed during .rd insertions. This is necessary to prevent scrambled output when input and output are attached to the terminal.

-t   Send output to the standard output, rather than directly to the typesetter. This option is often used inside a command script to send troff output to a postprocessor for a particular printer.

-a   Send an ASCII version of the output to the standard output. This option is useful for various purposes, including checking hyphenation without producing printed copy.

-p*N* Produce output in point size *N*. All spacing and character placement will be the same as the final copy. This option is useful for producing output quickly.

APPENDIX I

UNIX FOR MS-DOS USERS

MS-DOS and the UNIX system are much more similar than most pundits realize. Since Version 2.0, MS-DOS has been strongly influenced by the UNIX system, and many of its features have been taken directly from the UNIX system. Both systems feature a hierarchical file system, a line-oriented interface that is both a user interface and a programming language, and a similar set of base utilities for managing files. The added complexity of the UNIX system comes from its additional functionality—its support for multiple users and multiple tasks, its support for multiple terminal types and multiple terminal options settings, and its bundled applications programs such as electronic mail, text editing, and text formatting.

On MS-DOS the machine is ready to execute your commands as soon as it has been turned on and booted. However, on the UNIX system there is another stage—logging in. The login process identifies you to the system so that it knows which files you may access, where you should be placed in the filesystem, and perhaps who should be charged for your system usage. The login process in described in the Introduction.

Executing Programs

MS-DOS and the UNIX system obey similar conventions for running programs. In both systems there is no distinction (to a user) between the syntax for running a binary executable program and a command script. In the UNIX system command scripts may have any name, while in MS-DOS the extension of a command script is always .BAT. In both systems it is possible to pass command line information to a program. Most command line specifications are either *options*, which tell a program to behave in some alternate manner, or *filenames*, which specify the files that a program should use.

MS-DOS filenames are case insensitive. Filenames are displayed in upper case in directory listings, but any case may be entered on the command line. Although it is technically possible for MS-DOS programs to differentiate upper- vs. lower-case options, most do not do so. The UNIX tradition is for program names, filenames, and options to be lower case, but they are always case sensitive. In the following tables all MS-DOS names are in upper case, which is common, and UNIX names are lower case, which is nearly universal.

	MS-DOS	**UNIX**
Option Indicator	/	-
Option Grouping	Immediately following command name	Separated by spaces
Example	DIR/W	ls -l

In both MS-DOS and the UNIX system, an application program can either use or ignore command line information. As a result of the MS-DOS emphasis on supportive interactive user interfaces, many MS-DOS applications programs make little use of command line options. However, in the UNIX world most programs can be executed from within a script, so it is important for most features to be accessible on the command line.

Pathnames

Many UNIX features will be familiar to experienced MS-DOS users. For example, both DOS and the UNIX system have pathnames, the chief difference being that DOS uses the \ (backslash) to separate the elements of a pathname, and UNIX uses a / (slash). Both systems use the convention that the directory name . (dot) always refers to the current directory, and the name .. (dot dot) refers to the parent directory.

Because of its heritage in a floppy disk environment, MS-DOS pathnames often contain a prefix that names the particular disk where the file is located. This vestige is not present in the UNIX system, which references all file names to a common location called the *root directory*. In the UNIX system, only the system manager needs to know which physical disk actually contains a given file.

MS-DOS filenames can only contain eleven characters, an eight-character base name and a three-character extension. The UNIX system allows slightly longer filenames—fourteen characters on System V or 255 characters on Berkeley. The UNIX system doesn't force you to separate a filename into base and extension, although you may name your files that way if you wish.

	MS-DOS	**UNIX**
Component Separator	\	/
Example	C:\files\letters	/usr/janet/letters
Current Directory	.	.
Parent Directory	..	..
Change Directory	cd *dirname*	cd *dirname*
Print Directory Name	cd	pwd

These and other basic commands are discussed in the *General Utility Commands* section of this manual.

File Management

In both the UNIX system and MS-DOS individual users are reponsible for managing their own files. Directories should be created so that files are organized. Out-of-date files should be removed. Occasionally files need to be renamed, moved from one place to another, or copied, and both systems allow you do to those tasks.

	MS-DOS	**UNIX**
Create a Directory	MKDIR *dirname*	mkdir *dirname*
Remove a Directory	RMDIR *dirname*	rmdir *dirname*
Remove a file	DEL *filename*	rm *filename*
Copy a file	COPY *fromname toname*	cp *fromname toname*
Rename a file	REN *fromname toname*	mv *fromname toname*
List filenames	DIR/W	ls
List filenames sizes, dates, etc.	DIR	ls -l

The UNIX file management tools are discussed in the *File Management Commands* section of this manual.

Text Files

Both the UNIX system and MS-DOS have text files that can be displayed on the terminal or printed on an ordinary printer. In both systems a text file is structured into lines. In the UNIX system the <NL> character marks the ends of lines, and in MS-DOS a <CR> followed by a <NL> conventionally marks the ends of lines.

	MS-DOS	**UNIX**
Print a file	PRINT *filename*	lp *filename* lpr *filename*
Display a file on the terminal	TYPE *filename*	cat *filename*
Paginate a file on the terminal	MORE < *filename*	more *filename* pg *filename*
Compare two files	COMP *file1 file2*	diff *file1 file2*

These and other programs to manage text files are discussed in the *Text File Commands* section of this manual.

APPENDIX II

UNIX FOR RT-11 USERS

RT-11 is a single-user operating system for the Digital Equipment Corporation PDP-11 and LSI-11 computers. It was originally intended for real time tasks such as scientific laboratory data collection and industrial process control. However, RT-11 is also widely used for office automation tasks, mostly by those who also use it for real time applications.

RT-11 users shouldn't be intimidated by the size and scope of the UNIX system. Although the UNIX system does have a wealth of features, the UNIX system and RT-11 share a basically similar interactive approach to computing. In the beginning, you should concentrate on a few commands that accomplish the most important tasks. As your UNIX reflexes develop, you'll soon discover some regularity to the commands.

The added complexity of the UNIX system comes from its additional functionality—its support for multiple users and multiple tasks, its support for multiple terminal types and multiple terminal options settings, and its bundled applications programs such as electronic mail, text editing, and text formatting.

Although the extra functionality of the UNIX system usually makes it more compli-cated, there are some areas where the UNIX system is actually simpler than RT-11. For example, in RT-11 there are three separate syntaxes for executing commands, one for batch files, one for special commands (such as DIR) that are known to the operating system, and one for all other commands. In the UNIX system there is just one syntax for executing a program (which is described below). Another example is the RT-11 filesystem, which stores files contiguously. The simple RT-11 structure is great for speed and simplicity, but it makes it hard when a file needs to grow, and even harder when an application needs to have several growing files open at once. In the UNIX system files are stored in fragments (the UNIX system remembers where each piece is), and they can grow or shrink without wasting space. Although recent versions of RT-11 feature "logical devices" for organizing disks, the UNIX system has always had similar functionality, and the UNIX implementation is much smoother.

On RT-11 the machine is ready to execute your commands as soon as it has been turned on and booted. However, on the UNIX system there is another stage—logging in. The login process identifies you to the system so that it knows which files you may access, where you should be placed in the filesystem, and perhaps who should be charged for your system usage. The login process is described in the Introduction.

Executing Programs

Although the UNIX system has indirect files (which UNIX users call shell scripts), they are executed using the same syntax as executable files. You don't need a special indicator like the RT-11 @ to tell the UNIX system that the program is a script rather than a true executable. UNIX executable programs or command scripts may have any name, while in RT-11 the extension of an indirect file is usually .COM, and the extension of an executable is .SAV.

The UNIX syntax for executing programs is most like the RT-11 syntax for executing monitor commands such as DIR. A UNIX command consists of the command name, possibly followed by options, possibly followed by filenames. Most UNIX options are single-character mnemonics, unlike the complete words that are used in RT-11. You can specify filenames explicitly, or you can specify groups of files using wild cards.

RT-11 filenames are case insensitive. Filenames are displayed in upper case in directory listings, but either case may be entered on the command line. The UNIX tradition is for program names, filenames, and options to be lower case, but they are always case sensitive.

RT-11 filenames can contain only nine characters, a six-character base name and a three-character extension. The UNIX system allows slightly longer filenames—fourteen characters on System V or 255 characters on Berkeley. The UNIX system doesn't force you to separate a filename into base and extension, although you may name your files that way if you wish.

In the following tables, all RT-11 names are in upper case, which is common, and UNIX names are lower case, which is nearly universal.

	RT-11	**UNIX**
Option Indicator	/	-
Option Grouping	Immediately following command name	Separated by spaces
Example	DIR/BRIEF	ls -l

The RT-11 monitor knows which options and filenames a program expects. This feature enables RT-11 to prompt for missing information as needed. In the UNIX system the command interpreter, which is called the *shell*, has no idea which files or options are required by a program. Whatever information you enter on the command line is passed to the application program, which may either use or ignore that information.

Pathnames

You may find it easier to understand UNIX pathnames if you are familiar with the logical device feature of RT-11. Introduced in Version 5 of RT-11, a logical device is a way of subdividing a disk. For example, one logical device might reserve part of a disk for user's files, and then, within that user's region, additional logical devices might reserve space for each person who uses the machine.

The UNIX system has a similar, but more flexible feature. Each UNIX system contains a special directory, called the root directory, that contains a list of files and directories. Each directory can have subdirectories. One key advantage of UNIX directories over RT-11 logical devices is that you don't have to reserve space when you create a directory. Each disk (or disk partition) has a single pool of free blocks that is used by files in all of the directories. Another advantage is that the UNIX system has a flexible naming convention that makes it easy to refer to files. A pathname is a path from one directory to another that leads to the desired file. An *absolute* pathname starts in the root directory, while a *relative* pathname starts in the current directory. Another convention in the UNIX system is that the directory name . (dot) always refers to the current directory, and the name .. (dot dot) refers to the parent directory.

When a pathname starts with / (slash) it is an absolute pathname. Thus, the pathname '/usr/janet/letters' leads from the root directory to the 'usr' subdirectory, to the 'janet' subdirectory, and then finally to the 'letters' file. Pathnames that don't start with a / are relative pathnames; they start in the current directory. Thus, the pathname 'boots/docs/chqtr.s' leads from the current directory to the 'boots' subdirectory, to the 'docs' subdirectory, and then finally to the 'chqtr.s' file. You can use the name .. to ascend the filesystem paths. For example, the pathname '../resrch/lab2' leads from the current directory, to its parent directory, and from there to the 'resrch' subdirectory, and finally to the 'lab2' file.

Two of the most important commands that work with pathnames are cd, which moves to the given directory, and pwd, which prints the pathname of the current directory. These and other basic commands are discussed in the *General Utility Commands* section of this manual.

File Management

In the UNIX system individual users are responsible for managing their own files. Directories should be created so that files are organized. Out-of-date files should be removed. Occasionally files need to be renamed, moved from one place to another, or copied and both RT-11 and the UNIX system have commands for these tasks.

	RT-11	**UNIX**
Create a Directory		mkdir *dirname*
Remove a Directory		rmdir *dirname*
Remove a file	DELETE/NOQUERY *filename*	rm *filename*
Copy a file	COPY *fromname toname*	cp *fromname toname*
Rename a file	RENAME *fromname toname*	mv *fromname toname*
List filenames	DIR/BRIEF	ls
List filenames sizes dates, etc.	DIR	ls -l

The UNIX file management tools are discussed in the *File Management Commands* section of this manual.

Text Files

Both the UNIX system and RT-11 have text files that can be displayed on the terminal or printed on an ordinary printer. In both systems a text file is structured into lines, but in the UNIX system the <NL> character marks the ends of lines, whereas in RT-11 a <CR> followed by a <NL> conventionally marks the ends of lines.

	RT-11	**UNIX**
Print a file	PRINT *filename*	lp *filename*
Display a file on the terminal	TYPE *filename*	cat *filename*
Paginate a file on the terminal		more *filename* pg *filename*
Compare two files	DIFFERENCES *file1,file2*	diff *file1 file2*

These and other programs to manage text files are discussed in the *Text File Commands* section of this manual.

Keyboard Conventions

The *Keyboard Conventions* in the Introduction discussed some of the common UNIX system keyboard codes and their uses. It also mentioned that the UNIX system is very flexible in its keyboard assignments. Many of the special characters, such as the erase character that will erase your previously entered input, can be assigned to any keyboard character. It is even possible to adopt RT-11's keyboard conventions (erase, kill, and interrupt set to <DEL>, ^U and ^C; RT-11 style flow control using ^S and ^Q).

On UNIX System V the keyboard conventions can be enabled using the following commands:

```
$ stty erase '^?'
$ stty kill '^U'
$ stty intr '^C'
$ stty ixon
$ stty -ixany
$ _
```

Note that the UNIX `stty` command accepts two-character codes of *caret, letter* to specify a control character. Thus, in the preceding dialogue the notation ^U means a caret followed by a capital *U*. The quotes are necessary because older versions of the shell use the caret for a special purpose. On newer systems they may not be necessary. (The ^? is common UNIX notation for the <DEL> character.)

On Berkeley systems you can enable RT-11 keyboard conventions with the following command:

```
$ stty dec
$ _
```

The *dec* mode is built into the Berkeley handler; it establishes the same conventions as the five System V `stty` commands shown above.

Depending upon your system, one of these two command sequences should be placed in your '.profile' file in your home directory if you want the UNIX terminal handler to work like the RT-11 keyboard handler.

APPENDIX III

UNIX FOR VAX/VMS USERS

VMS is a multiuser operating system for the Digital Equipment Corporation VAX computers. It features the DCL command language, which has its roots in earlier Digital Equipment Corp. operating systems. VMS is widely used in commerce, industry, and academia.

Executing Programs

The UNIX syntax for executing programs resembles the VMS command syntax. You type the command name, followed by the options, followed by the files. Most UNIX options are single-character mnemonics, unlike the complete words that are used in VMS. You can specify filenames explicitly, or you can specify groups of files using wild cards.

VMS filenames are case insensitive. Filenames are displayed in upper case in directory listings, but either case may be entered on the command line. The UNIX tradition is for program names, filenames, and options to be lower case, but they are always case sensitive.

VMS filenames can contain twelve characters, a nine-character base name and a three-character extension. The UNIX system allows slightly longer filenames—fourteen characters on System V, or 255 characters on Berkeley. The UNIX system doesn't force you to separate a filename into base and extension, although you may name your files that way if you wish.

In the following tables, all VMS names are in upper case, which is common, and UNIX names are lower case, which is nearly universal.

	VMS	UNIX
Option Indicator	/	-
Option Grouping	Immediately following command name	Separated by spaces
Example:	DIR/FULL	ls -l

The UNIX command interpreter, which is called the *shell*, has no idea what files or options are required by a program. Whatever information you enter on the command line is passed to the application program, which may either use or ignore that information.

Pathnames

The UNIX system has a simpler syntax for pathnames than VMS. Each UNIX system contains a special directory, called the root directory, that contains a list of files and directories. Like VMS, each UNIX directory can have subdirectories. The UNIX system has two types of pathnames, *absolute* pathnames and *relative* pathnames. An absolute pathname starts in the root directory, while a relative pathname starts in the current directory. Another convention in the UNIX system is that the directory name . (dot) always refers to the current directory, and the name .. (dot dot) refers to the parent directory.

In the UNIX system the / (slash) character separates the elements of a pathname, unlike the . (dot) that VMS uses. It is not necessary to bracket the directories in a UNIX pathname; in the UNIX system, all but the rightmost component of a pathname must be a directory, and the rightmost component may be any file type including a directory file. In the UNIX system, it is also unnecessary to use a device prefix. Only the system manager (or systems programmer) needs to keep track of which device stores which files.

The UNIX system does not automatically maintain multiple versions of a file. Although UNIX programs are free to make a copy of a file each time it is updated, few do so. For example, the UNIX editor doesn't automatically maintain a backup copy of the files that you edit. This simplifies some aspects of managing your files, but you must be very careful.

When a UNIX pathname starts with / it is an absolute pathname. Thus, the pathname '/usr/janet/letters' leads from the root directory to the 'usr' subdirectory, to the 'janet' subdirectory, and then finally to the 'letters' file. Pathnames that don't start with a / are relative pathnames; they start in the current directory. Thus, the pathname 'boots/docs/chqtr.s' leads from the current directory to the 'boots' subdirectory, to the 'docs' subdirectory, and then finally to the 'chqtr.s' file. You can use the name .. to ascend the filesystem paths. For example, the pathname

'../resrch/lab2' leads from the current directory, to its parent directory, and from there to the 'resrch' subdirectory, and finally to the 'lab2' file.

	VMS	**UNIX**
Change Directory	SET DEFAULT [*dirname*]	cd *dirname*
Print Directory Name	SHOW DEFAULT	pwd

These and other basic commands are discussed in the *General Utility Commands* section of this manual.

File Management

In the UNIX system individual users are responsible for managing their own files. Directories should be created so that files are organized. Out-of-date files should be removed. Occasionally files need to be renamed, moved from one place to another, or copied, and both systems have commands for these tasks.

	VMS	**UNIX**
Create a Directory	CREATE/DIRECTORY *dirname*	mkdir *dirname*
Remove a Directory	DELETE/NOQUERY *dirname*	rmdir *dirname*
Remove a file	DELETE/NOQUERY *filename*	rm *filename*
Copy a file	COPY *fromname toname*	cp *fromname toname*
Rename a file	RENAME *fromname toname*	mv *fromname toname*
List filenames	DIR/BRIEF	ls
List filenames sizes, dates, etc.	DIR/FULL	ls -l

The UNIX file management tools are discussed in the *File Management Commands* section of this manual.

APPENDIXES

Text Files

Both the UNIX system and VMS have text files that can be displayed on the terminal or printed on an ordinary printer. In both systems a text file is structured into lines, but in the UNIX system the <NL> character marks the ends of lines, whereas in VMS a <CR> followed by a <NL> conventionally marks the ends of lines.

	VMS	**UNIX**
Print a file	PRINT *filename*	lp *filename*
Display a file on the terminal	TYPE *filename*	cat *filename*
Paginate a file on the terminal		more *filename* pg *filename*
Compare two files	DIFFERENCES *file1,file2*	diff *file1 file2*

These and other programs to manage text files are discussed in the *Text File Commands* section of this manual.

Keyboard Conventions

The commands to make the UNIX system terminal handler follow the VMS or RT-11 keyboard conventions were presented at the end of Appendix II. Although it is possible to map the UNIX system's end of file character to <Ctrl-Z>, which is the VMS usage, few users do so. The UNIX system usage of <Ctrl-D> is pervasive and should probably be maintained.

INDEX